GLOBAL MEDIA, CUL
IDENTITY

D0143572

This edited volume examines the ways that global media shapes relations between place, culture, and identity. Through the included essays, Chopra and Gajjala offer a mix of theoretical reflections and empirical case studies that will help readers understand how the media can shape cultural identities and, conversely, how cultural formations can influence the political economy of global media. The interdisciplinary, international scholars gathered here push the discussion of what it means to do global media studies beyond uncritical celebrations of global media technologies (or globalization) as well as beyond perspectives that are a priori dismissive of the possibilities of global media.

Some of the key questions and themes that the international contributors explore within the text include: Is the global audience of global television the same as the global audience of the internet? Can we conceptualize the global culture–media–identity dynamic beyond the discourse of postcolonialism? How does the globalization of media affect feelings of nationalism? How is the growth of a consumer "global middle class" spread, and resisted, through media? *Global Media, Culture, and Identity* takes a comparative media approach to addressing these, and other, issues across media forms including print, television, film, and new media.

Rohit Chopra is Assistant Professor of Communication at Santa Clara University. He is author of *Technology and Nationalism in India: Cultural Negotiations from Colonialism to Cyberspace* (Cambria Press, 2008).

Radhika Gajjala is Professor of American Culture Studies and Communication Studies at Bowling Green State University. She is author of *Cyber Selves: Feminist Ethnographies of South Asian Women* (Altamira Press, 2004) and co-editor of *South Asian Technospaces* (Peter Lang, 2008).

GLOBAL MEDIA, CULTURE, AND IDENTITY

Theory, Cases, and Approaches

edited by Rohit Chopra and
Radhika Gajjala

Routledge
Taylor & Francis Group

NEW YORK AND LONDON

First published 2011
by Routledge
711 Third Avenue, New York, NY 10017

Simultaneously published in the UK
by Routledge
2 Park Square, Milton Park, Abingdon, Oxon OX14 4RN

Routledge is an imprint of the Taylor & Francis Group, an informa business

© 2011 Taylor & Francis

Typeset in Minion by Book Now Ltd, London
Printed by Walsworth Publishing Company, Marceline, MO

Library of Congress Cataloging in Publication Data
Global media, culture, and identity: theory, cases, and approaches / [edited by] Rohit
Chopra and Radhika Gajjala.
    p. cm.
Includes bibliographical references and index.
1. Communication, International. 2. Mass media and culture. 3. Popular culture and
globalization. 4. Technological innovations—Social aspects. I. Gajjala, Radhika, 1960–
P96.I5G55 2011
302.2—dc22   2010042960

ISBN13: 978–0–415–87790–9 (hbk)
ISBN13: 978–0–415–87791–6 (pbk)

Contents

Figures

Foreword

EMILE McANANY

This volume edited by Rohit Chopra and Radhika Gajjala is both a contribution to the future of global media studies and a legacy of the past. The legacy is partly acknowledged by Chopra in his thoughtful introduction with references to theoretical influences from critical theory, poststructuralism, postcolonial theory, and other recent influences on media studies. The summaries of the chapters refer us to more recent analyses of how identity, culture, media, and globalization can be understood in our constantly changing media contexts. My reference to legacy, however, suggests that this current volume can be seen in an even larger historical context of media studies.

It is worth remembering that media studies had its roots in the field of communication that itself was "invented" in the past century, 1948 to be precise, at the University of Illinois. Wilbur Schramm created the first graduate degree course in mass communication in that year and began a study of the mass media that would become a formal field of study called communication. The global aspect of media studies in the United States at least would be part of the government's Cold War struggle with the Soviet Union to win the hearts and minds of the so-called Third World in the 1950s. Daniel Lerner's *The Passing of Traditional Society* in 1958 became the first link of media studies with modernization theory in what would be called international communication but would over the coming decades morph into global communication/media studies.[1] The cultural studies aspect of media studies can be traced to the United Kingdom where both Raymond Williams and the Media Group in Birmingham's Centre for Contemporary Cultural Studies with Stuart Hall brought media studies into the cultural studies orbit in the 1970s. Finally, *Global Culture*, a seminal book edited by British sociologist Mike Featherstone in 1990, introduced the idea of the "global" into media studies, also seen in Arjun Appadurai's often cited chapter on "Disjuncture and Difference in the Global Cultural Economy."[2] Appadurai also suggested that identities were shaped by the global flow of media images and technologies. This suggestion led researchers such as Chris Barker and James Lull to in-depth studies of identity and media a few years later.[3]

If this is the legacy, then what will be the future? That question, as Chopra so forthrightly asserts, is harder to predict. There is in current postcolonial studies, for example, a blending of

> a materialist, Marxist conception of power as rooted in material inequities . . . and a Foucauldian conception of power as simultaneously productive and regulatory though not necessarily repressive. Such tensions are singularly pertinent to global media studies. They remind us that the complex realities of social life—especially those of a global world—always exceed the reach of theory even as they provoke theory to extend its grasp.

The chapters of this volume reflect both the ambiguity and the reach of theory suggested by Chopra. There are a variety of topics, approaches, and theories that populate the contributions. I shall highlight only three that point the way to a future media studies.

One of the things that will strike the reader of this book is the sheer diversity of theory and methodology. There are theories of postmodernism, postcolonialism, political economy (rather fewer), media/cultural production, globalization, feminism, film, and more. The most regularly cited authors are probably Arjun Appadurai and Benedict Anderson, though Edward Said and Roland Barthes also appear. Ethnographic methods are evident in several of the studies (Ivan Kwek in Chapter 8 and Damien Stankiewicz in Chapter 11), but textual and image analysis is prevalent (David Kenley in Chapter 5, Nayantara Sheoran in Chapter 6, Frederike Felcht in Chapter 7, image and text in Aalok Khandekar and Grant Jun Otsuki in Chapter 9, Hudson Moura in Chapter 13, and digital texts in Matthew Heinz and Hsin-I Cheng in Chapter 14), the latter by far the most common. Though clear academic identities are not apparent, the studies make it clear that the authors come from a variety of backgrounds other than just media studies, including history, cultural anthropology, health sciences, and literature. What are we to make of this diversity? We could conclude that there is no focus in the book or that it simply reflects the confused picture of media studies. On more careful reading of this and other current publishing in the field, we might better conclude that the field that began more than 60 years ago in mass communication studies has evolved to reflect the globalizing context of our everyday lives, as the technologies of communication have moved to the center in our global societies. The line between confusion and richness is a thin one, but one that Chopra's Introduction carefully defines for the reader.

The second observation to make is that there are represented here a global list of authors. The field of communication research began with Americans and a few European immigrants in the 1940s and 1950s[4] but has gradually globalized over the past five or six decades. There remains today a hegemony of English language authors, theories, and methodologies, but this volume suggests that the global community of media studies needs representation of authors and topics that better reflect their diversity of concerns and interests. The sites of the studies represent not only the United States but also China, India, Singapore, Denmark, France, Germany, Canada, and Taiwan, as well as ethnic, sexual, gender, and class minorities/ majorities who still suffer from unequal power and resources. This latter phenomenon is a constant theme throughout this volume.

A final comment is that this diverse collection of research suggests an unarticulated element in the analysis of the global system of media technologies and images: the direction of change (are disparities lessening or not?) and what role the media scholar has in the larger scheme of global mediated societies. If it is true that we live in a globalizing and increasingly mediated world, there should be some role for those who are trained in analysis of this world to be public intellectuals who promote ideas for change and a narrowing of the power disparities among various identity communities where we live. There are hints in the chapters for a greater democratization of action in Chinese filmmaking, sexual identities, and digital empowerments, among others. Perhaps a clearer role for media scholars in this democratization of diversity of all kinds will be part of the future of media studies throughout the globe.

Endnotes

1. Daniel Lerner, *The Passing of Traditional Society: Modernizing the Middle East* (New York, NY: Free Press, 1964).
2. Arjun Appadurai, "Disjuncture and Difference in the Global Cultural Economy," in *Global Culture: Nationalism, Globalization and Modernity*, ed. Mike Featherstone (London: Sage Publications, 1990), 295–310.
3. Chris Barker, *Global Television* (Malden, MA: Blackwell, 1997); James Lull, *Media, Communication, Culture: A Global Approach* (New York, NY: Columbia University Press, 1995).
4. Everett M. Rogers, *A History of Communication Study: A Biographical Approach* (New York, NY: Free Press, 1994).

Acknowledgments

We would like to express our thanks to the many who have made this volume possible. It has been a pleasure working with Matthew Byrnie at Routledge, and we are enormously grateful for his support. The insightful suggestions of the anonymous reviewers of the manuscript improved the book tremendously. Thanks also to Carolann Madden at Routledge for all her help with the manuscript. Anca Birzescu, Franklin Yartey, and Yeon Ju Oh provided superb research assistance at all stages of the project.

Rohit Chopra would like to thank his colleagues at the Department of Communication at Santa Clara University, in the course of conversations with whom the idea for this volume materialized. He would also like to thank Dean Atom Yee and the Provost's Office at Santa Clara University for research grants that enabled the volume to become a reality. Gitanjali Shahani has been an important contributor to the project in all kinds of ways. And little Arihaan Shahani Chopra, by being a joyous distraction, provided a sense of much-needed perspective that enormously enriched the work.

Contributors

Paul Longley Arthur is Deputy Director of the National Centre of Biography and Deputy General Editor of the Australian Dictionary of Biography at the Australian National University. He has held research fellowships at universities in Europe, North America, and Australia and published widely on the history of technology, media, travel, and empire, including *Virtual Voyages: Travel Writing and the Antipodes 1605–1837* (2010) and *History and New Media* (forthcoming 2012). An authority on digital research methods in the humanities and social sciences, Paul Arthur is a series editor of Anthem Scholarship in the Digital Age (Anthem Press, London and New York).

Anca Birzescu is a doctoral candidate in Communication Studies at Bowling Green State University, Ohio. Her research interests include postcolonial theory, feminist cultural studies, ethnic identity, gender and communication, and mass media discourse in Eastern and Central European transitional societies. Her current doctoral research focuses on Roma minority identity negotiation in post-communist Romania.

Hsin-I Cheng is an Assistant Professor of Communication at Santa Clara University. Her research interests include culture and identity, immigration, diasporic communities, and border crossing in the context of transnationalism. Specifically, she is interested in unpacking various interactive processes of identity crafting (e.g., intersections of ethnicity, class, gender, race, nationality, etc.) in relationship to geopolitical arrangements (e.g., colonial and imperial legacies, neoliberal consumerism). She is the author of *Culturing*

Interface: Identity, Communication, and Chinese Transnationalism (2008). Her research has appeared in the *Journal of International and Intercultural Communication*, and *Intercultural Communication and Language*.

Rohit Chopra is an Assistant Professor in the Department of Communication at Santa Clara University. He is the author of *Technology and Nationalism in India: Cultural Negotiations from Colonialism to Cyberspace* (Cambria, 2008) and editor (with Aniket Alam) of "Empire Redux," a special issue of the *Economic and Political Weekly* (forthcoming). He has published in several journals, including *Cultural Studies, New Media and Society, First Monday,* and the *Journal of International Law and Policy*. His research interests include global media and technologies, new media, South Asian history, and postcolonial theory. His current projects address violence and communication and failures of communication.

Frederike Felcht holds an M.A. in Cultural Studies, Scandinavian Studies, and Philosophy from Humboldt University, Berlin. She is currently writing her dissertation on Hans Christian Andersen from a global perspective at the graduate program "Formations of the Global," an interdisciplinary research forum in the Humanities Division at the University of Mannheim, Germany. She has been awarded several grants to conduct research in Denmark. Her research fields are globalization, Scandinavian literature, the theory of things, the history of the nineteenth century, and the philosophy of history.

Radhika Gajjala is Director of American Culture Studies and Professor of Communication and Cultural Studies at Bowling Green State University, Ohio. Her book *Cyberselves: Feminist Ethnographies of South Asian Women* (2004) was published by Altamira Press. She is also the coeditor of *South Asian Technospaces* (Peter Lang, 2008) and *Webbing Cyberfeminist Practice* (Hampton Press, 2009). Radhika is currently working on a couple of book length projects: one on "Technocultural Agency: Production of Identity at the Interface" and the other on "Affect and Placement in Indian Digital Diasporas." More details about her work can be found at http://personal.bgsu.edu/~radhik.

Matthew Heinz is a Professor in the School of Communication and Culture and Associate Dean of the Faculty of Social and Applied Sciences at Royal Roads University in Victoria, British Columbia, Canada. Originally from Germany, he obtained his Ph.D. in Communication Studies from the University of Nebraska-Lincoln (1998) and has held faculty appointments at Bowling Green (Ohio) State University and the University of North Dakota. His scholarship in culture and communication focuses on the intersections of language, gender identity, sexual orientation, and culture. His current research project consists of leading a community-based transgender needs assessment for Vancouver Island.

Michael Jenson is an Associate Professor of Architecture and director of undergraduate architectural studies at the University of Colorado. He has published in *Open House International, Drain Magazine, The Journal of Architecture, The Journal of Utopian Studies,* and *MONU (Magazine on Urbanism)* as well as contributed to the book *Design Studio Pedagogy: Horizons for the Future.* Professor Jenson received a Ph.D. in Philosophy from the University of Edinburgh, a Master of Architecture from Columbia University, and a Bachelor of Science in Architecture from the University of Texas at Arlington.

David Kenley (Ph.D., University of Hawaii) is an Associate Professor of Chinese History at Elizabethtown College in Pennsylvania. He is the author of *New Culture in a New World* (Routledge, 2003) and other works dealing with Chinese intellectual history and diasporas in world history. He is currently researching the Chinese-language press in Cuba during the early twentieth century.

Aalok Khandekar has received his Ph.D. in Science and Technology Studies at the Rensselaer Polytechnic Institute in Troy, NY. His dissertation, entitled "Engineering the Global Indian: Skills, Cosmopolitanism, and Families in Circuits of High-Tech Migrations between India and the United States," is an ethnographic exploration of the cultural logics of transnational mobility among Indian engineering students and professionals. Speaking directly to the need for globally focused studies of science, technology, and culture, Aalok's research analyzes the experiences of transnational migration among Indian technomigrants and the historically and culturally specific political economies in which they are embedded.

Ivan Kwek, a former producer and director of current affairs and documentaries of over 15 years, is currently a Ph.D. candidate at the School of Oriental and African Studies, University of London. For his doctoral research, he conducted ethnographic fieldwork at a minority Malay-language television channel in Singapore, focusing on how production practices at the channel intersect with the attempts to use television to encourage particular worldviews, change mindsets, sustain "cultural values," and to re-vision Singapore Malays into "modern" subjectivities, loyal to the state, and ready for the new economy.

Emile McAnany began his communication career with a Ph.D. at Stanford University (1970) where he remained until 1978 as a research associate and lecturer. He moved to the University of Texas at Austin in 1979 and had a joint appointment in the College of Communication and the Institute of Latin American Studies. He moved to Santa Clara University in 1997 and was chair of the Department of Communication from 1997 through 2002.

He held the Schmidt Professorship in Communication at the university until starting a phased retirement in 2009. He has published nine books and a large number of journal articles and chapters over his career.

Nolwenn Mingant is an Associate Professor in American Studies at the Université Sorbonne Nouvelle-Paris 3. In 2008, she defended her thesis entitled "Les Stratégies d'exportation du cinéma hollywoodien (1966–2004)" at the Université Paris X-Nanterre. She cofounded the research group CinEcoSa (Cinema, Economy and English-Speaking Society), which aims at developing studies of the film industry from a cultural angle. Her current fields of interest are the relationship between Hollywood and the Middle East and the presence of foreign languages in recent Hollywood movies. She recently published *Hollywood à la conquête du monde: Marchés, stratégies, influences* (CNRS Editions, 2010).

Hudson Moura is a Canadian-Brazilian film scholar. He acquired his Ph.D. in Literature and Film from the University of Montreal and has completed his postdoctoral research in intercultural cinema at Simon Fraser University. Before joining Ryerson University's faculty Dr. Moura taught at several universities including the University of British Columbia, Simon Fraser University, and the University of Montreal in Canada; the Federal University of São Carlos in Brazil; and the University of Algarve in Portugal. He has presented his research at several film and media conferences. Dr. Moura has published his written work in English, French, and Portuguese in journals and books.

Grant Jun Otsuki is a Ph.D. candidate in social-cultural anthropology at the University of Toronto. He received his B.Sc. Hons. in Science, Technology, and Society from the University of Calgary, Canada, and his M.S. in Science and Technology Studies from Rensselaer Polytechnic Institute, United States. His dissertation research focuses on transhumanism in Japan and North America and investigates the construction of understandings of nature, culture, and the human in relationship to emerging technoscientific interventions into the human body.

Cindy Patton holds the Canada Research Chair in Community, Culture and Health at Simon Fraser University (Vancouver, Canada), where she is a Professor of Sociology and Anthropology. Her wide-ranging work includes social aspects of HIV, including critique of media coverage; history of sexuality; and ethnographic works on medical practice in different clinical settings.

Joseph Sciorra is an Associate Director for Academic and Cultural Programs at Queens College's John D. Calandra Italian American Institute. As a folklorist, he has published on religious practices, cultural landscapes, and popular music. He is the editor of the social science journal, *Italian American Review*. He is the author of *R.I.P.: Memorial Wall Art* (1994; 2002), the coeditor of poet Vincenzo Ancona's *Malidittu la lingua/ Damned Language* (1990; 2010), and the editor of *Italian Folk: Vernacular Culture in Italian-American Lives* (Fordham University Press, 2011). As the avatar "Joey Skee," Sciorra maintains the blog, "Occhio contro occhio," at http://www.i-italy.org.

Nayantara Sheoran is a Ph.D. candidate in Cultural Studies. Her research interests include Science, Technology, and Medicine (STM); critical communication theories; consumer culture with a particular interest in media advertising; and the production, consumption, reception, and regulation of media texts. She is also interested in pharmaceutical cultures from a transnational perspective, "postliberalization" India, and the visual manifestations of commoditization of health. From July 2010, she will be traveling in India for her dissertation research which has been supported by the National Science Foundation.

Damien Stankiewicz is completing a Ph.D. in New York University's Department of Anthropology. Damien completed the department's Program in Culture and Media in 2006, which included training both in the ethnography of media and in digital video production. His research explores the role that producers of media are playing in the negotiation of national, regional, and global identities in Europe. Although his fieldwork research primarily examined the French–German and European cultural television station ARTE, he has also conducted ethnography with the staff of EuroNews, cafebabel.com, and several other European media outlets. Parts of his graduate research have been funded by the Social Science Research Council, the National Science Foundation, and the Wenner-Gren Foundation for Anthropological Research.

Daya Thussu is a Professor of International Communication and Founder Codirector of the India Media Centre at the University of Westminster in London. He is the Founder and Managing Editor of the Sage journal *Global Media and Communication*. Among his main publications are *Electronic Empires: Global Media and Local Resistance* (1998); *War and the Media: Reporting Conflict 24/7* (2003); *International Communication: Continuity and Change*, second edition (2006); *Media on the Move: Global Flow and Contra-flow* (2007); *News as Entertainment: The Rise of Global Infotainment* (2007); and *Internationalizing Media Studies* (2009).

Franklin N. A. Yartey received his Bachelor of Arts degree from Northwestern College, IA and Master of Arts degree from Indiana State

University. He is currently pursuing a Ph.D. in Communications at Bowling Green State University, in Ohio, focusing on digital media and globalization. His primary research interests include microfinance and women in developing countries, the representation of Third World bodies in the media and on the internet, media ethics, citizen journalism, and globalization. He has been elected to the Phi Kappa Phi national collegiate honors society. He was also a fellow at the 2008 Colloquium on Media Ethics & Economics, Colorado.

CHAPTER 1

Introduction

Media, Culture, and Identity in the Time of the Global

ROHIT CHOPRA

Chapter Description

The introductory chapter to the volume presents a case for the significance of the relationship between media, culture, and identity in our global times. Identifying some challenges posed by each of these terms, and engaging with relevant scholarship from media studies and other disciplines, the chapter outlines a theoretical approach for the study of global media, culture, and identity. This approach rests on three related propositions. One, that global media are central to the production of cultural identity in the present historical moment; two, that cultural identification is a key driver of logics and content of global media flows; and three, that expressions of cultural identity in media texts can be read as reflecting a global awareness. The chapter also highlights the distinctive contributions of the volume and presents the key thematic, theoretical, and methodological focus of each chapter.

* * *

On November 4, 2008, Barack Obama was elected the first global President of the United States. Much of what happens in American public life qualifies as a global event, from episodes in the lives of celebrities to the excesses of Wall Street. But the excitement generated by the Obama campaign far exceeded the usual level of international interest in events American.[1] To make this observation is not to be seduced by the utopian appeal of a

1

remarkable historical moment. It is, rather, to recognize that the global attention on Obama, significantly fostered by the media, unsettles the usual patterns of cultural identification in our times. On television, the internet, and in print, in national and transnational conversations, Barack Obama's story emerged against the backdrop of an intricate set of relationships between the realms of media, culture, and identity.

Biracial but marked as African American, Obama brought out into the light of day the complicated meanings of race in contemporary American society, even as he promised to transform these meanings into more inclusive definitions of Americanness. Globally, Obama stood for the same promise. In the words of *Washington Post* columnist, Eugene Robinson, Obama was

> both an African American and the biracial son of a black Kenyan father and a white American mother; both a product of the streets of Chicago, where he worked as a community organizer, and a son of the streets of Jakarta, where he played as a kid.[2]

Obama, as Robinson put it, was the very "personification of 'both-and.'"[3] His "both-and" story was played out in a simultaneously national and global media space, with key moments in the narrative consisting of his famous "Race Speech,"[4] his victory speech, and the inauguration. Obama's victory brought centerstage the issue of minority rights in other nations too. With Obama's election, European nations were compelled to reflect on their professed claims that minorities could realistically hope to occupy the highest political office in their societies.[5]

But there were other, less salubrious, reactions within the United States to Obama's identity. Though Obama repeatedly affirmed his Christian faith during the campaign, he was demonized for the fact of possessing a "Muslim" name.[6] The implied claim that a Muslim was unfit to be a president was itself made possible by the construction of Islam as a violent faith in American public discourse. This characterization of Islam was significantly shaped by the American media in the aftermath of the September 11, 2001 attacks and during the occupation of Afghanistan and Iraq.

Media have been central to the processes by which the world and Obama have come to know each other. Obama's mediated engagement with the world has been marked by elisions and inclusiveness. His media persona, for instance, has been carefully managed to prevent too close an association with certain demographics, such as hijab-clad Muslim women.[7] Obama reflects the relevance of identity politics, with all its attendant complications, in our present-day world. Indeed, an astonishing number of communities across the globe have claimed Obama as one of their own. The list includes, at the very least, Americans, African Americans, white Americans, individuals with biracial identities, immigrants, Kenyans, Africans, academics, activists, Grammy award winners, lawyers, Harvard alumni, Indonesians, Chicagoans, and residents of Hyde Park. Obama's identity has also provoked racist reactions, anti-Muslim hysteria, and a host of anxieties about criteria of belonging in national and transnational communities. The Obama phenomenon, in numerous ways, embodies the media-culture-identity problematic in the time of the global and highlights the need for critically investigating it. Accordingly, each of these categories—culture, media, identity, and the global—deserves closer examination.

Culture, Identity, Media, and the Global

The entry for the term "culture" in *New Keywords*, an updated version of Raymond Williams' classic work, *Keywords*, begins with a revealing anecdote:

> There is now a great deal of hesitancy over the word **culture**. "I don't know how many times," Raymond Williams once said, "I've wished that I had never heard the damned word" (R. Williams 1979: 154), registering his frustration that its complexity defied the tasks of ordinary analysis.[8]

Williams' frustration may be recognized as reflective of the dizzyingly broad and often contradictory uses of the term, including the anthropological definition of culture as a general way of life, the highest form of aesthetic expression of a people, the primary marker of human difference, the basis for a shared humanity, a realm of human activity predicated on economic life, and a basic human drive fundamental to social existence. Similar stories might be charted for the terms "identity," "media," and "global."

In the past few decades, the academic world has witnessed an explosion of interest in identity. Cooper and Brubakers argue that the phenomenon is emblematic of broader developments within the United States, notably the articulation of social and political claims by groups in the vocabulary of identity.[9] They assert that the excessive theoretical burden placed on the term render it meaningless for academic analysis.

The term media also encompasses a wide range of meanings that might expose it to similar charges of inexactitude. Williams is instructive here, clarifying the valences of the word as vehicle, medium, material, technology, and process.[10] Williams also reminds us of the necessity of thinking about media in a manner that defies technological determinism.[11]

Once arguably a largely descriptive adjective, the term global now brings with it an undertow of associated questions that mark it as an evaluative term.

The term has been given a new lease of life by the debate on globalization.[12] When does the global start? Does it indicate any kind of cultural contact between societies or should it be used only to signal the unprecedented changes in telecommunications, finance, and media that have locked nations into complex patterns of interdependence in the past few decades? If the global implies a certain vision of the universal, how do we approach invocations of the global in light of the powerful critique of universalism launched within the academy?[13]

Each term, then, has taken on a slipperiness of meaning through its extensive use. The pervasiveness of the terms reflects their abidingness in everyday language, media conversations, and public discourse. Although this confirms the value of the terms as objects of inquiry, it also points to challenges in articulating them as analytic categories.

Theoretical Approach

Any investigation of the culture-media-identity problematic must be responsive to the range of meanings that these terms take on in the era of the global, while being attuned to contingency of outcomes and identifiable patterns in which the problematic manifests itself. Such an analysis must also categorically articulate some general relationships between media, culture, identity, and the global that can serve as a frame for scholarly analysis. I outline elements of such a theoretical frame, following a discussion of relevant perspectives in media studies, postcolonial studies, and poststructuralist theory that are already in conversation with Marxist perspectives. The framework outlined below is not meant as a prescriptive model but as a general schematic model suggesting directions for further examination.

Global Media Studies After Marxist, Postcolonial, and Poststructuralist Theory

The "cultural imperialism" theory is a natural starting point for any discussion of global media. Global media scholarship has extensively focused on the thesis, which analyzes media as an instrument of cultural domination, reflecting unequal power relationships between nations that dominate the production of global media and those that import such media.[14] The main limitations of the thesis are a simplification of complex flows of communication to a two-way relationship, its neglect of adaptations of global products to local conditions, the simplistic conception of a native culture under threat from the West, and assumptions of passivity on the part of the audience.[15] Taking these criticisms into account, Morley argues that the theory still retains value for the study of media. For, even in a multipolar world, some locations are more powerful than others. Furthermore, an emphasis on the agency of audiences should not be misread as the ability of viewers to immunize themselves from any media influence.

Sreberny-Mohammadi has critiqued the use of the concept by scholars for its equation of imperialism and Americanization, its conflation of cultural imperialism and media imperialism, and its reductive focus on imperialism as a post-World War II phenomenon.[16] She argues that scholars such as Said, Tomlinson, and Hall have privileged "the realm of the discursive" in their assessments of cultural imperialism, which has had the effect of obfuscating the multifaceted nature of cultural contact.[17] She calls, instead, for analyses of cultural imperialism based on an anthropological view of culture as the practice of everyday life.

As these perspectives indicate, treatments of imperialism within media studies have not always converged with the powerful critiques of imperialism proposed by postcolonial studies. One reason may be that the basic modes of analysis of imperialism within media studies have been "heavily indebted to the works of Marx, Lenin, and Rosa Luxemburg" or reliant on Marxist-inspired frameworks such as dependency theory.[18] Postcolonial studies, on the other hand, stands in an ambivalent relationship to Marxism.[19] But there are obvious overlaps between the postcolonial studies and media studies. The influence of postcolonial studies on media studies, for instance, may be recognized in scholarship that centers on media representations of Others—national, racial, ethnic, sexual—and on processes of Othering. Shohat and Stam's work, *Unthinking Eurocentrism*, exemplifies the point. It represents a radically new perspective on mediated exchanges between Europe and its Others.[20] Presenting "a theorized and historicized discussion of Eurocentrism as shaped and challenged by the media," Shohat and Stam seek to replace that Eurocentric lens with a "polycentric multiculturalism."[21] They clearly do not view polycentric multiculturalism as a postcolonial perspective.[22] Nonetheless, their critique of Eurocentric epistemologies and their description of racial difference as fundamentally constitutive of colonialism reveal close affinities with the project of postcolonial studies. Shome and Hegde argue that the distinct value of postcolonial studies for the field of communication lies in its contextualization of cultural power in historical and international perspective; its location of the national in broader "histories and geographies of global power and culture"; and its embedding of the problematics of race, class, gender, and sexuality in concrete historical manifestations of modernity.[23] The arguments in several contributions in Parks and Kumar's important volume on global television may be interpreted as broadly reflecting such imperatives. Luckett's essay on the television series *Goodness Gracious Me* and the South Asian diaspora in Britain whose experience it voiced demonstrates how the show confounds a model of media production and consumption for a conventionally understood national audience.[24] Schwoch's essay conceptualizes Russian audiences as a new horizon against which Chechen national identities were "imagined" through the televisual coverage of Russian–Chechnya political conflict.[25] Although the Chechens had hoped to gain the attention of the West through the "CNN Defense"—holding out against an adversary till the attention of the Western world could be mobilized—it was Russian and Chechen audiences, instead, who became the audiences of any "national" narratives contained within the telecast.[26]

Poststructuralist diagnoses have assessed media technologies and media representations as instruments and embodiments of late capitalist and late modern or postmodern culture. They have also provided analytic techniques and concepts that have been useful for the analysis of media. Some poststructuralist contributions that have been especially influential for the study of media are Lyotard's conception of postmodern social existence in a technologized world as fundamentally characterized by the lack of grand narratives, Baudrillard's ruminations on the simulated nature of reality itself, Foucault's concepts of discourse and the panopticon, Derrida's method of deconstruction to reveal the always-already unraveling threads of signification underlying apparently stable meanings in texts, and Bourdieu's work on how television authorizes a narrow vision of the world that masquerades as an objective picture of reality.[27]

Critical differences between poststructuralist and Marxist frameworks also bear noting here. There is a much stronger emphasis on questions of representation in the former compared with the Marxist focus on political economy. Marxist analyses center on ideology as the repository of culture while poststructuralist work often focuses on discourse as an object of cultural analysis. There is a more sustained engagement with forms of social difference other than class, especially gender and sexuality, in poststructuralist scholarship. Furthermore, in contrast to the evaluative-normative framework proposed by Marxism, poststructuralist readings usually take the form of a descriptive enterprise.

Postcolonial studies has sought to straddle—fruitfully, if often uneasily—the Marxist and poststructuralist paradigms. For instance, Said employs the Foucauldian concept of discourse in his landmark work, *Orientalism*, yet seeks to preserve a humanistic conception of agency, which may appear contradictory to the thrust of Foucault's method.[28] As noted earlier, postcolonial studies bears a complicated relationship to Marxist scholarship. Indeed, postcolonial scholarship often works with two conceptions of power: a materialist, Marxist conception of power as rooted in material inequities and related to the ownership of modes of production, and a

Foucauldian conception of power as simultaneously productive and regulatory though not necessarily repressive.[29] Such tensions are singularly pertinent for global media studies. They remind us that the complex realities of social life—especially those of a global world—always exceed the reach of theory even as they provoke theory to extend its grasp. They demand theoretical frameworks that are at once flexible and reflexive, although being attuned to historical and sociological particularities.

Elements of a Theory for the Study of Global Media, Culture, and Identity

Existing in the contested space shaped by the theoretical debates described earlier, this volume is informed by the following three theoretical propositions about the relationship between global media, culture, and identity.

a) *Global media flows, structures, and processes are central to the production of cultural identity in the present historical moment.* Appadurai's concept of mediascapes and Castells's notion of flows in the network society are helpful in grasping the dynamics of such arrangements pertaining to global media. The term mediascapes refers to both

> the distribution of the electronic capabilities to produce and disseminate information (newspapers, magazines, television stations, and film-production studios), which are now available to a growing number of private and public interests throughout the world, and to the images of the world created by these media.[30]

In addition to mediascapes, Appadurai theorizes the global cultural economy as structured by several other scapes; these are, respectively, transnational flows of people (ethnoscapes), capital (finanscapes), technology (technoscapes), and ideological themes (ideoscapes). Each of these scapes functions according to an internal logic, often in disjuncture with the others. Flows, as Castells conceptualizes them, are fundamental to the "network society" that has crystallized over the second half of the twentieth century, thanks to innovations in computing and telecommunications, transformations in the nature of work, and the social impact of the mass media.[31] Practically, every dimension of the contemporary network society operates in terms of flows: of capital, information, technology, and images, sights, and sounds.[32] Like Appadurai, Castells acknowledges an unevenness in the forms of global society that correspond to the current ecumene; logics of flows have created new elites and subalterns, structured new centers and hinterlands, and fostered divisions between those who are an integral part of the network society and those who are excluded from it.[33]

b) *Conversely, forms of cultural identification and affiliation are key drivers of logics and content of global media flows.* As Shohat and Stam suggest, the contemporary media "now exist close to the very core of identity production."[34] Thus, although Hindu, Muslim, Jewish, and Christian fundamentalist groups use the Internet to stake majoritarian claims, the American cable television channel Fox News frames the interests of conservative, largely white, groups as synonymous with the American national good. As Nicholas Kristof writes in the *New York Times* about the moral obligations of citizens of developed nations to protect the rights of oppressed women in developing nations, media in countries with Muslim populations routinely conjure the specter of a West out to attack Islam. Assertions of cultural difference and identity—whether they be images of exotic Others; ugly forms of prejudice, such as anti-semitism and anti-immigrant sentiment; nationalist anxieties; historical narratives of newly independent nations; or new kinds of political communities imagining themselves into being—significantly inform streams of media content that crisscross the globe and are consumed within and across national boundaries.

c) *Expressions of cultural identity in media texts can be read as embodying a sense or awareness of the global.* This awareness is a function of two characteristics about global media. One, that media content is increasingly produced through transnational financial, technological, and creative arrangements, as the analyses of Appadurai and Castells indicate, and two, that such media content also increasingly assumes a global audience. The sense of the global implied here, however, is neither that of an even playing field in which participants from different locations contribute on an equal footing nor that of a monolithic global audience that consumes content in predictably identical fashion. The recent Oscar-winning film *Slumdog Millionaire* is a case in point. An international collaboration, involving creative and corporate interests from the United Kingdom, the United States, and India, the film was successful in the West but ran to less than packed houses in India.[35] The Oscar victory celebrations were also marred by the controversy that the Indian children acting in the film were paid a meager amount for their work.[36] The controversy raised uncomfortable questions about power relationships in global systems of media production and the unequal value of the labor of agents from various locations in global media markets. Taking these factors into account, media texts produced in locations across the globe can be seen as engaged with a range of cultural groups, imagined as insiders or outsiders. The varied critical receptions of media texts across global locations are arguably reflective of pressures on the texts to be in conversation with a number of communities, each of which may possess a different level of familiarity with the cultural codes in the text.

Paying attention to the realities of unequal global power relationships between and among state and nonstate actors, this volume seeks to go beyond dichotomies of West versus rest, global versus local, and elites versus subalterns. Sensitive to the complex role of media in constructing and communicating global threats, public anxieties, and narratives of emancipation, the volume questions the commonsense perception of media as vectors of progressive modernity and enlightened political consciousness. The general approach taken here recognizes that the remapping of the world through globalization calls for analyses of media production, consumption, and circulation beyond the frame of the nation. However, the emphasis on global networks, circuits, and flows does not ignore the continuing importance of the nation-state as one locus of political identification. Rather, the assumption is that the category of the national itself has been profoundly altered in a global world, and media both contribute to and reflect this change. The theoretical framework of the volume accommodates the possibility of multiple temporal trajectories of the global in its more immediate as well as longer historical variants. It seeks to identify both what is new about the present form of the global media-culture-identity relationship and the ways in which earlier patterns of mediated transnational cultural exchanges and community formation both anticipate and differ from current-day manifestations.

The theoretical schematic of the volume does not locate any identity category as foundational but is attentive to the way in which national identity, ethnicity, gender, race, and sexual identity interact under specific conditions. It does not posit the material and discursive as opposed. It reflects the view that the global, as, indeed, the signifieds of identity, media, and culture, are discursively produced, that is, they do not exist in any fixed universal form as a given prediscursive reality. Responding to new developments in televisual, digital, and online media, the volume asks us to rethink what materiality means and how social relationships are articulated in such circuits of communication.

Finally, an edited volume, as a collaborative scholarly venture, is an ideal forum for an interdisciplinary examination of the relationships between global media, culture, and identity. Individual chapters in the volume exemplify concrete engagements with diverse disciplinary and interdisciplinary traditions in the humanities and social sciences. The chapters reflect various models of scholarly inquiry, including case studies, primarily theoretical and philosophical reflections, and historical assessments. Cumulatively, the chapters employ a range of methods, including ethnography, textual analysis, discourse analysis, and historical and historiographical analysis. At the same time, the chapters are united by a basic theoretical commitment of taking a critical stance toward one or more of the categories of culture, media, identity, and "the global," such that their meanings are expanded or defamiliarized.

Structure of the Volume

Part I: Geographies and Currents of Global Media and Identity

Cindy Patton's essay, "Endemic Reporting: Calibrating the 'News' and 'Normal Disease,'" inaugurates the volume. Patton argues that media coverage of the H1N1 virus provides a stark case study of the problems of medical reporting in a world with proliferating communication systems. Patton shows how the tiny virus and the gigantic epidemic each operate at their own speed and in incommensurable spaces, and are intercepted and complicated by vaccines and treatments on the cellular/actual level and by information campaigns on the global/virtual level. H1N1 coverage shows how the mainstream media pretends to criticize disease management while protecting medicine's master narrative of triumph over disease and the bodies that carry that disease.

In his chapter, "The Mediascape of Hip-Wop: Alterity and Authenticity in Italian North American Hip-Hop," Joseph Sciorra explores how Italian American and Italian Canadian rappers reproduce racial and ethnic identities within hip-hop culture. White Italian rappers have positioned themselves by conjuring a mediated ethnicity of cinematic mafiosi to lay claims to authenticity within the gangsta rap genre. The chapter examines musical, textual, and visual elements in the development of a translocal ethnoscape and mediascape within a global hip-hop culture.

Michael Jenson's chapter, "The Global Nomad: Navigating Mediated Space at a Global Scale," engages with the ways in which global communication technologies are eroding our traditional conceptual foundations of space. Jenson posits that many questions concerning our modern existence have emerged within contexts explicitly connected to the transformation of our spatial logic by the global media. He argues that the relevance of space to our quality of life rests on how we respond to the rapid transformation of our means to negotiate space by the increasingly powerful technologies of global mediation.

David Kenley's chapter, "Overseas Print Capitalism and Chinese Nationalism in the Early Twentieth Century," investigates the role the overseas Chinese press played in the nation-building process. It demonstrates the methods by which newspapers highlighted existing cultural codes and at the same time challenged concepts of collective national identity. The chapter examines the Chinese community in Tokyo, the role of San Francisco in the debate over Chinese national identity, and publications produced by Paris's diasporic Chinese population.

Part II: Entanglements of the Global, Regional, National, and Local

In the chapter, "Reading the i-pill Advertisement: The Pleasures and Pressures of Contemporary Contraceptive Advertising in India," Nayantara Sheoran focuses on the advertising campaign for one pharmaceutical product—the i-pill, an emergency contraceptive launched in India by Cipla, an Indian pharmaceutical company, in 2007. Sheoran argues that the campaign is symptomatic of a cultural shift in understandings of health and "self," contributing to a contradictory imagined identity for the contemporary Indian woman.

In "The Fetishistic Challenge: Things in Nineteenth-Century Danish Literature as Mediators of Identity," Frederike Felcht analyzes how "things" in nineteenth-century Scandinavian literature are signifiers of the global as well as mediators between local, regional, national, and global concepts of identity. As literature became part of a global market in the mid-nineteenth century to early twentieth century, it simultaneously played a central role in the formation of emergent national identities. The imaginary of the global was involved in these contestations, taking shape not as exotic locations or non-European Others, but in the world of things.

Based on ethnographic fieldwork at a television channel in Singapore, Ivan Kwek's chapter, "How Far to the Global? Producing Television at the Margins as Lived Experiences," considers how the global and regional are intertwined with the cultural politics behind the establishment of Surya, a minority Malay-language channel in Singapore, that was launched in 2000 by the state. The channel's producers, mostly ethnic Malays, are caught between regional affinities and the demands of the state. The chapter demonstrates how the global, regional, and local are contested terrains over which the marginality of a minority channel is produced or challenged.

The chapter, "Remediation and Scaling: The Making of 'Global' Identities," by Aalok Khandekar and Grant Jun Otsuki draws on an understanding of globalization as scale-making and the concept of remediation, that is, the simultaneous erasure of media through its multiplication. Khandekar and Otsuki examine two distinct sets of case studies that involve claims to global identities: among diasporic Indians and among Hapas (in North America). Through a critical focus on media portrayals of the global and local, the chapter illuminates how identities become universals through processes of "scale-making" and remediation.

Nolwenn Mingant's chapter, "A New Hollywood Genre: The Global–Local Film," examines the cultural consequences of globalization on the Hollywood majors and on the Hollywood big-budget film. Focusing on the "global–local film," Mingant argues that it combines traditional Hollywood elements such as stars, action-adventure, and special effects (which she terms the strategy of the spectacular) and foreign elements such as foreign themes, locations, actors, and director (which she terms the strategy of the familiar). The result is a more complex Hollywood film open to diverse interpretations and well adapted to the diversification of distribution channels.

Damien Stankiewicz's chapter, "The Discursive Disjunctions of Globalizing Media: Scalar Claims and Tensions at the French–German and European Television Channel ARTE," examines how television producers and programmers at the French–German and European television channel ARTE understand the channel's identity. There are two discourses of culture at ARTE: a predominantly European sense of high culture and a broader view of culture as an all-encompassing whole. The chapter examines whether ARTE opposes European culture to global culture, thus tying European identity to problematic notions of civilization.

Part III: Digital Mediations in the Global Era

Paul Longley Arthur in "Toward a Global Digital History" describes how technological innovation in the early twenty-first century is transforming the study of the past. Global interconnections enabled by digital media are a central factor in these transformations. People everywhere are studying the past with a new degree of sophistication and are using digital tools to tell their own stories and track their own histories. This is creating new sorts of primary documents that will form the records for future historians.

Hudson Moura, in the chapter, "Subtitling Jia Zhangke's Films: Intermediality, Digital Technology, and the Varieties of Foreignness in Global Cinema," examines the new possibilities that globalization and new technical filming devices bring to contemporary Chinese cinema. Jia Zhangke's films, such as *The World*, *Still Life*, *Dong*, *Useless*, and *24 City*, create a new approach to subjectivity in global cinema, which draw on the use of subtitles and digital media. This approach creates new narratives that correspond with the experiences of new generations living through and connecting via media.

The chapter, "Women Seeking Women: Identity Constructions in German and Taiwanese Online Personal Ads," by Matthew Heinz and Hsin-I Cheng analyzes the locality and universality of global queer discourse as manifested in LGBTQ personal ads posted on Web sites originating in Germany and Taiwan during the summers of 2003 and 2007. The authors argue that personal ads can be perceived as a discourse that encourages idiosyncratic linguistic expressions and representations, which are simultaneously molded by salient social and cultural values. Critically analyzing these ads may assist with discerning the dynamics of individual, social, and cultural ideology formations.

Radhika Gajjala, Anca Birzescu, and Franklin N. A. Yartey provide the final chapter, "Marketing Empowerment? Commodifying the 'Other' through Online Microfinance," in this volume. The chapter focuses on the online microfinance site, Kiva.org. The authors argue for the need to interrogate the marketing paradigm through transnational feminist lenses to critically explore development movements and social actors in developing countries who access and participate in online network cultures such as Kiva.

Conclusion

On November 26, 2008, an event, unfortunately all too familiar in the present, began unfolding—a terrorist attack on the city of Mumbai that would last for 3 days and that would kill and wound scores of people. It was obvious that the terrorists wanted not just international attention but also international *media* attention. Their choice of locations included highly visible symbols of the city: sites, such as the Taj Hotel, frequented by foreigners; an iconic local railway station; and a Jewish prayer house. Media coverage of the event was relentless. During the pitched battle between terrorists and Indian security forces, it was rumored that associates of the terrorists situated in Pakistan were drawing on the news coverage from Indian television channels and relaying information to the terrorists within the hotel.

Social media, such as blogs and Twitter, provided a steady stream of information that served as an alternative to both mainstream media and official state accounts. In the days that followed, the drama concerning the identity of the lone accused terrorist captured by Indian forces, Ajmal Amir Kasab, filled the pages of national dailies and exercised the imagination of bloggers, with the Pakistani state eventually confirming that he was a Pakistani national. In the *New York Times*, the Indian writer Amitav Ghosh commented on whether 26/11, as it came to be known, should be considered India's 9/11 or not, given that many in India were describing it as such.[37] The Indian media's reactions to the event ranged from nationalist hysteria to anguished soul-searching. Analysts offered any number of explanations from the tortured history of the subcontinent to the war in Iraq as reasons for the killings. These reactions inserted Indian politics, the actions of the terrorists, and the potential reaction of the Indian state into the global narrative of the war on terror.

14 • Rohit Chopra

The tragedy of 26/11, a commingling of political violence and identity politics in which global media became witness and interlocutor, may be seen as the antithesis to that other global media event a few weeks earlier, which appeared to so many as a moment of hope—the election victory of Barack Obama in the United States. These events are radically different instances of ways that networks and discourses of global media, culture, and identity constantly overlap, collide, and connect with each other. It is in the nature of the networks and discourses that the variables keep shifting in meaning, which makes them difficult to define and study. However, we may have no choice but to attempt to do so, if only to discern the ways in which these colliding and colluding networks and forces influence our lives. For we may then begin imagining a shared global culture, a conception of the common good, and a global media sensitive to such a vision of humanity.

Endnotes

1. "The Inauguration of President Barack Obama," *Boston Globe*, January 21, 2009, http://www.boston.com/bigpicture/2009/01/the_inauguration_of_president.html (accessed February 2, 2009).
2. Eugene Robinson, "The Moment for This Messenger?" *Washington Post*, March 13, 2007, http://www.washingtonpost.com/wp-dyn/content/article/2007/03/12/AR2007031200983.html (accessed January 19, 2007).
3. Ibid.
4. "Obama Race Speech," *Huffington Post*, March 18, 2008, http://www.huffingtonpost.com/2008/03/18/obama-race-speech-read-th_n_92077.html (accessed February 2, 2009).
5. Steve Erlanger, "After U.S. Breakthrough, Europe Looks in Mirror," *New York Times*, November 11, 2008, http://www.nytimes.com/2008/11/12/world/europe/12europe.html?_r=1&scp=3&sq=europe%20on%20obama%20victory&st=cse (accessed February 7, 2009).
6. Perry Bacon Jr., "Foes Use Obama's Muslim Ties to Fuel Rumors About Him," *Washington Post*, November 29, 2007, http://www.washingtonpost.com/wp-dyn/content/article/2007/11/28/AR2007112802757.html (accessed February 2, 2009).
7. Ben Smith, "Muslims Barred from Picture at Obama Event," *Politico*, June 18, 2006, http://www.politico.com/news/stories/0608/11168.html (accessed February 3, 2009).
8. Tony Bennett, Lawrence Grossberg, and Meaghan Morris, eds., *New Keywords: A Revised Vocabulary of Culture and Society* (Malden, MA: Blackwell, 2005), 63, emphasis in original. See the entry "Culture" at 63–9. See also "Culture" in Raymond Williams, *Keywords: A Vocabulary of Culture and Society*, rev. ed. (New York, NY: Oxford University Press, 1983), 87.
9. Frederick Cooper (with Rogers Brubakers), "Identity," in Frederick Cooper, *Colonialism in Question: Theory, Knowledge, History* (Berkeley: University of California Press, 2005), 83.
10. See the entry "Media" in Raymond Williams, *Keywords: A Vocabulary of Culture and Society*, rev. ed. (New York, NY: Oxford University Press, 1983), 203–4; "From Medium to Social Practice" in Raymond Williams, *Marxism and Literature* (New York, NY: Oxford University Press, 1977), 158–64; "Cinema and Socialism" in Raymond Williams, *Politics of Modernism: Against the New Conformists* (London: Verso, 2007), 107–18; "Culture and Technology" in Williams, *Politics of Modernism*, 119–39.
11. Williams, *Politics of Modernism*, 120–1.

12. An excellent selection of perspectives on globalization can be found in Frank J. Lechner and John Boli, eds., *The Globalization Reader*, 3rd ed. (Malden, MA: Blackwell, 2008).

13. For Wallerstein, the present, global, form of the world-system has its roots in the sixteenth century (55). Immanuel Wallerstein, "The Modern World-System as a Capitalist World-Economy," in *The Globalization Reader*, ed. Frank J. Lechner and John Boli, 3rd ed. (Malden, MA: Blackwell, 2008), 55–61. Robertson describes the period of roughly the 1870s to the mid-1920s as the "take-off period of modern globalization" (93). Ronald Robertson, "Globalization as a Problem," in *The Globalization Reader*, ed. Frank J. Lechner and John Boli, 3rd ed. (Malden, MA: Blackwell, 2008), 87–94. Appadurai observes that although the concept of the world as "a congeries of large-scale interactions for many centuries" is part of common academic knowledge, the global world is "an interactive system that is strikingly new" (27). Arjun Appadurai, *Modernity at Large: Cultural Dimensions of Globalization* (Minnesota: University of Minnesota Press, 1996), 27–47.

14. For a comprehensive and nuanced survey of perspectives on global media, see Emile McAnany, "Globalization and the Media: The Debate Continues," *Communication Research Trends* 21, no. 4 (2003): 3–19. For an empirically rich and theoretically robust mapping of key aspects of the global communications landscape, see chapter 5, "Communication and Cultural Globalization," in Daya Kishan Thussu, *International Communication: Continuity and Change* (London: Arnold, 2000), 167–99. For a discussion of cultural imperialism, see John Tomlinson, *Cultural Imperialism: A Critical Introduction* (Baltimore, MD: Johns Hopkins Press, 1991).

15. David Morley, "Globalisation and Cultural Imperialism Reconsidered: Old Questions in New Guises," in *Media and Cultural Theory*, ed. James Curran and David Morley (New York, NY: Routledge, 2006), 30–42.

16. Annabelle Sreberny-Mohammadi, "The Many Cultural Faces of Imperialism," in *Beyond Cultural Imperialism: Globalization, Communication and the New International Order*, ed. Peter Golding and Phil Harris (London: Sage, 1997), 49–68.

17. Ibid.

18. Oliver Boyd-Barrett, "Media Imperialism Reformulated," in *Electronic Empires: Global Media and Local Resistance*, ed. Daya Kishan Thussu (London: Arnold, 1998), 157–76.

19. Robert J. C. Young, *Postcolonialism: An Historical Introduction* (Oxford: Blackwell, 2001), 167–81, 308–11. For a postcolonial critique of Marxism, see Edward Said, *Orientalism* (New York, NY: Vintage, 1994), 153–6.

20. Ella Shohat and Robert Stam, *Unthinking Eurocentrism: Multiculturalism and the Media* (New York: Routledge, 1994), 3, 13–54.

21. Ibid., 7, 8, 46–59.

22. Ibid., 37–46.

23. Raka Shome and Radha S. Hegde, "Postcolonial Approaches to Communication: Charting the Terrain, Engaging the Intersections," in *International Communication: A Reader*, ed. Daya Kishan Thussu (New York, NY: Routledge, 2010), 91–2.

24. Moya Luckett, "Postnational Television: *Goodness Gracious Me* and the Britasian Diaspora," in *Planet TV: A Global Television Reader*, ed. Lisa Parks and Shanti Kumar (New York: New York University Press, 2003), 402–22.

25. James Schwoch, "Television, Chechnya, and National Identity after the Cold War: Whose Imagined Community?" in *Planet TV: A Global Television Reader*, ed. Lisa Parks and Shanti Kumar (New York: New York University Press, 2003), 226–42.

26. Ibid., 230.

27. Jean-François Lyotard, *The Postmodern Condition: A Report on Knowledge*, trans. Geoff Bennington and Brian Massumi (Minneapolis: University of Minnesota, 1984); Jean Baudrillard, *Jean Baudrillard, Selected Writings*, ed. Mark Poster (Stanford, CA: Stanford University Press, 1988); Michel Foucault, *The Order of Things: An Archaeology of the Human Sciences*, 2nd ed. (New York, NY: Routledge, 2001); Michel Foucault, *Discipline*

and Punish: The Birth of the Prison, 2nd ed. (New York, NY: Vintage, 1995); Jacques Derrida, *Of Grammatology*, trans. Gayatri Chakravorty Spivak (Baltimore, MA: Johns Hopkins University Press, 1998); Pierre Bourdieu, *On Television*, trans. Priscilla Parkhurst Ferguson (New York, NY: The New Press, 1999).

28. Foucault eschews the idea of the "human" as the subject and object of history. I am not arguing that Foucault denies agency to human subjects. A detailed discussion of Foucauldian politics is beyond the scope of this introduction, but the point may be made that politics in Foucault are configured in a manner that does not require a conception of the human agent.

29. Foucault, *History of Sexuality*, Vol. 1 (New York, NY: Vintage, 1990), 8–13, 68–73.

30. Appadurai, *Modernity at Large*, 35.

31. Manuel Castells, *The Rise of the Network Society*, 2nd ed. (Oxford: Blackwell, 2000).

32. Ibid., 442.

33. Ibid., 442, 443, 436.

34. Shohat and Stam, *Unthinking Eurocentrism*, 6–7. Appadurai argues that the twin forces of electronic mediation and mass migration significantly structure the dynamics of global cultural economy (2–11). The theoretical proposition presented here applies to the media and cultural identity more broadly, with due acknowledgment of Appadurai's point about the significance of electronic mediation in global media flows and of migratory and diasporic communities in shaping of cultural identities in the present.

35. Madhur Singh, "*Slumdog Millionaire*, an Oscar Favorite, Is No Hit in India," *Time*, January 26, 2009, http://www.time.com/time/arts/article/0,8599,1873926,00.html (accessed May 11, 2009).

36. Hannah Ingberger Win, "'Slumdog Millionaire' Payment Controversy Provokes Union Debate," *Huffington Post*, January 28, 2009, http://www.huffingtonpost.com/2009/01/28/slumdog-millionaire-payme_n_161954.html (accessed May 11, 2009).

37. Amitav Ghosh, "India's 9/11? Not Exactly," *New York Times*, December 2, 2008, http://www.nytimes.com/2008/12/03/opinion/03ghosh.html (accessed February 4, 2010).

PART I

Geographies and Currents of Global Media and Identity

CHAPTER 2

Endemic Reporting

Calibrating the "News" and "Normal Disease"

CINDY PATTON

Chapter Description

Critiques of the media coverage of the 2009–2010 H1N1 flu season identi-fied poor terminology ("swine flu") and sensational reporting of isolated cases as the potential cause of public misunderstanding and/or failure to adopt precautions. In addition, conspiracy theorists argued that govern-ment officials had erroneously declared an epidemic to aid drug companies in marketing their flu vaccines and medications. Aligned with a social stud-ies in medicine approach, this chapter considers changes in the medical-reporting industry in the context of the evolving role of internet sources in promulgating medical information. These may have contributed to some poor reporting, but this chapter argues that the major problem was not at the level of factual errors but at the level of misunderstanding, and therefore failing to explain, how disease modeling and epidemic monitoring occurs.

* * *

The New York Times, January 4, 2010. Although it is too early to write the obituary for swine flu, medical experts, already assessing how the first pan-demic in 40 years has been handled, have found that although luck played a part, a series of rapid but conservative decisions by federal officials worked out better than many had dared hope.

Imagined Reporter: Influenza. What a stupid, boring disease! How to make news out of a common ailment? "Vaccine time again!" . . . blah! Didn't millions die of flu in 1918? That was News! Maybe this is only the beginning . . . Let's treat public health officials' early assessment of potential for an unusual flu season as the beginning of a catastrophe. Win-win, either death beyond imaging or proof that government scientists are in control of our fate.

Mainstream coverage of H1N1, the preferred scientific name of the 2009–2010 influenza strain, fell prey to many of the same explanatory failures that characterized AIDS coverage of the 1980s and 1990s, reportage heavily criticized in cultural studies of media, and which has served as a negative case study for student journalists ever since.[1] Although there is much to say about these flaws, the focus of this chapter is the underlying conceptual problems that reporters either cause or fail to correct. In particular, reporters' confusion about how epidemiologic modeling is accomplished and how local epidemiology is incorporated into meso-scale models, which are then used by global health management organizations such as the World Health Organization (WHO), the Red Cross/Red Crescent, and Doctors Without Borders/Medecine Sans Frontier, resulted in: intermittently hysterical reporting on single, local cases; unfounded critique of government actions; and claims that those very actions had staved off an epidemic that reporters themselves extrapolated from their own hysterical reporting on the individual cases.

The increasingly diminished ranks of medical writers who tried to explain the flu undermined their credibility through misuse of technical terms, exacerbated by "viral" communication forms that provided quicker updates and a vast terrain on which science skeptics could criticize both reporters and the government. To some extent, reporters' problem was that endemic disease is not really news, but it might be the baseline for future news: missing the opening salvo of a severe acute respiratory syndrome-like incident or a massive-casualty flu epidemic would be professional suicide. But, spread thin to cover a wide range of medical stories, reporters in the new millennium must be vigilant to avoid becoming recyclers of slick drug company press releases. Not only must medical reporters understand the science behind the disease but also they must understand drug approval and marketing processes. In theory, editorial processes serve as a check on reportorial exuberance (and ambition). However, in the 1980s, three changes in the traditional editorial structure of newspapers and of medical/scientific journals degraded the credibility of popular medical reporting: (1) increased role of wire services; (2) fast-tracking of research on particular disease scenarios in medical/scientific journals, essentially lowering the threshold of certainty for published research on those topics; and (3) the advent of niche market desktop publishing.

First, there was a shift in the role of wire services,[2] which had once enabled small town and regional newspapers to get credible national and international news for their pages, but still retain their focus on local angles, issues, and events. This relationship had some reciprocity: wire services enlisted local reporters as stringers to cover stories that could then be shaped and sent out to small- or medium-sized papers around the world. But as national, regional, and international conglomerates (most famously, Rupert Murdoch's empire) bought smaller entities and folded them into, essentially, news franchises, the idea of a direct relationship between "localizable" newspapers and "local" sources broke down, and the wire service—with no fixed locale and a mix of staff and stringers scattered around the world—became the model for newspaper reporting in general. The editorial function remained intact through this deterritorialization of reporting but created two new problems. Because the relationship between writer and editor was now more often virtual, editor's role as enforcer of journalism's professional standards declined. With fewer crusty editors yelling across the newsroom floor to sharpen the skills of potentially brilliant young reporters, the relationship between editorial staff and reporters became more marketized: naïve reporters wanted to sell their stories but were isolated from the newsroom habitus that only sometimes now turns writers into reporters. Second, news was now automatically conduited to multiple newspapers simultaneously, and with fewer reporters and editors of the traditional ethos on the receiving end, the process of adding local information to global stories—sometimes with almost no fact-checking or rewrite at the receiving outlet—enabled initially well-crafted news to be badly reframed.

The editorial function at major medical and science journals also changed, although in relationship to different pressures. Citing the quick research response to Legionnaire's disease in 1976, and toxic shock syndrome in 1978, AIDS activists and AIDS researchers implored scientific journals to streamline the process of publishing promising research results on the new disease syndrome. In fact, in the case of Legionnaire's disease, several journals had actually decided to fast-track research on that topic. Using that experience as a positive precedent,[3] the journals lowered the threshold for publication of AIDS-related research, a change widely debated at AIDS conferences, but little understood outside the initially small circle of clinicians and researchers working in the field. As Steven Epstein (1998) elaborates in his *Impure Science*, the effect of the streamlining was simultaneously to raise hopes for those with the new disease and their clinicians and to create a sense among activists that they could intervene in the scientific process, perhaps forever altering the dynamic process of establishing scientific credibility.

Finally, the miniaturization of computers enabled medical writer/ entrepreneurs to launch cost-effective specialty medical newsletters aimed primarily at professionals in technical and minor applied research areas whose interests were not represented in the major medical and research discipline-based journals. These newsletters primarily recycled stories from press releases, and although they often included greater detail to explain how particular innovations or discoveries were relevant to the target biomedical/technical audience, writers were rarely in a position to challenge suspect research outside their own area of expertise. In the context of the large journals' lowered standards for publishing research on specific diseases and the devolution of reporting to wire services and stringers, the rise of desktop medical specialty publishing enabled a potential multiplier effect in the (mis)construction of scientific facts: the same press release might generate parallel stories in different kinds of journals, which newsletter writers used to check or second-source their own stories. This created the appearance of independent verification, when, in fact, all the sources could be traced to a single source. Elsewhere (Patton forthcoming), I have documented a particularly extreme example of this process, made worse by the cross-over between biomedical and social science. In this case, a series of press-release rewrites of a small (and methodologically dubious) study of crystal methamphetamine effects appeared widely in small specialty newsletters and a few newspapers. A close examination of the least rewritten shows us tell-tale original language that appears in slightly different form in more rewritten versions, some of which contain quotes that reporters acquired, apparently, by calling the researcher. These quotes go far beyond the conclusions that could be supported by the actual study (available in a fairly obscure academic journal). Those comments were then taken up in bigger stories, as if the study supported these "facts," which were then widely circulated in policy circles, so that bureaucrats were soon quoting these facts as if unequivocally true. No further citation of the original study or its author for readers was now needed, and it became quite difficult to track down the source of these facts, which were astonishingly and quickly merged with folklore about gay men and crystal meth.

Local News, Global Science

- WHO works with a wide range of individuals to obtain the input needed for WHO to address public health issues. WHO has systems in place to safeguard against potential conflicts of interest by experts in its advisory groups.

- WHO requires all experts advising the organization to declare all professional and financial interests, including funding received from pharmaceutical companies or consultancies or other forms of professional involvement with pharmaceutical companies. This information is shared with other members of the advisory group and taken into account by WHO in determining whether the experts concerned should continue to provide advice to the organization.
- Allegations of undeclared conflicts of interest are taken very seriously by WHO, and investigated immediately.

(January 11, 2010 WHO Press Release responding to allegations by European member states that the H1N1 epidemic was "faked")

It might seem that issues related to American media and American scientific journals are a parochial matter, but they have global implications. Calculating research output is difficult, not least because some discoveries represent a huge leap in knowledge, whereas most represent only modest refinements of the "already known," and thus an article or conference presentation of the same "size" may represent more or less work, more or less net gain in knowledge. Nevertheless, using as crude a measure as articles published, several authors have tried to identify where the centers of research productivity are located. Most authors (e.g., May 2009), regardless of research strategy, identify the United States as the single largest producer of scientific knowledge at about one-third of all articles over the past three decades or about the same volume as the next five countries combined (United Kingdom, Japan, Germany, France, and Russia). A similar analysis (National Science Board 2004) of publication trends showed a higher percentage in those years (38%), with a flattening of the US production between 1995 and 2004, but still shows the United States at 30% of the world's research publication volume at 2004. These broad stroke trends are important to consider, because they suggest that not only does the United States have a large scientific workforce and (capitalist style) investment in research and development but also the method of scientific proof—refuting established research with new research or replicating accepted work in new contexts—means that the United States both holds down a high volume of big ticket "truths" (e.g., major research findings representing leaps in knowledge) and is able to cast a wide net to chip away at problems that represent smaller increases in knowledge. To claim a corner of world scientific output, all the other countries must contest the knowledge developed (if not in its initial breakthrough, then in its phase of refinement) generated by a single dominant player.

But the US-centrism in the volume of medical publication is even more complicated in the context of global exchange of scientific information, disregarding a reader's ability to understand scientific information. Even the most nimble fingered internet searcher can access only a small proportion of this official scientific output because most academic and quasi-academic journals require subscriptions or membership at a university that holds an institutional subscription. Although non-US scientists are producing their work against the tide of US research empire dominance (intertwined with the work product of transnational pharmaceutical companies), their publics are indirectly accessing the debate about science that is occurring outside formal channels. This includes not only the detailed definition of terms and explanations of biochemical and biomechanical processes that underlie diseases, which are helpful to readers anywhere, but it also includes writings of science skeptics and conspiracy theorists. There is no more poignant example than that of South Africa's former President Mbeki, who decided to take up the work of Peter Duesberg, the most famous of the scientist conspiracy theorists who believe that AIDS is not caused by HIV, or that if it is, that HIV was invented in a US biological weapons lab. Mbeki defied his own board of medical advisors and blocked the implementation of what would likely have been epidemic-mitigating policies—both anti-HIV drug dispensing and safe sex campaigns. Similar accusations[4] surround the origin and probable deadliness of H1N1, although there do not seem to have been any countries that blocked WHO recommendations based on these conspiracy theories.

Science and health science educators have developed a sophisticated mix of Web resources, incorporating an earlier generation of simplified health promotion messages by adding reference pages that can be navigated as user-driven curriculum. Careful searchers who regard their universities and governments as generally reliable sources of this type of information can fairly and readily identify these Web sites, although conspiracy theorists sometimes create logos and domain names that resemble those of "official" sources. Government and university Web sites are often primary and referenced sources for information found on Wikipedia, widely recognized as at least the equivalent of the old fashioned print encyclopedia, only faster with updates and new topics, and space for scientifically controversial materials to be signaled by contributors. This openness of the internet allows for a kind of "third way": the location of quite a lot of "science-based" science but with a room for antagonistic points of view, from science skeptics (creationists, etc.) to science conspiracy theorists (left and right wingers who accept science's science but believe that government twists facts to suit political or capitalist ends or that government manufactures germs for use against its other or its own population). University and government information is fairly and internally consistent—"scientific"—and antagonists more often attack these sources than do official scientists respond to their critics, rendering the challengers more scattered than their targets. To some extent, the challengers try to mimic the ongoing and vital debates about scientific fact that occurs within conventional scientific proof processes, which include the use of verifiable procedures and review by journal or grant committees of scientific peers; they see themselves as bringing debate about science (if less often "scientific debate") into the public domain. But few internet perusers have the training in the history and philosophy of scientific verification that would enable them to make sense of the challengers, who do not have the means to independently reproduce studies and, thus, can only attack studies' methods or rely on the research of renegade scientists who are outside the routines of "normal science."[5]

In this open sea of translated science, challenge, and, recently, counter-challenge, it is quite easy for Web searchers to get conflicting information that they have little or no background to sort through. Thus, although the WHO's (2010) anti-disinformation campaign press releases—unique in the speed at which they sought to defend the science behind their policies—were forceful, immediate, and, on my reading, credible, the biggest problem was not information and disinformation but failure to correct the confused or erroneous background assumptions and concepts that direct (if not determine) *how* individuals interpret facts that they discover online.

Some blogs include spaces for readers to interact with the bloggers and other readers—many of whom have a fairly high degree of science knowledge, including credible academic degrees—allowing for discussion of scientific assumptions and ethical responsibility by people with some science training. But unlike, say, the letters to the editors pages in a science or medical journal, which serve the role of giving space to alternative theories by publishing the opinions of credentialed skeptics, blogs frequently devolve into *ad hominem* attacks on the intelligence of individuals or on their ability to do "good science." Avid readers of such blogs (some written as follow-ups to mainstream science writers' own print articles) probably gravitate toward the assumptions explicitly or implicitly promoted by their favorite blog writers, anchoring an interpretive framework for any actual information offered by that blog writer. Thus, bloggers writing against conspiracy theories have to grapple with the understanding of biology and of the relationship of science to government held by the conspiracy theorists; those responding to a *New York Times* science writer have to trade in questions of access to official science and whether newspapers (with their financial ties to advertisers) have reason to lie, situationally or in general. We might say that when information is offered on these two different kinds of blogs, the reader has to gain interpretive traction against the tide of an underlying battle over expertise. Individuals who only intermittently search the Web for information about a disease they fear they might get do not necessarily take the time to read through blogs; most likely, they gravitate toward what appear to be self-help sites, recognizable by quick access to superficial facts, with structured links to more complex information. Naïve searchers may not quickly recognize the tropism of health sites that are either very close to government policy makers or very close to science skeptics and conspiracy theorists.

Bad Words or Bad Ideas?

Self-critique by reporters, analyses in the professional journalism press, and corrective educational seminars for reporters hosted by health agencies focused on two issues: languaging problems, mainly the use of swine flu rather than the technical term H1N1, and sensationalism in reporting on individual cases, which most critics believed stemmed from novice reporters' lack of understanding of disease monitoring processes. Underlying these critiques and the consensus about how to "fix" the medical reporting problem is an assumption that disease on both the individual and global level is transparently real (as opposed to a complex socioscientific construction of a biochemical phenomenon made visible through scientific tests, voiced experience of symptoms, and shared notions of the nature of disease) and that reporters' sole obligation is to be accurate and objective. This understanding of the translation problem in science (just as a matter of providing the common term for the scientific one) flies in the face of almost a century of philosophical, theoretical, and empirical research on the construction of facts within science, on the modes of proof and falsification in the several research sciences, and on the nature and feasibility of explaining "expert" knowledge to "public" minds.[6] Even if we look only at recent research on viral and viral-like infections, one can hardly argue that reporters simply got the story right or wrong, because scientific disciplines themselves (especially genomics, informatics, and virology) are subdividing and morphing into new research areas. For example, proteomics is the new, "post-genomics" subdiscipline that studies the nature and function of proteins. A subset of these proteins are classified as virus or virus-like matter, creating multiple confusions for lay persons, who imagine a protein to be a substance to build muscles, and who were likely taught in high school that viruses are not "alive" in the same way as bacteria or protozoa because they cannot independently reproduce. But after the advent of genomics, we now know that viruses sustain their lines by inserting themselves into the genetic material of other organisms, sometimes attaching to bacteria, sometimes to humans, cows, pigs, and so on. For protemicists, that counts as alive.

For them, the current "nonliving" biological matter is the hypothesized prion—a hunk of protein lacking DNA or RNA and, thus, incapable of distinguishing self from nonself; under this understanding, "living" is defined as self-knowing rather than reproducing independently, an interesting philosophical point for those who like to make moral analogies from nature. A prion is the hypothesized agent in Bovine Spongiform Encephalopathy (BSE)—a still poorly understood syndrome whose reportage was also horribly flawed and is probably one of the backdrops against which frightened readers interpret the term swine flu in the current round of disease stories. But unlike the concerted and largely successful media effort to turn "mad cow" disease into BSE, swine flu remains, well, swine flu.

Endemic, Epidemic, and Pandemic

The tiny virus (a material entity) and the gigantic epidemic (a statistical simulation) each operate at their own speed and in incommensurable spaces; they are intercepted and complicated on the cellular level by vaccines and treatments and on the global/virtual level by information campaigns and conflicting mandates from national versus supra-national health authorities. All-too-close and inconceivably far, the cellular and global are complexly knit together with a wide range of distance-management practices—from covering one's mouth and washing one's hands to border closures and quarantine—and discourses—from associating disease with particular places or animals to incorporating culturally and historically laden terms such as "epidemic" and "pandemic" without regard for their technical meaning in the health sciences. As we saw in the opening quote, media sources such as the *Times* invent the problem—an epidemic—that they ultimately report as solved, and they do this by failing to distinguish between common and technical meanings of the term epidemic.

In common parlance, epidemic means "a lot of cases" (e.g., "an epidemic of home invasions") or, more poetically, "an onslaught" of some collective malady ("an epidemic of bad driving"). Similarly, pandemic is hazily used to suggest something even bigger and more extensive than an epidemic. While capturing the idea of the sudden appearance of something unwanted on either a medium or gigantic scale, epidemic and pandemic have quite specific definitions in the world of population health. From the scientific point of view, an epidemic is more cases in a defined group or community or area than expected within a defined time period. Although the idea of epidemic arose in the eighteenth century in relationship to infectious diseases (in particular, cholera, typhoid, and malaria), the term is currently used by the US Centers for Disease Control (CDC) and other disease monitoring bodies and researchers to describe socio-pathological phenomena other than infectious diseases, for example, environmentally linked cancers, obesity, and, controversially, violence.

It is important to pause here and consider the significance of the reality that declaring an epidemic depends on an expectation, on a model of what is the normal occurrence of a disease. How far out of the norm the case count must go depends on the character of the disease as well as on the type of people perceived to be subjected to a disease. For emergent disease (e.g., "new," mystery, or reoccurant but once eradicated diseases), even very small numbers are cause for intensive investigation and declaration of an epidemic. But deciding that observed cases are "more than expected" also depends on who gets the disease. AIDS provides a good example (Patton 1985, 1990): in 1978, there was a spike in cases of pneumonia among drug injectors in New York City, a phenomenon that was noticed but not extensively investigated. The phenomenon was given a name—"junky pneumonia"—but because drug injectors were perceived to be routinely susceptible to respiratory ailments, the increased incidence did not trigger concern about an epidemic. Only a few years later, a tiny number of otherwise healthy gay men in several cities suddenly became very sick and died of pneumonia. If the doctors who saw these patients had held right-wing views about homosexuality—that they were physically inferior and susceptible to disease—then it is unlikely that what we now recognize as the AIDS epidemic would have been reported so early in its trajectory. But liberal doctors who viewed their gay patients as healthy adults could find no explanation for their patients' health decline and quickly reported these cases to the CDC. Thus, in identifying and defining AIDS, the perceived health status of those affected was an important part of the "expectation" about whether new disease should be investigated as an epidemic.

Scientists who devote their research to modelling influenza consider the disease endemic but with the potential to become epidemic. For influenza—caused by a class of viruses that vary in their attack characteristics—the number of cases must exceed by a statistically significant amount the modeled fluctuations, which include factors such as incubation period, mechanism and rate of spread, success rate of treatments, and environmental factors (can the etiologic agent survive on surfaces, in the water or ground under the heat, cold, or humidity of the environment?). Influenza is a cyclical disease that routinely results in death and sick days in vulnerable groups. Modelers consider both the morbidity (sickness that disrupts normal life) and mortality of influenza to determine total cost of disease, as well as monitoring changes in the ratio of sickness to death. This is an important aspect of modeling the expectation of endemic diseases caused by multiple strains of an agent because higher or lower ratios can predict epidemics—a higher death to illness rate may indicate a particularly virulent strain of influenza, whereas a lower death to illness rate might indicate a longer incubation period, and hence, if infections are not checked, an epidemic further down the road.

Therefore, despite reporters' implications that public health officials were either alarmist or pandering to drug companies when they equivocated about declaring an H1N1 epidemic, disease monitoring is a rather complex matter. If we want to evaluate how difficult taking such a decision might be, we need to only look at the 2009 North American flu season. For example, it is easy to look at the information that public health officials were evaluating, as they considered the differences between Fall 2009 and a "normal" flu season.[7] Among the charts and graphs in the reports from the CDC, we see one with parallel wave-like lines, representing the "seasonal baseline" and "epidemic threshold" for pneumonia and influenza death. These are the normal deaths attributed to these two complaints, which are symptomatically similar (many diseases are described as "flu-like" or having symptoms similar to flu—in fact, early HIV cases were described in this way) and, thus, must be confirmed by medical testing, to differentiate individuals who might have pneumonia (a syndrome, which may be caused by bacteria, protozoa, or fungi) from those who might have influenza (a more specific disease with a narrower range of etiologies, all of which are viruses). How do the scientists decide when there are more cases than expected beyond applying a threshold number by rote? Scientists adjust their models to be more sensitive to information about specific viruses (this year, H1N1) that differ in who they affect, how likely the infected are to infect others, how long it takes the virus to go from infecting to replicating and being available to infect another host, and how quickly vaccines can protect those who have not yet been infected.[8] At the global level, the confusion about what an epidemic is impeded the WHO's ability to promulgate recommendations—there is a technical definition of pandemic, too, that relies on even more complex statistical modeling than epidemics, and is complicated by the fact that "world health" is administered on a geopolitical basis by "health regions."[9] Inattentive science reporting in 2005 meant that very few reporters had followed the innovations in flu tracking by competing modeling teams, so public health officials in 2009 debated which model was most appropriate for H1N1. Reporters (and some public health officials) reported (erroneously) that the WHO had changed its disease model, opening the door for conspiracy theorists to claim that the WHO had caved into the pharmaceutical industry, which wanted to hype the flu to sell more tamiflu and flu vaccine. Lost in this claim was the very interesting story (reported widely in the medical press during the summer of 2009) of how innovations in theoretical statistics and increasingly sophisticated means of testing for influenza enabled researchers to propose more fine grained estimates—models—of number of flu cases per flu death, adjustable for the different endemic and epidemic behavior of different forms of influenza.

The WHO, navigating the differences in disease surveillance systems—which are partly international collaborations among scientists—and health response infrastructures that are under the aegis of sovereign nations of varying capacities, developed a fairly narrow definition of pandemic, which emphasizes space as a marker of time. Dealing only with infectious disease, the WHO telescopes the scientific definition of epidemic outward in a series of phases. A pandemic as an infectious disease with documented "human–human spread" in

> at least two countries in one WHO region. While most countries will not be affected at this stage, the declaration of Phase 5 is a strong signal that a pandemic is imminent and that the time to finalize the organization, communication, and implementation of the planned mitigation measures is short.
>
> (WHO 2010)

The big debate at the WHO—and the thing for which it was criticized—was the decision to declare H1N1 "Phase 6" pandemic, that is "characterized by community level outbreaks in at least one other country in a different WHO region in addition to the criteria defined in Phase 5. Designation of this phase will indicate that a global pandemic is under way." It is not surprising that there might be controversy surrounding this decision, which triggered both national responses (which might include border closures, quarantine, and other civilly problematic public health actions) and supranational activation of drug company production and government and nongovernment organization distribution networks. But reporters did virtually nothing to explain the complexity of extrapolating a natural phenomenon (an epidemic disease) over unnaturally—geopolitically—divided space. Declaring a pandemic is both contingent on and wholly different than declaring an epidemic: to declare pandemic, you must have more cases than expected (dots on a map of disease) that are superimposed on the artificial geography that is the WHO's regional health administration system, these contingent on European colonial and postcolonial history in Europe and Africa and on Japanese, British, and American imperial history in the American and Pacific Rim.

Are There Real People in This Population?

The failure to adequately explain the relationship between disease modeling, disease observation, and the declaration of an epidemic and pandemic enabled the conditions for an exaggerated initial story that invoked the 1918 flu pandemic. Reporters did not explain that to a great extent, the H1N1 epidemic was declared based on the early timing of flu deaths and not on a large number of deaths. It is still anyone's guess what effect government action had in North America and elsewhere—this will be an interesting modeling question to be put to statisticians in years to come. But the larger question is the relationship between "real people" and "real disease." Epidemiologists do not deal with real people, they offer maps of the movement of disease across bodies: we are all just dots holding "disease" in place on a larger simulation of germ vectors. We need epidemiologists and sensible public health agents to interpret what they see. But in order for their science to help people, we need reporters who can translate the meaning of science, giving us sufficient background information to interpret what we can, and the confidence in their abilities to accept as credible what we cannot evaluate on our own. In the H1N1 case, what we got was reporting that tried to make a sensational story out of a reality that was alarming for those who "got the flu" but was fairly remote for the rest of us. Instead of trying to convince us that washing our hands and covering our mouths was sufficient against a 1918-like wave of disease, reporters might have just calmly explained how the scientists know what they know, and how most of us can use simple daily procedures to calmly minimize our risk. But then, that is not news.

Endnotes

1. One could develop a full syllabus of cultural studies work of the first decade and a half of the AIDS epidemic. Of particular note is the work on media, including Simon Watney's *Policing Desire: Pornography, AIDS, and the Media* (London: Cassell, 1986), my *Inventing AIDS* (New York, NY: Routledge, 1990), and Douglas Crimp, "AIDS: Cultural Analysis, Cultural Activism," the special issue of *October*, 43 (1987); Paula Triechler's *How to Have Theory in an Epidemic: Cultural Chronicles of AIDS* (Durham, NC: Duke University Press, 1999) would be a good starting point for understanding how several branches of the emergent field of cultural studies intertwined to provide a coherent analysis of the early phases of the first modern pandemic of a new disease.

2. Wire services have a long and very interesting history, rooted in the development of the telegraph in the mid-1800s. Reuters, established in London by a German entrepreneur, was the first international wire service and is owned by the global conglomerate Thompson. Associated Press (AP), in the United States, was established as a cooperative with subscribing newspapers and remains independent today. AP launched an iPhone news feed application in 2008, reestablishing the direct relationship between news writers and readers that characterized the earliest newspapers. The Scripts newspaper property called United Press (UP) emerged in 1907 when the older AP refused to syndicate to Scripts newspapers. In 1958, UP bought the comparable Hearst papers wire service—International News Service— and formed United Press International (UPI). In 2000, UPI was sold to the Unification Church, which had been acquiring US media outlets for two decades.

3. Toxic shock syndrome (TSS), though not fast tracked, might have served as a cautionary counterexample, because much of the early and widely reported research proved to be incorrect. Indeed, TSS is now one among many targets of the science conspiracy theorists.

4. Conspiracy theorist and retired nurse Shelley Penney, who hosts her own Web site (www. SwineFlu-Information.com), says:

> The longer we have observed the FAUX-pandemic the more convinced I am that this was a virus, genetically engineered and dropped in Mexico City. The likelihood is that it was released in a busy mall, arena, or station somewhere where there were a LOT of people.

5. Thomas Kuhn argued that, within science, there are periods of time when almost all scientists accept a theoretical framework as correct and largely work within it—what he calls normal science—and rare periods of time when basic assumptions are up for grabs—what he calls "scientific revolution." See Thomas Kuhn, *The Structure of Scientific Revolutions*, 3rd ed. (Chicago: University of Chicago Press, 1996).

6. There is a lively debate about how scientists learn to "think like" scientists and how knowledge mediators—educators, reporters, and so on—identify cultural metaphors for explaining scientific concepts. Much of the current poststructuralist work in this area is influenced by Ludwick Fleck's posthumously rediscovered *The Genesis and Development of a Scientific Fact*, written in the 1930s but only available in the late 1970s. Fleck argues that scientists form a community of thinking which possesses a "thoughtstyle" (a concept he may have drawn from Karl Mannheim's German writings). Becoming a member of an "expert culture" entails incrementally coming to see specialized concepts as natural and real. Extending this framework to consider how the public relates to expert knowledge, researchers in the Social Study of Science and Medicine (including myself) suggest that knowledge mediators are neither fully within the expert culture nor the public culture, but rather haphazardly (if sincerely) try to find metaphors that link expert and public conceptualizations. In this way, for example, newspaper writers ought to have immediately realized that calling H1N1 swine flu would unhelpfully agitate cultural memory of the 1978 swine flu vaccine debacle (when the vaccine was alleged—probably incorrectly—of killing people who took it).

7. The CDC provides a weekly flu update: www.cdc.gov/flu/weekly; I wrote this essay initially in relationship to the update reviewing cases through week 51—December 26, 2009—because this seems to be the report to which the *Times* writer refers. However, the epidemiologic curves did not change in the subsequent months.

8. Even vaccination is complicated by the social factors that make up infection rates: officials target vaccination to particular groups both because some people are more susceptible to dramatic sequelae of disease (e.g., death) and because some groups are able to indirectly protect those who were not vaccinated. For example, a health care worker is highly likely to become infected but also to pass on an infection to highly susceptible people (because they work directly with vulnerable persons). In addition, some groups automatically remove themselves from settings where they may infect others—adults often simply go home, but college students do not, creating mini-epidemics so often seen on campuses. Reciprocally, parents of young children—especially young children in day care who are exposed to many other young children—have higher rates of infection with common diseases than non-parents. Therefore, social mobility is a major consideration in modeling infection rates and calculating vaccination rates. From an individual point of view, vaccination usually prevents (or mitigates) disease. But from a population health point of view, vaccination intends to reduce disease across a population. Modelers try to predict the percentage of and type of people who need to be vaccinated to achieve "herd immunity," that is, to reduce the level of an etiologic agent below the threshold where it will be commonly encountered.

9. I have written extensively elsewhere about the geopolitics and health administration problems that result from the need to divide the world's health by government and region. In short, the regions are not constructed using the same definition, so that, for example, Europe is a single health region, whereas Africa is divided in two, with Asia housing three different regions. See Patton, *Globalizing AIDS* (2002).

CHAPTER 3

The Mediascape of Hip-Wop
Alterity and Authenticity in Italian American Rap

JOSEPH SCIORRA*

Chapter Description

This chapter examines the musical, textual, and visual elements of contemporary rap music produced by Italian American artists. "Hip-wop" practitioners have forged their artistic personae from the alluring gangster image—the dominant narrative of the Italian experience in the United States in the popular imagination—found at the confluence of film, television, music, and the Internet. Italian American rappers make a proprietary and authoritative claim to the gangster figure in an attempt to negotiate their positions as "white rappers" within a musical form associated with and dominated by African Americans. Claims of authenticity are reinforced through a series of cultural references that include the Italian language, Italian musical styles, and other objects and behaviors that contribute

*This essay greatly benefited from the comments I received after presenting earlier versions at conferences sponsored by the American Folklore Society, the American Italian Historical Association, the American Studies Association, and the John D. Calandra Italian American Institute. I would like to thank Lisa Cicchetti, Lucia Grillo, and Carmine Pizzirusso of the Calandra Institute for their generous assistance in preparing the PowerPoint component of my conference papers and Tommaso Cuccia, a former Calandra Institute intern, who assisted me. I am grateful to Rosangela Briscese, Thomas Ferraro, John Gennari, Goffredo Plastino, and Laura Ruberto for their insightful critiques to earlier versions. To all the artists who provided me with material and answered my endless questions, *grazie mille*.

to the establishment of an Italian American Hip-hop sensibility. Finally, these artists are attuned to the possibilities of deterritorialized affiliations, as they use the Internet to communicate and collaborate in a youth centric, transnational dialogue of reinvented community that forges a diasporic consciousness linking points on a global Italian cartography.

* * *

Louie: Yeah. He calls himself Ghost Dog. I don't know, a lot of these black guys today, these gangster type guys, they all got names like that they make up for themselves.

Ray: Is that true?

Sonny: Sure. He means like the rappers. You know, the rappers, they all got names like that: Snoop Doggy Dogg, Ice Cube, Q-Tip, Method Man. My favorite was always Flavor Flav from Public Enemy. You got the funky fresh fly flavor. "Live lyrics from the bank of reality. I kick da flyest dope with my maneuver technicality. To a dope track." I love that guy.

(*Ghost Dog: The Way of the Samurai* 2001)

On the semiotic battlefield that is Italian American cultural production, the media image of the mafioso is the looming target of innumerable discursive skirmishes. Middle and upper middle-class ethnic brokers, organized in national chapter associations and positioned as self-appointed spokespeople for the imagined community called "Italian American," wage a relentless crusade at the national and increasingly international levels, not against the mafia, but its celluloid and cathode specters. Combat breaks out persistently along a binary battle front of "negative" versus "positive" imagery. These antidefamation campaigns, what many people characterize as misguided, self-serving, and ultimately failing, are conducted to a large degree in the name of "Italian American youths" who are deemed vulnerable to the potentially pernicious impact of these undeniably pervasive and puissant images. The persistent trepidation for these guardians of expressive propriety is that Italian American youths will embrace these media mobsters in the formation of their ethnic consciousness.[1] Entering the fray that is the cultural politics of mob entertainment and white ethnic identity are the proponents of what is being called "hip-wop."[2]

American rap artists who self-identify as "Italian" are using hip-hop to engage, negotiate, and comment on identity, race, and masculinity·in a mediascape of the Italian American imagination. Mediascapes, according to Arjun Appadurai,

> tend to be image-centered, narrative-based accounts of strips of reality [that] offer to those who experience and transform them . . .

a series of elements (such as characters, plots, and textual forms) out of which scripts can be formed of imagined lives, their own as well as those of others living in other places.[3]

To a large degree, the elements in question for hip-wop revolve around the figure of the gangster, from the historical Al Capone to the fictional Tony Soprano, who has become the dominant narrative of the Italian experience in the United States in the popular imagination. Working in dynamic tension with and against the gangster image, Italian American youths in the twenty-first century are interpreting and reconfiguring media depictions of white ethnicity and masculinity so as to produce sonic narratives about the Italian American imaginary within a musical form associated with and dominated by African Americans. The creative engagement young Italian Americans have with this racially keyed art form is a vexing one as they seek a proprietary and authoritative stake of the mafioso image in the ever-shifting racial and ethnic funhouse of alterity and mimesis "in which not only images chase images in a vast, perhaps infinitely extended chain of images, but also become matter."[4] In their search for success, hip-wop artists strategically employ rap's codified aesthetic principle of verbal confrontation and claims of authenticity to negotiate and exploit these infinitely refracted reflections within and across convergent mediascapes.

As part of this artistic initiative, the dynamic and multivalent public space that is the World Wide Web, opens lines of communication across the Italian diaspora in a youth centric, transnational dialogue of reinvented community. As Appadurai observes, "The link between the imagination and social life, I would suggest, is increasingly a global and deterritorialized one."[5] Hip-wop artists are attuned to the possibilities of deterritorialized affiliations, as they use rap and the Internet to engender an Italian diasporic consciousness with links across the United States, as well as with their counterparts in Italy and at other points on the global Italian cartography. For example, the "Italian Hip Hop Movement" on myspace.com is part of hip-wop's ever expansive "diasporic public spheres"[6] that has forged associations between hundreds (there are 2,176 "friends" as of May 2010) of artists and fans across the globe, with West Coast, Midwest, Southern, New Jersey, Wisconsin, and European "chapters." In 2007, the site became a meeting place for sixteen "Italian" MCs from Chicago, Detroit, Montréal, New York City, Paris, and Rome (Italy) who produced the song "The Movement (Who the Fuck Are You?)" by emailing digital files of their vocal tracks to each other and distributing the finished version online.[7] Mikie Da Poet of Chicago cites his efforts, along with others, in creating the Italian Hip Hop Movement so as to bring "ITALIANS TOGETHER IN A CAUSE TO MAKE OUR MUSIC MAINSTREAM."[8]

For this study of hip-wop's musical, textual, and visual elements, I looked at forty-seven contemporary rappers and hip-hop groups from the United States who self-identified as Italian, ultimately focusing on those artists who addressed Italian identity in a sustained manner. Not discussed in this essay are biracial rappers, who, while they reference their Italian or Italian American backgrounds on their respective websites, do not do so in their music.[9] I identified five Italian American women artists out of the forty-seven surveyed, two of whom were part of separate trios (rapper Spero, formerly Guinea Love, of Northern State from Dix Hills, New York, and singer Bella Nicole of the disbanded Real Goombattas of Aliquippa, Pennsylvania). Out of these five, it was only the latter trio, with Bella Nicole providing backup vocals, which actively dealt with issues of *italianità* (Italianness) in any recurrent fashion. The lack of women rappers addressing Italian themes may be attributed, in part, to the media mafia persona's highly gender-specific coding and the lack of commercially viable imagery of empowered Italian American women in general.[10] As a result, my presentation focuses on male, heterosexual (at least not openly gay) rappers. In addition, because the focus of my investigation is the professed ethnic identity of the rappers and the content of their music, it does not take into consideration hip-hop's aesthetic criteria, and as a result, my study, artistically speaking, is ecumenical in scope. Thus, this chapter includes MCs respected within the larger hip-hop scene for their creative skills of rhyming and flow, as well as others who would be summarily dismissed as talentless "wannabes" and "toys."[11]

The creative work of Italian American rappers operates within the cultural and economic matrix of black cultural production and proprietorship, in particular black-operated music companies such as Violator and Ruff Ryders. Hip-wop emerged in the late 1990s in the shadow of previous white artists such as 3rd Bass, Marky Mark, Vanilla Ice, and others whose artistic merits were questioned and/or derided by critics and fans.[12] As such, the conjoined issue of whiteness and credentials is a pervasive theme for hip-wop artists. In "Big Shot," Genovese of Yonkers, New York, links his skills to that of sounding "black," an idea of racial passing with a long history in American music:

> And when I first came out
> nobody knew I was white.
> I was a black rapper to most
> till my face hit the light.
> So don't put me in that white rapper fad.
> It's a gimmick to me
> for the jails, and the corners, and it's all living with me.[13]

Staten Islander JoJo Pellegrino's adroit sampling of Rosemary Clooney's 1954 "Mambo Italiano" in his online video "Mambo" plays with the historical notion of southern Italian racial ambiguity:[14]

> Introducin' the rap guinea,
> spit at dudes like a mac millie.
> Naw, I ain't Sicilian
> but one listen and you'd swear
> that there's black in me.

In a reformulation of the theory of limited good, some aspiring and struggling Italian American MCs hold the view that the success of a white artist is achieved at the expense of another, as Genovese declares in his song "Doin' For the Love":

> Cuz white rappers fucked up the game for me.
> Maybe I fucked up the game for them.
> I don't know.
> Maybe I'm just helping them.

JoJo Pellegrino articulates the professional jealousies between white rappers, what he characterizes as "white-on-white animosity," in this way:

> There seems to be these things with white rappers, they seem to all hate each other. Because they're all fighting over who's black and who's not. "I'm blacker than you are." I'm not like that. I already know for a fact these other rappers haven't seen or been around the shit I've been around. Which doesn't make me a gangsta or a killer or Black. I don't walk around fighting with white rappers over who's black.[15]

Distinguishing one's self beyond the category "white rapper" thus entails eliciting a distinct set of identifiable traits in the pursuit of a successful hip-hop career.

Italian American MCs are negotiating their position as white rappers, a category that has been marketed by musical niches organized around notions of class, region, and ethnicity. Thus exists Eminem as trailer park white trash, the Beastie Boys as the sophomoric Jewish suburban cutups, the Irish American brawling hooligans that were House of Pain, good ol' boy MC Bubba Sparxxx from Georgia, and on and on.[16] Hip-wop artists assert a distinctiveness that Laura Cook Kenna terms "not merely white," in which group identity is configured and expressed at the intersect of an American bifurcated racial system set against both an Anglo-Saxon white mainstream and African Americans.[17] In the wake of the popular and critical success of HBO's television program *The Sopranos*, a reinvigorated media notion of "Italianness" became a potent marketing tool, a branding device for establishing a valid hip-hop persona for Italian American artists. The Real Goombattas' promotional material reads, in part: "These three paisons deliver the unique and incredibly hot brand of Rap Music (Hip Wop) while capitalizing on the phenomenal marketability of American Italian Culture." It was Violator's A&R person Eric Nicks who suggested to JoJo Pellegrino that he used the phrase "fogedaboudid" in a rap. "When JoJo came in, I was so impressed by his freestyling skills. He had this real Italian feel, so I said, 'Let's keep this original.'"[18] Given the cultural economy of ethnic marketing, it comes as no surprise that Pellegrino is not the rapper's birth name but is, in fact, his paternal grandmother's maiden name that he embraced when he "had to find [his] own identity" beyond that of yet another white rapper.[19] His underground career has been dogged by accusations that he is, in fact, not Italian but "fugazy," a wannabe, an imposter.[20]

Establishing hip-wop's distinctiveness and validity involves the use of standard Italian, Italian dialect, and Italian American keyed words and phrases woven into rap's rhythmic delivery and complexity. Hip-hop monikers range from Italian names (e.g., Marco Polo, Ritrovato, Vesuvio) to Italian American ones (e.g., Tone Fazools, Italian Ice, OC the Street Pizon, The Real Goombattas), to those referencing Italian/Italian American mafiosi (e.g., Al Capo & Tommy Guns, Don Pigro, Nicky Scarfo aka The Chopfather, Teflon Johnny). The Italian nome d'arte of Cost' Ovest ("West Coast") from Oakland, California, underscores the issue of language use for Italian American rappers. This third-generation MC's raps are acts of reclamation for he rhymes not in Italian but Sicilian (as well as English), which he studiously learned from his elderly grandmother before her death, as he narrates in "Ameri-Sicula":

> Since she never taught her kids,
> I knew I needed to learn,
> and what she tried so hard to forget,
> I unearthed and returned.

The artist's transcription of his self-titled, macaronic piece "Cost' Ovest" contains no less than forty-two footnotes of translations and glosses of sometimes esoteric Southern Italian allusions and references.[21] Rapping in Italian is rare and clearly has a limited appeal in the United States.

Hip-wop's lingua franca is neither a standard Italian nor an Italian dialect but, in fact, "Brooklynese," as the Alpha Male Gorillas of Marlboro, New York, note in their comical "Bleed Marinara":

I bleed marinara.
It's "rigott'" not "recatta."
Our thing, we never
sing the "bing" without the "bada."

Ey! How ya doin'?
In Brooklynese I'm fluent.
Pardon me, let me finish
the gabagol' that I'm chewin'.

The Real Goombattas' promotional literature is a revealing document for understanding language use:

> [MC] Primo's style exemplifies the Hip-Wop concept. Using Rap as a vehicle, he successfully translates the American-Italian experience to the masses. His lyrics are peppered with just enough Italian slang to add authenticity and represent his passions without alienating The Real Goombattas' non-Italian fan base.

The common knowledge of things Italian American allows artists to have hits, albeit underground, as with JoJo Pellegrino's brilliantly crafted and executed songs "Fogedaboudid" and "Bah Dah Bing Bah Dah Boom," and G Fella's (Ardsley, New York) one-minute freestyle on the monosyllabic yet polysemous expression that is the elongated vowel "Ohhhh!":

You know we're Italian when you hear us say
Ohhhh!
You don't understand there's lots of meanings for
Ohhhh!
You can be happy or sad when we say
Ohhhh!
You can be surprised or mad when we say
Ohhhh!
Like we find the body of a rat, they're like
Ohhhh!
Say something out of line, we like
Ohhhh!
See a bad broad walkin' by, we like
Ohhhh!
Ain't seen a dude in a long time, you're like
Ohhhh!
Pull up in that brand new whip, they're like
Ohhhh!

Thus, language is an integral part of that cultural space whereby an Italian structure of feeling is interconnected with mainstream public knowledge, a place where once esoteric southern Italian dialect words and phrases, such as *agita*, *skeeve*, and *u' gazz'*, as well as their proper pronunciation, are now familiar to the viewers of *The Sopranos*, the web surfers of urbandictionary. com, and the readership of *The Wall Street Journal* and *The New York Times*, whose editors are no longer compelled to gloss once foreign words and concepts.

In addition to Italian-coded language, hip-wop artists incorporate various Italian and Italian American musical references to the aural pastiche of their work, most commonly incorporating the ethnically marked and emblematic strains of mandolins and accordions (e.g., Genovese's "Sit Down," G Fella's "Broken English," JoJo Pellegrino's "Sunnyside Up"). Cost' Ovest, on the other hand, is by far the most knowledgeable of the Italian American MCs about Italian folk and popular musical traditions, reflected in the titles of the two songs "Tarantella Rap" and "Malafemmina," the latter being the name of the 1951 hit from the Neapolitan song canon. Cost' Ovest takes his musical cues from artists in Italy such as Almanegretta who during the 1990s "contaminated" their music by welding Italian folk music such as *tammurriata* to rap, reggae, and dub. His mash-ups of Sicilian *musica popolare* and rap's percussive beats are part of an agenda of "folklore reclamation," to quote Sabina Magliocco, whereby "aspects of folk tradition previously stigmatized by a dominant discourse" are salvaged and ascribed with positive value.[22] His songs stand apart from the work of other MCs in the United States with its mining of the rich opus of field recordings of Sicilian folk music, from the rural carter's melismatic lament to the percussive beats of the frame drum, all mixed with a hip-hop producer's deft hand. As with his Sicilian rapping, Cost' Ovest's musical work is highly idiosyncratic and unique in the larger hip-wop scene.

The "Italian" musical referent of choice is the melodic singing style of the Neapolitan song tradition and, in particular, American crooners. JoJo Pellegrino's "Sunnyside Up" begins with Calabrian singer Otello Profazio's song "Amuri" with its accordion accompaniment, floating above the DJ's cross fader beat, and the MC's proclamation "Ol' Blue Eyes is back, reincarnated." The fact that an ethnic perennial such as "Mambo Italiano," a bouncy tune with its own hybridic history that has appeared on movie soundtracks from *Married to the Mob* (1988) to *Big Night* (1996), has been sampled by no less than three rappers—JoJo Pellegrino, The Real Goombattas, and Marco Polo of Detroit—is a musical assertion of Italian American identity based on an endlessly recycled mass media entity from a period in which Italian American performers and cultural products asserted themselves into national and international spheres. This imagined past evokes a time and a longing in which Italian Americans are perceived to have reached a cultural apex of ethnic dominance, especially on the musical front.

Rap's grounding of an artist's persona to a specific spatial entity—"the extreme local" of regional and neighborhood affiliations—is evident in many works by Italian American MCs.[23] Street names and local hangouts in Chicago, Detroit, and Oakland are evoked in a portrait of lived experiences, as in First Cousins' "The Corner" and "My Block." The duo Cold Heat—Jak Danielz and Johnny Walker—trade-off a series of New York place names and associated neighborhoods strongly identified with Italian Americans in the opening of "Wops":

Fresh Pond Road
    Ridgewood
18th Avenue
    Bensonhurst
Spaghetti Park
    Corona
Cross Bay Boulevard
    Howard Beach
Pleasant Avenue
    Harlem . . .

Music videos are shot in urban neighborhoods with overt signs of Italian American identity, including restaurants, tri-colored flags, and the festivalized spaces of street fairs. These geographic citations mask the fact that the vast majority of Italian American MCs live in suburban areas far from historical Italian urban neighborhoods: Marco Polo comes not from Detroit but from the suburb Mt. Clemens, and Cost' Ovest lives in Oakland's more exclusive Montclair section and not his deceased grandmother's Temescal neighborhood. The conjuring of a specific cultural landscape is informed by the chronotope of the "old neighborhood" and infused with hip-hop's sentimental temporality of "back in the day." This image is most evident in the cultural production of The Lordz, a rap-rock group that wears their nostalgia for the good old days in Brooklyn on their sleeveless T-shirts. From their repeated references to precrack weapons such as brass knuckles and switchblades to their guise of fedoras and Pro-Keds sneakers, from their web posting of images from photographer Bruce Davidson's 1959 opus *Brooklyn Gang* to their use of the 1961 film *The Young Savages* about gang violence for their music video "People Who Died," The Lordz situate themselves in the beguiling realm of front stoops and street corners, candy stores and social clubs, Sunday dinners in kitchen basements, and other working-class urban landmarks on the mythic topography of the Italian imaginary. Physical dislocation and loss of community haunts hip-wop as its artists map older topographies and establish new sites of affinity online.

For many Italian American MCs, rap's appropriation of the violent and economically successful mafioso provides an entry point into the music market. Hip-hop, especially in its gangsta guise and its subgenre "Mafioso Rap," has contributed to the romanticized and mythologized image of the American mafia through its wholehearted embrace and replication.[24] African American use of the media mafia began in the 1970s with "blaxploitation" films *Black Caesar* (1973) and *The Black Godfather* (1974) in which "Italian-ness signified access to power and privilege that included whiteness but also boasted its own language, style of dress, and criminal organization."[25] Enacting a "black/Italian crossover fantasy"[26] has resulted in African American and Latino artists adopting a plethora of mob-related hip-hop monikers, for example, Triple 6 Mafia, Lil' Gotti Gambino, The Chicano Gambinos, and The Black Sopranos. Songs such as Lil' Kim's "Queen Bitch," Kool G Rap and DJ Polo's "Mobsta Lyrics," and Nas's "Street Dreams" and the associated videos feature the African American appropriation of the Italian American mafioso imagery. This mimetic (re)masking is best exemplified by *The Sopranos* star Frank Vincent coaching black rappers on mafiosi kinesics and couture in their attempt to emulate Italian American gangsters.[27]

Rap's mafioso simulacrum illustrates how the Italian American subject has become a common referent in media representation that complicates the ways in which Italian American identity and knowledge is reproduced. Literary scholar Thomas Ferraro notes:

> Italian American self-understanding and the portrayal of Italians in American culture at large . . . moved closer together, to the point where the feelings Italian Americans have for themselves, the feelings non-Italians have for Italian Americans, and the feelings they both have for the role of Italianness in America intertwine and interpenetrate.[28]

Italian American MCs rely on the full repertoire of mafia imagery and commoditized ethnic identity in their attempt to distinguish themselves from other rappers.[29] Myriad cinematic references are interspersed, juxtaposed, and layered in an infinite looping of ethnic intertextuality, as with JoJo Pellegrino's boastful encounter in his underground hit "Fogedaboudid":

> Met this beauty uptown by Carvel.
> She said she wants a *Goodfella*.

I put it in the *Bronx Tale*.
Jungle Fever like De Niro,
rob you like Pesci,
drama like Pacino,
snipe you like Wesley.
All you need is some 15s in your trunk and you're good.
Tell your boys "Fogedaboudid."
Let it bump in your hood.

In "Do You Know," G Fella exploits rap's self-referential swagger and uber individualism, the "'I' of me,"[30] embodying mediated ethnicity with a Whitmanesque litany of foodstuffs, fashion brands, and other pop references that are markers of collective Italian attributes:

I'm the show you run home at 9 on Sunday to see [*The Sopranos*].
I'm that movie everybody got 1, 2, and 3 [*The Godfather*].
I'm Joey from *Friends*.
Yep, I'm Ray Romano
and *Everybody Loves Raymond*
and Versace and Movado.

It should come as no surprise that both artists refer to themselves as "Tony Soprano" in their songs. The replicating and self-referential media mafia is most evident in G Fella's unreleased feature film *Crew* in which the Westchester rapper plays a mobster trying to leave the criminal life by becoming a rapper.

Many hip-wop artists struggle rhetorically to regain control of the gangster image as a way of devising a distinctive rap persona in the hip-hop world, as JoJo Pellegrino acknowledges:

When I first got on, I was trying to come from a 'hood standpoint.
I wasn't talking about this Italian thing. All these other rappers were trying to play it off like they were young Italian mobsters. I figured if somebody was going to make money, it might as well be me.[31]

MC Genovese dismisses ersatz gangsters in "Fuck Y'all" who access their mob knowledge from TV: "Y'all are living in a fantasy/You don't know nothin about the mob/You all watchin' A&E." Italian American artists repeatedly assert their claim to being "O.G.," that is, "the original gangster." In his song "They Wanna Be Like Us," Genovese avows a genetic advantage in his challenge to black rappers' legitimacy in the face of ethnic/racial imitation and masquerading:

You want to be like us,
wear our clothes,
use our names for reasons unknown.
And you know once we come through the door
Your mob shit ain't real no mo'.

. . .

And what's all these ads in the magazines?
You ain't the mob.
It ain't in your genes.
You ain't connected
cuz you know a bunch of Italian actors.
Recognize the root, the underlying factors.

Shifting between a first-person narrative and the communal in "Do You Know," G Fella explicitly names, in an itemized list, those reified entities deemed appropriated by gangsta rappers that were purportedly originated and now collectively "owned" by mafiosi, and one would conclude Italian Americans as well, given the non-crime-related objects mentioned:

Let's think.
Gangsta. That's ours.
Big jewelry. That's ours.
Drive bys. That's ours.
Lincoln and Caddy cars.
Chuck Zito from "Oz."
Smoke from the fine cigars.
Oooh, this thing of ours.
Can't forget behind bars.

I'm Fort Dix [Federal Prison].
I'm Green Haven [Correctional Facility].
I'm MCC [Metropolitan Correctional Center].
I'm Valhalla [Correctional Center].
I'm Rikers [Prison Complex].
I'm MDC [Metropolitan Detention Center].

Hip-wop's verbal confrontation is in keeping with rap's aesthetics that camouflage the artistic and commercial collaboration between Italian American MCs, DJs, and producers and African American artists and business people who are instrumental in developing and promoting hip-wop. Musical partnerships take the form of Busta Rhymes of the famed Wu-Tang Clan rapping in JoJo Pellegrino's "Built Like That" and Genovese's "Made Man" featuring Nature.

Claims of veracity are integral to rappers' rhetorical strategies and Italian American MCs are no different. They situate themselves within an art form created and artistically dominated by African Americans by invoking the language of authenticity—what rappers refer to as "keepin' it real"—and asserting an inherited and unbroken legacy of a bounded and incontrovertible cultural identity. As G Fella told me, "We grew up with this," leaving the pronoun's subject conspicuously unspecified.[32] JoJo Pellegrino shifts the locus of rap from the hood to the suburban South Shore of Staten Island in "Where I'm From," with the opening refrain "How real is this?" repeated four times:

> I'm like twenty lights around the corner
> and down the street
> from where they dumped Luciano
> when the feds found their heat.
> I'm two blocks from where Gravano
> use to ground his beef.
> I'm five minutes from where the Castellanos is sound asleep.
> I'm from where the cugines meet and greet with a kiss on their cheek,
> where little boys discover bodies taking a piss in the creek.
> I'm from where the people hold their speech if they witness the
> grief.

Thus the depiction of a professed lived reality, made common knowledge through enumerable media representations, is conflated with a sense of place to render the speaker, if not a direct eye witness, then certainly a member of a community that engages in the reported behaviors.

For some, the search for a place at the rap table is based on biological predeterminants, as OC the Street Pizon of Kenosha, Wisconsin, notes in his "Bloodline"—"I'm a gangsta by blood, and a hustler by mind"—thereby linking Italian identity and criminality in an essentialist paradigm unwittingly harkening back to anti-immigrant racism from the latter part of the nineteenth century. Italian American MCs, in particular Genovese and now a reality show star Carmine Gotti aka C-Gotti, invoke a direct patrimonial legacy of infamous mafiosi progenitors. In the song "The Movement (Who the Fuck Are You?)," which is performed by sixteen rappers, Little Joe CEO states his gangster credentials while marveling at the opportunity to share musical space with the infamous John Gotti's grandson:

> The Sicilian kid, so real, so cocky.
> Little Joe CEO.
> I'm so hard body.

As a baby, taught to load and pump the shottie.
It's Bensonhurst, Brooklyn,
I was growin' up with Gotti.
The last real don, was the man John,
My uncle ran the streets with Mr. Teflon,
now me on a beat with his grandson.
I'm a smoking gun.
Shoot eight bars and I'm done.

History is precedent for establishing authority and obtaining status within hip-hop.

Hip-wop mirrors and replicates public debates surrounding media depictions of Italian American gangsters, from the position that such images are in keeping with artistic expression to the opposition of representations deemed stereotypical and ultimately harmful. As with their film and television counterparts, Martin Scorsese and David Chase, to name but two young rappers, maintain that the mobster figure is an element that can be used artistically to tell a story, paint a portrait, evoke a mood, or convey an emotion. JoJo Pellegrino states "I'm not a criminal, I'm just a rapper displaying the raw" in his song "Built Like That." G Fella's rap "Do You Know" is in keeping with this artistic position:

I'm AC [Atlantic City].
I'm Vegas.
I'm entertainment.
I'm G Fella the underdog
but still I'm the favorite.

Like other hip-hop artists, Italian American MCs are constantly negotiating theatrical projection and cultural and personal veracity as part of their creative enterprise.[33]

Hip-wop also includes voices challenging the mafioso character as means for Italian American male identity. Alpha Male Gorillas' tongue-in-check "Bleed Marinara" undermines media-generated clichéd behaviors and mannerisms by mischievously reveling in them:

My hair's slicked back and jet black
I can't speak without my hands
but what the broads can't resist
is the year round tan.

So what's with all the hype?
I'm a stereotype.

No spaghetti [unclear]
You baccalas live the life.

And whatsamatta you?
You disgraced my calamari.
You try and feed me that ragu?
But that shit comes from a jar!

It is non-New York artists such as The Real Goombattas who speak directly to their cohorts about modeling themselves on real and media gangsters, as in their song "Nothin' Nice":

Don't you know there's nothin' nice about this life we lead?
Don't believe those mafiosi on the movie screen.

The trio's "Doc Melfi" is a tragic-comic routine featuring "one very whacky wiseguy" who lives in a "delusional world" in which the fictional characters from *The Sopranos* actually exist, providing wry commentary on the power of media mafia. Cost' Ovest declares his aversion to the gangster image in "Limoncello":

I don't buy into the Mob, cause I'm nobody's dog.
No one's my master, but I'm nobody's god.
So I'm free of the strings of stereotypes.

In "Paizon," Vocab Malone of Phoenix, a self-proclaimed Christian rapper—his MySpace profile states that he is the "The Donnie Osmond for the Hip Hop generation, the Italian underground version of Will Smith"—goads producers of mob imagery:

Showin' our people as evil ain't equal
Godfather Dons in a Regal livin' illegal?
Movies are fecal matter that don't matter.
Instead of watchin' an actor
you should read another chapter!
My name's not Guido, Dago, Luigi.
I don't say "AY YO" like a boxer Rocky
Not Pavarotti or Soprano family
No oregano on my bowl of Cheerios
Bada-Boom-Bada-Bing?
Boy, ya betta doubt it.
Try to cliche me?
Ya betta fagetitaboutit!

It is these rappers who move beyond self-referential and self-promotional lyrics to content that is historical in nature, encompassing the immigrant past. Cost' Ovest references and narrates the exploitation of the Sicilian rural poor and Italian immigrant proletariat with his songs "Abbanniaru" and "Carusi." The defunct Real Goombattas demonstrate a particularly keen understanding of history, especially in relationship to people of color in the song "B.O.K.":

> Our people were so poor, yo.
> They packed their bags and said, "Buon giorno."
> Jumped on the ships at every port, yo,
> and exited straight out the Mezzogiorno.
> Youse called us WOPs, an acronym for people "without papers."
> Without papers, it's hard to find labor,
> the reason that our people even started the mob;
> had to drop the vowels off their name for a job.
> Youse can't compare it to the blacks and Natives,
> but still we was degraded,
> race discriminated,
> second class citizens,
> under compensated,
> worked as hard as the next mother
> for less wages.
> Black handers
> got what they demanded.
> If you ain't a goomba, you would not understand it.
> So underhanded,
> preyed on their own kind;
> immigrant Italians
> got no peace of mind.

For this hip-wop group, a white ethnic subjectivity is imagined as one formed not in opposition or competition with people of color and cognizant of white privilege for the descendants of European immigrants.[34]

Hip-wop practitioners have forged artistic personae from the alluring gangster image found at the confluence of film, television, music, and the Internet. They reconfigure the "gangster" to develop and express a contemporary, youth-based identity grounded in an African American-associated musical form that is globally embraced. Italian American artists are using social networking and direct merchandising websites to advance the hip-wop "movement's" transnational visibility and ongoing affiliations. However, for these rappers, this artistic identity and cultural work are sources of constant negotiation as JoJo Pellegrino observes:

People are always telling me that I go too hard with the Italian thing . . . [F]ans are quick to criticize me doing "that corny Italian shit." At the same time, that's the thing that separates me from everybody else.[35]

The dilemma of conflicting fan interest may be the source troubling Italian American artists' search for commercial success that continues to elude them. Several of the rappers discussed in this chapter have had contracts with established labels, but only The Lordz have released a commercial recording.[36] If both gangsta rap and *The Sopranos* emerged at a time when the social reality of the American mafia was experiencing a significant decline, then to what degree can hip-wop succeed commercially in the aftermath of the popular television series' conclusion and the (perpetually pronounced) demise of gangsta rap?[37] For now, the incessantly refracted media gangster is a site where these artists and their fans communicate and work out the meanings of style, difference, and identity.

Endnotes

1. The "Image & Identity" page of the National Italian American Foundation's website states, "Let us not forget that educating our Youth needs to remain our focus and will advance our efforts to promote a positive image the furthest," http://www.niaf.org/image_identity/summer2004.asp (accessed April 29, 2010. No longer active as of January 18, 2011). For discussion of antidefamation initiatives, see Philip V. Cannistraro, "The Duce and the Prominenti: Fascism and the Crisis of Italian American Leadership," *Altreitalie* 31 (2005): 76–86; Laura Cook Kenna, "Dangerous Men, Dangerous Media: Constructing Ethnicity, Race, and Media's Impact Through the Gangster Image, 1959–2007" (PhD diss., George Washington University, 2008); George De Stefano, *An Offer We Can't Refuse: The Mafia in the Mind of America* (New York, NY: Faber & Faber, 2006); Libero Della Piana, "Are Italians the New Anti-Racist Front?" RaceWire blog, 2004, http://www.arc.org/racewire/041006l_piana.html (accessed April 4, 2006).

2. The term "hip-wop" is a reappropriation of the derogatory ethnic epithet "wop." Also written "hip whop" and known as "Italian rap." The first known rap recording by an Italian American with an explicit Italian American theme was Guido MC's 1987 "Guido Rap" and "Bensonhurst, 86th Street" (Beeyoik Records, #BRD-1200). See Donald Tricarico, "Guido: Fashioning an Italian American Youth Subculture," *The Journal of Ethnic Studies* 19, no. 1 (Spring 1991): 41–66.

3. Arjun Appadurai, *Modernity at Large: Cultural Dimensions of Globalization* (Minneapolis: University of Minnesota Press, 2003), 35.

4. Michael Taussig, *Mimesis and Alterity: A Particular History of the Senses* (New York, NY: Routledge, 1993), 43.

5. Appadurai, *Modernity at Large*, 55.

6. Ibid., 21.

7. Because of space limitations, I am unable to fully address the digital diasporic consciousness of "Italian rap." For further elaboration, see my article "'Hip Hop from Italy and the Italian Diaspora': A Report from the 41st Parallel," *Altreitalie* 24 (January to June 2002): 86–104 and my unpublished conference paper, "'Took a Bird to the Boot': Hip Hop Expressions of Italian Diasporic Consciousness" (2008).

8. Mikie Da Poet, "Interview," Original Italian Soul MySpace blog, January 6, 2008, http://blogs.myspace.com/originalitaliansoul (accessed May 28, 2009).

9. For example, Lyrics Born ("half-Japanese-American half-Italian American hip hop MC") from San Francisco, Italian-born Marco Polo (aka Marco Aleandro Zambito, whose father is Italian and whose mother is African American) from Ft. Worth, and DJ Kid Capri (aka David Anthony Love, whose mother is Italian American and whose father is African American).

10. It is beyond the scope of this article to address hip-wop's representations of women as wives, lovers, mothers, and daughters.

11. The term has its roots in graffiti but is applicable across hip-hop to mean a novice with limited skills.

12. Armond White, "Who Wants to See Ten Niggers Play Basketball?" in *Droppin' Science: Critical Essays on Rap Music and Hip Hop Culture*, ed. William Eric Perkins (Philadelphia, PA: Temple University Press, 1996), 192–208.

13. The digital distribution of many of the songs analyzed here, some of which have not been issued on CD, makes dating and citation difficult at best, and subsequently, I have not created a separate discography for this paper. I transcribed all raps quoted in this paper, often with the generous assistance of the artists, except for those of Cost' Ovest, who graciously provided the full texts.

14. *Are Italians White?: How Race is Made in America*, ed. Jennifer Guglielmo and Salvatore Salerno (New York, NY: Routledge, 2003).

15. Brian Kayser, "Interview with JoJo Pellegrino," *Hip Hop Game*, March 17, 2008, http://www.hiphopgame.com/index2.php3?pahe=jjp (accessed March 18, 2008). See also da MetroGnome, "Interview with JoJo Pellegrino," *SoundSlam*, http://soundslam.com/articles/print_page.php?id=in_jojope&type=interviews (accessed October 3, 2007).

16. William Eric Perkins, "The Rap Attack: An Introduction," in *Droppin' Science: Critical Essays on Rap Music and Hip Hop Culture*, ed. William Eric Perkins (Philadelphia, PA: Temple University Press, 1995), 35–8. It is interesting to note JoJo Pellegrino's repeated assertions that he was marginalized at Violator Records, where he had a contract, when white performer Bubba Sparxxx was signed (Kayser 2008).

17. Kenna, 2008, 22–5, 180–7.

18. Jessica Koslow, "JoJo Pellegrino," *The Source* (October 2000): 104.

19. JoJo Pellegrino, "About JoJo Pellegrino 'Pella,'" *MySpace*, November 11, 2007, http://profile.myspace.com/index .cfm?fuseaction =user.viewprofile&friendid=44584748 (accessed March 18, 2008. No longer active as of January 18, 2011).

20. Troy D, "Jo Jo Pellegrino," *Rap Scene*, http://www.rapscene.com/JOJO.htm (accessed October 12, 2007. No longer active as of January 18, 2011).

21. Personal communication, emailed February 2, 2009.

22. Sabina Magliocco, "Imagining the Strega: Folklore Reclamation and the Construction of Italian-American Witchcraft," *The Italian American Review* 8, no. 2 (2001): 58.

23. Murray Forman, *The 'Hood Comes First: Race, Space, and Place in Rap and Hip-Hop* (Middletown, CT: Wesleyan University Press, 2002), xvii.

24. Wikipedia contributors, "Gangsta rap," *Wikipedia, The Free Encyclopedia*, http://en.wikipedia.org/wiki/Gangsta_rap (accessed May 28, 2009).

25. Kenna, 2008, 228.

26. John Gennari, "Passing for Italian: Crooners and Gangsters in Crossover Culture," in *Frank Sinatra: History, Identity, and Italian American Culture*, ed. Stanislao G. Pugliese (New York, NY: Palgrave, 2004), 149.

27. Personal conversation with Marylou Tibaldo-Bongiorno and Jerome Bongiorno, June 28, 2007.

28. Thomas J. Ferraro, *Feeling Italian: The Art of Ethnicity in America* (New York: New York University Press, 2005), 4.

29. Micaela di Leonardo, *The Varieties of Ethnic Experience: Kinship, Class, and Gender among California Italian-Americans* (Ithaca, NY: Cornell University Press, 1984), 178–80.

30. Nelson George, *Hip Hop America* (New York, NY: Penguin Books, 1998), 50–5.
31. JoJo Pellegrino, "JoJo Pellegrino Journal," July 30, 2007, *Hip Hop Game*, http://www.hiphopgame.com/index2.php3?page=jojojournal (accessed October 12, 2007).
32. Personal conversation, September 20, 2007.
33. Hugh Barker and Yuval Taylor, *Faking It: The Quest for Authenticity in Popular Music* (New York, NY: W. W. Norton & Company, 2007), x, 244.
34. David R. Roediger, *Colored White: Transcending the Racial Past* (Berkeley: University of California Press, 2002), 212–40; Ingrid Walker Fields, "Family Values and Feudal Codes: The Social Politics of America's Twenty-First Century Gangster," *The Journal of Popular Culture* 37, no. 4 (2004): 611–33.
35. JoJo Pellegrino, "JoJo Pellegrino Journal," July 30, 2007, *Hip Hop Game*, http://www.hiphopgame.com/index2.php3?page=jojojournal (accessed October 12, 2007).
36. As a music writer noted, the group's first CD *All in the Family* "was one of the best hip hop albums of the '90s, even if nobody noticed." Chuck Eddy, "Spaghetti Eastern," *Village Voice* (August 23–29, 2006).
37. De Stefano, 2006; Fields, 2004; Fred L. Gardaphé, *From Wiseguys to Wise Men: The Gangster and Italian American Masculinities* (New York, NY: Routledge, 2006), 209–14.

CHAPTER 4

The Global Nomad

Navigating Mediated Space at a Global Scale

MICHAEL JENSON

Chapter Description

The effects of globalization over the past several decades are best captured through the term *deterritorialization*—a conception of the territorial where social, economic, and political spaces are no longer necessarily geographic. For the first time in history, cultural spaces are developing which have no tangible connection to geographical places. Technological advances in global media are major contributors to this spatial transformation. Because the perception of space provides the underlying context for our actions and events, the ubiquitous effects of such advances will only increase as global communication technologies integrate into our daily lives and erode our conceptual conventions of space.

The premise of this chapter is that the status, relevance, and defining role of space rests on how we mitigate the rapid transformation of spatial perception and navigate the increasingly powerful technologies of global mediation. This chapter investigates the relationship of space to mediated space, in three parts. The first part examines the conventional conception of space and its meaning within the existence of the everyday. The second part explores how the media technologies of globalization have deterritorialized our world by creating a *supraterritorialism* that forces the transformation of our spatial imagination. The final part speculates about the potential of a spatial interaction more akin to the way traditional nomadic cultures related to and conceived of space.

* * *

Figure 4.1 Between Two Worlds
Source: Reproduced with permission of Wikimedia Commons.

> As for the twenty-first century there is a big question mark hanging over it. Perhaps it will answer that question, because the "unlimited possibilities" are all there, whether in biology, communications, or the conquest of space, both cosmic and terrestrial. One of the great problems of the near future will be the dramatic shrinking space of earth, of life-size reality. The effect of being enclosed which Foucault noted in the eighteenth century will in fact characterize the twenty-first. What will human space be like in a world reduced to nothing by supersonic and instantaneous communications? Space as emptiness will be unlimited and space as fullness drastically limited. There will be a new interface between the solid and the fluid, except now the terrestrial littoral is vertical!
> (Paul Virilio,"Interview—Landscape of Events Seen at Speed"[1])

In this volume's introduction, a metaphor for envisioning the profound effects of rapid globalization is presented that equates the political success and worldwide influence of an African American—as illustrated in Barack Obama's ascension to the American presidency—as symbolic of the nuanced, simultaneous, and complex atmosphere surrounding identity in our globalizing world (Figure 4.1). Obama's success rested on persuading the electorate of his legitimacy as both "unmarked *and* African American."[2] In other words, as Eugene Robinson points out, "Obama is the personification of "both-and.""[3]

Space has gone through a similar transformation compelling individuals to define their identity differently. For millennia, identity was largely derived from the landscapes and geographic locales one inhabited. Envisioning identity was impossible detached from the part of the world that one (and their ancestors) resided. Languages reinforced this, as one was always seen in relationship to a native city, region, or nation. Periodically, there were changes in this attitude. For example, with the discovery of the new world, hyphenated descriptions of ethnic or national groups such as Irish, Italian, or Polish American became common. The recent rise of global telecommunications has only exacerbated this cultural/geographic merging, as globalized technological advancement has forced our spatial experience into Robinson's identity paradigm of "both-and."[4]

Globalization is often described in a multitude of ways, from its being a process of *liberalization*, of *universalization*, or *westernization* to a form of *internationalization*. None captures the enormity of globalization's impact better than the term *deterritorialization*—a conception of the territorial where social, economic, and political spaces are no longer necessarily geographic. For the first time in history, cultural spaces are developing, that have no tangible connection to geographical places. This state is radically altering our traditional territorial logic and forces the adoption of new methods of conceptualizing space/geography.[5]

Along with cultural and economic forces, two additional contributors to this spatial transformation have emerged—technological advances in transportation and global telecommunication. Because our perception of space provides the context for most actions and events, the wide-ranging effects of these advances are overwhelming in their complexity. This will only increase, as global communication technologies become more ubiquitous to our daily lives and continue to erode our conventional conceptualization of space.

Though these technologies' transformation of reality through the mass production of images does not destroy our perception of the world, Paul Virilio asserts their distortions appear bent on replacing it and describes this state as "videoscopy," whose "repercussions will make themselves felt through the constitution of an age of instantaneous, interactive 'space-time' having nothing in common with the topographical space of geographical or even geometrical distance."[6] The most disturbing aspect here is that, with this technologically driven desire for a global "reality replacement" based on the instantaneous connectivity of our social/political landscapes, a "switch" is being thrust on societies still unaware of the consequences.[7]

Jonathan Crary stretches this scenario further by describing a new age of perceptual machines that not only allow incredible new visual terrains to be experienced but also simultaneously calibrate and distance the viewer from the viewed in a rigidly uniformed manner. This calibration provides a "straightjacket" that conditions our perception of the world generically as well as allowing objects and actions to be experienced "out of context." Though a visual field emerges that is unprecedented in scale, autonomy, reach, and flexibility, it is one disassociated from "the unified field of geometric perspective" that has dominated our theories of vision and representation since the time of the Renaissance.[8]

Though this technologically mediated *supraterritorial* realm[9] is distinct from the immediate material reality surrounding us, it is reliant on the events occurring within this sphere and is indicative of an age where the mediated processes of globalization present serious challenges to the traditional logic underlying space/place relationships. Such technologies erode the clarity of our spatial connection to cultural identity as all forms of human contact, relationships of social power, and historical forms of domination are stretched globally at an increasingly accelerated rate, thus deepening their impact exponentially. These circumstances invite questions concerning our cultural ability to retain, reconstruct, or recall our traditional structures of meaning, especially those associated with our spatial understanding of the world.

The discussion surrounding this spatial reconceptualization necessarily centers on alternatives to ending the envisioning of space as a mythologized and exclusionary form. If it is always considered as a series of internally coherent constructs that inherently constitute "closed" worlds, space in relationship to place will be consistently challenged and undermined by globalization. As Doreen Massey observes,

> If places are thought of as settled, coherent worlds of their own, then they are surely under challenge in an age when everywhere seems to be opened up to wider forces. The constant interconnections—of economics, culture, ecology—mean that any notion of an internally generated uniqueness of place is hard to sustain.[10]

In the wake of this disruption, a contemporary "geographical imagination" must be cultivated that embraces the cosmopolitanism necessary to navigate the complexities of a globalized world, yet remains rooted in our traditional understanding of space. What is needed is a mentality that simultaneously accepts the gains of globalization as a universal force yet retains a connection to the values, traditions, and cultural dictates connected to specific locales. This will allow a healthy global identity that merges a universal spatiality with one that remains geographically understandable. Ricoeur underscores this seemingly paradoxical move with the question: "how to become modern and return to sources; how to revive an old, dormant civilization and take part in universal civilization?"[11]

Virilio presents a possible method for navigating this "split" with the notion of a stereoscopic or double vision where individuals "maintain one eye on the physical world and one eye on the virtual world." If successful, extraordinary opportunities can emerge, but the "tearing up of Being" and its "awkward consequences" to our traditional spatial logic must be confronted as the primacy of the material world dissolves. Embracing these new opportunities is possible only if an awareness of their consequences is also understood. The real and the virtual must coexist as twenty-first century modernity becomes a matter of simultaneous existence—part situated in the "real time of our immediate activities" overlayed by a mediated realm that "privileges the *now* . . . to the detriment of the *here*."[12]

Consequently, the premise here asserts that the status, relevance, and influence of material space rests on how the transformation of our means of navigating it is mediated. In a world where our traditional conceptions of space/place—once considered the epitome of stability and connection to the natural environment—are being radically reconceptualized, what constitutes the criteria for assessing the significance of space? In other words, how does globalized media enhance or detract from our experience of the immediate landscapes/places we inhabit?

To understand the relationship of these dueling spatial realms, the concept of space must be examined in all of its nuanced complexity. As a guide, the metaphor of the "modern nomad" will be used to explore how Virilio's call for the development of a stereoscopic perceptual capacity might manifest. The implications of this endeavor will be studied in three parts.

The first will examine the conventional conception of "space," its meaning within the existence of the everyday, and the effect that the universalized spatiality of globalism has on it. The second will explore how global media is *deterritorializing* our world through the creation of a *supraterritorialism*. The final section will define a relationship to geography where space and identity are conceived in a similar fashion to many nomadic cultures. By transforming conventional modes of spatial thinking in relationship to the logic of a more technologically advanced visual realm, a more fluid and flexible conceptual platform for perceiving space can be developed. This flexibility can better align with the constant technological transformation facing our spatial boundaries while maintaining connections to the spaces and places founding our cultural identity. In other words, a new form of technologically enhanced geographical imagination[13] might be defined that can navigate both worlds seamlessly to the benefit of our modern existence.

Concrete Versus Abstract: Space, Placelessness, and the Modern Technological Landscape

What is the conventional view of the space/place relationship and why is it so fundamental to human existence? In short, its meaning rests within the imagination of its inhabitants and the concrete nature of space as constituted by everyday phenomena.[14] The breadth of experience shaping our mental picture of place can range from a mountain vista to a shadow's passage over a threshold. Coupled with concrete experience are ephemeral qualities, such as memories and imagination. Space is the totality of experiences—emotional, rational, and spiritual—encountered in a particular locale with a "materiality" emerging through characteristics such as shape, color, texture, temperature, and light. These are the "given" content of existence and differ radically from the quantitative abstractions constituting the logic of global technologies of mediation that routinely elevate the importance of these abstractions above the "life-world" of our surroundings.[15]

By Virilio's argument, these technologies induce a "picnolepsy"[16] or state of awareness where real-time/real-space events are lost because of an overexposure to mediated visualization techniques. These create a disorientation where the perceptual boundaries between real time/space and image time/space are blurred beyond recognition. This "industrialization" of images elevates our visual intensity to the point that even familiar objects appear unfamiliar and encourages over attentiveness to the most banal of objects. With this, the hierarchy of our traditional spatial logic collapses, thus causing the "crucial and the incidental" to become confused under a barrage of random informational imagery. In addition, this hypervisual state has made the unstructured pursuit of informational detail an end-in-itself.[17]

This visual state is so influential that, like the pollution of air or water, there is now "a dromospheric and chronoscopic pollution—the gradual reduction of space/time by the various tools of instantaneous, ubiquitous visualization"[18] attacking the nuanced qualities of space as well as elevating the temporal over the spatial. Our perceptual abilities are displaced through the presentation of both the near and the far simultaneously within the technologies of instantaneous communication.

Space is more integral, varied, and complex in its richness than the conventions of scientific enquiry can describe or visual technologies can reproduce. It is more than a "flattened" reference to an abstract locale, for it reveals its character in highly nuanced atmospheric qualities. Its power is its emergence as a complete phenomenon whose attributes constantly and subtly change with the passage of time. These nuances are lost if reduced to singular aspects, such as image, and described only in terms of function within the global system. Also, space can be neither "frozen" nor extracted from time. The temporality of its subtle and constant transformations is a key to comprehend its unique character. Though related to time, space constitutes more than time itself.

Our material landscapes often seem fixed and unchanging but are constantly changing in relationship to the passage of time. Space intricately references place, as each experience is interpreted differently by each individual "viewer." Each subsequent experience changes both the inhabitant and the space itself, as both are caught in a state of constant "Becoming." The flattened and distance-less world of globalization often leads to a profound sense of loss because it can only describe part of the picture. Space, then, is composed of and determined by a multitude of qualitative experiences that play out over time. Its complexity cannot be reduced to a specific set of descriptions based solely on the quantifiable agendas of science or economics. The gamut of existence comprises an integral web of concrete experience, multiscalar in nature, and ranges from the crossing of a door step to globally significant events viewed on television or the Internet.[19]

The "vision machines" of global telecommunication underlie much of the current attack on the unique qualities of space. The ubiquitous nature of the industrialized landscape, our need for efficient travel, and our desire for instant communication have radically transformed the ways of experiencing our surroundings. Though the environments created by industry are often condemned for their generic qualities, life before the advent of these technologies was neither long nor idyllic. Materially, our quality of life has greatly improved and has afforded profound transformations to our existence. The trade-off has been the loss of many of our traditional aesthetic, cultural, and spiritual values associated with space and its unique relationship to place.

This trade-off underlies the powerful sense of loss often felt when experiencing many landscapes that now constitute our surroundings. Intellectually, their worth can be accepted, but emotionally, the loss they represent is hard to rectify. Ted Relph describes this state as:

> Modern landscapes are profoundly ambivalent. On the one hand, they are obvious manifestations of technical accomplishments and widespread material prosperity—obvious because we know and appreciate them for these qualities in daily life. On the other hand, they reflect aesthetic confusion, ethical poverty and a disturbing

dependence on technical expertise, but these are subtle and can only be identified by a deliberate effort of observation and reflection. The source of this ambivalence can be traced directly to humanism, the philosophical perspective which encourages the exercise of human reason for human benefit.[20]

The benefits of this process are distinct and calculable, for its transformational power emerges tangibly. Its associated losses are more subtle because they are less tangible and defy conventional measure. Thus, the paradox of modernity presents itself as a series of ambivalent gains and losses.

This ambivalence cannot be overcome by rejecting the benefits of technological progress for some return to a romanticized preindustrial past. Defining how modernization might support the creation of meaningful spaces as well as material benefit is a more sound strategy. It is not sensible, nor possible, to reject globalization or the dromospheric reality it creates for a vision of a pre-industrial, craft-based society arbitrarily chosen and artificially manifested. Both aspects are utopian and extremely dangerous. However, Relph correctly believes that "we have enough technical knowledge. It is time to reconsider matters of quality, value, and distribution."[21]

The challenge lies in the development of a mode of operation that critiques the mediated effects of globalization through a system of values supporting a more authentic way of inhabiting and building. This system must wholeheartedly accept the uncertainty and change that future technology brings yet demand more than a superficial reality based purely on mediated images. Society must insist that the qualitative attributes of particular environments temper the universal forces of technology and globalization. Only then can we maintain the "rootedness" so imperative to our cultural identity. Individuals must still be from a specific place while operating within the emergent spatial logic of the vision machines driving globalization.

Speed, Collapse, and the Emergence of Supraterritorialism

In the essay, "Environment Control," Virilio profoundly asks,

> What are the implications for the transparency of air, water, and glass, for the "real space" of the things surrounding us, when the "real-time" interface supersedes the classical interval, and distance suddenly gives way to power of emission and instant reception?[22]

In answering, the author describes a transparency based on the derangement of both sense-appearances and transparency itself. Here, derangement is considered a transparent state with zero materiality because nothing lies beyond the image nor is there a material density approaching that of the concrete world. This type of transparency refers to the ephemeral apparitions transmitted instantly over distance. Both Virilio's question and subsequent answer indicate an emergence of another simultaneous realm existing in parallel to our life world. Though detached from our world, it still transforms and blurs our perceptions of it.

In the "Over-exposed City," Virilio indicates how qualities of spatial boundary have been transformed from stone façade to "screen" and then from screen to electronic interface. The contemporary metropolis has lost the traditional defining oppositions of "city/country . . . centre/periphery . . . localized/axial" as well. These dichotomies have collapsed with the revolutions of transport, telecommunications,[23] and virtuality; globalism has been brought into the domicile through interfaces devoid of any real depth. Through electronic transmission, they create a "kind of distance, a depth of field of a new kind of representation, a visibility without any face to face encounter . . ."[24] Amazingly, immense vistas appear within the perspectives displayed within the immaterial depth of a flat-screen monitor and what appears as miles in our concrete world are presented on a screen no more than a few inches deep.

Terms such as near and far are no longer relevant because the difference between macro and micro is extended to fantastic bounds through devices such as the electron microscope and satellite camera.[25] Virilio concludes, "At the end of the twentieth century, urban space loses its geopolitical reality to the exclusive benefit of systems of instantaneous deportation whose technological intensity ceaselessly upsets all of our social structures."[26] Our computerized window to the world brings absolutely everything to the same place, simultaneously. It is a place that is "no place" in the classical sense because it is a location with no physicality. It exhausts both natural and physical description because of its existence in all locations and positions simultaneously. The ultimate measure of this realm is that of speed-distance whose virtuality obliterates physical distance to the point that all conventional spatial characteristics seem to be interchangeable at will.[27]

Contemporary global culture has become *hypervisual* where comprehending what is perceived is beyond our capacity to understand as reference points and conventional cultural indicators are dislocated from their traditional locales.[28] Though greater transmission speed of information and imagery is taken for granted as an outcome of globalization, at times it seems a motivating force because it occurs in a spatial realm where questions of social or environmental concerns are easily pushed aside.

Virilio describes this unchecked manifestation of speed as "dromology" or the largely unchecked acceleration of social, political, and economic worlds globally. This informational acceleration encourages the emergence of a technological superficiality as the transference of people, objects, images, and ideas become exceedingly more rapid and compressed. In addition, the creation of a unified global media system where political debate will increasingly occur within communication outlets controlled by conglomerates and other highly organized institutions such as government will occur. Time, space, and conversation needed for the consensus building founding a strong democratic process will disappear as the line between governments and media outlets blur. Even as democracies continue to emerge and then merge and blur, the outcome will be the control of debate or dissent before it even begins.[29]

This distance-less realm of the temporal instance, where the flattened image is more powerful than the dimensional object, and the actual as well as the mediated are barely distinguishable, constitutes the *supraterritorial*. Here, money and power structures move around the globe instantaneously as the abstractions that underlie them are broken into bits of information and transported in a flash. It is a world devoid of history and contains only a transient connection to our material world. An "infosphere" with its own set of operations and ethical standards that often only tangently reflect those of this world. At once connected yet detached, at other times concrete and permanent in appearance, while being able to transform into something unrecognizable instantaneously. A realm that is both simultaneously frightening and fascinating.

Potentially negative effects aside, the possibilities for this space are as limitless, as its structure is boundless. If the potential for grand vistas is used benevolently, the ability to centralize information and connect the dots between problems or issues will be unrivaled. It is its detachment and tangential connection to the life world that makes for a powerful tool of observation with the possibility to become anything or anyone imaginable within this realm being its curse and its blessing. When all histories and cultural hierarchies become neutralized, infinite possibilities to analyze and construct new traditions, identities, or cultural grounds quickly come to the forefront.

Modern societies must adapt and exist fluently between the territory of our world and the *supraterritory* of virtual media. As the metaphor of the modern nomad comes into focus, it is imperative to follow the advice of Yi Fu Tuan and remember: "The visual media, even as they open our eyes, blind us to other realities."[30] The emergence of a supraterritorial logic of instant transport and telecommunications within the wake of globalization is as unstoppable as turning back the clock is impossible, so how one chooses to navigate both realms is the only power an individual can control. It is the sole means of avoiding being overwhelmed by the homogenizing onslaught of the *supraterritorial* and will take the development of a modern geographical imagination to master it.

The Stereotopic Geographical Imagination: Connecting Lived to Mediated Space

In undertaking the speculative development of a modern geographical imagination that contemporizes our conceptual understanding of space, discerning the spaces of representation from the representations of space and the benevolent potential of both realms is imperative.[31] After this primary step, connections between the two realms can be made for the necessary development of a "stereoscopic" vision (one side ocular and one side mediated). However, several misconceptions must be overcome before this step can be undertaken.

The first concerns the erroneous perception that virtual technologies can recreate our present world in such detail as to replace it. This idea was prevalent in the earliest stages of the development of virtual reality technologies. To insist on this possibility is to deny the multivalent spatiality and temporality of our surroundings. The experiential quality of our existing reality is so varied and complex that any attempt to recreate it through mediation could only produce a superficial facsimile. Though our technology becomes more sophisticated, its foundation is largely one of the surfaces and can only mimic the nuances of our reality and not truly reproduce its richness. This leads to the second misconception that a concerted resistance or "turning away" from the destructive forces of globalization and its stepchildren—virtual and telecommunication technologies—is possible. This mistaken attitude must make way for more measured and careful deliberation of their authentic role, meaning, and utility. We must acknowledge the benefits that these technologies bring while ceasing to accept their increasing influence with a passive distrust.

New methods of interpreting the connections of these technologies to our existing landscapes must be developed comprehending the full impact of space on the human psyche. Ruskin indicates how this *change in attitude* might emerge: "Every advance in our acuteness of perception will show us something new, but the old and first discerned thing will still be not falsified, only modified and enriched by the new perception."[32] This indicates the possibility of a multivalent and multiscalar process of interpreting space that incorporates these mediated vision technologies with our history and tradition. It outlines a multidimensional attitude toward space that can serve as a foundation for the interpretation of its meaning through the utilization of the perceptual strengths afforded by each realm.

David Harvey describes the transient and complex nature of spatial configurations in a manner very relevant to this discussion in his call to connect our social and geographical imaginations:

> Space is neither absolute, relative or relational in itself, but it can become one or all simultaneously depending on the circumstances. The problem of the proper conceptualization of space is resolved through human practice with respect to it. In other words, there are no philosophical answers to philosophical questions that rise over the nature of space—the answers lie in human practice. The question "what is space?" is therefore replaced by the question "how is it that different human practices create and make of distinctive conceptualizations of space?"[33]

The "meaning" of real space must be evaluated but not just in its physical and formal manifestations. Their connections to human activity, which give meaning to space, afford the best avenue to conceive of the space place relationship to identity.

To encounter space with an unprejudiced attitude, modes of perception that appreciate "everything" in its connectedness must emerge. This "seeing" must omit as little detail as possible and avoid the imposition of a preordained agenda on the encountered. It must seek to comprehend the given world in its entirety, while also attending to the particular characteristics that make a location a unique space.[34] A humility acknowledging essences defining space while being open to the diversity of individual ecologies and varieties of human actions/accomplishments that underlie experience. It is an inherently open, inclusive, and varied viewpoint that comprehends the quality of individual place while avoiding the imposition of a singularly fixed or ideologically closed viewpoint. It must value the characteristics of individual spaces by acknowledging the fragility of their existence and search for the distinctive within the continuous. To understand how an element simultaneously emerges as a specific outcome and contributing factor in the process of the appearance of the world would be its greatest and lasting benefit.[35] We must relearn how to appreciate the tapestry constituting our material, social, and historical worlds.

It is here that the global vision machine's power for seeing the world with an objective gaze that can seek meaningful connections within spatial encounters becomes most apparent. By returning "to things," in the form of a deeper, detailed method of observing, the complexity and fluidity of the world can manifest from a much broader viewpoint. Because this type of perception can be random, the transient nature of space can be appreciated as its spirit emerges through myriad scales and cultural structures. These new vision technologies can bring to light many of the commonality and universal aspects of our existence.

For balance, an open and continual process of evaluating the meaning of mediated images can offset the rapid transformations and temporal/spatial collapse brought about by globalization to continually reassert the primacy of the spatial logic of this world in the face of these forces. Globalization is largely based on ideological agendas that are one-dimensional readings of natural and social processes. These serve as the basis for the alignment of processes that construct the hyperefficient strategies of modern industry. The power and achievement of these techniques are undeniable; however, they are based on abstractions that may provide only a partial picture of the material world.

Such universals allow logic and precision to serve as the foundation for the technological society that is globalizing our world to continually materialize, so information can be accumulated and organized rapidly. This affords the ability to construct conceptual frames of understanding and perception, which allow connections between cultures, economies, and disciplines to be made. However, these frames are superficially precise, and though our vision machines have great potential in interpreting and providing meaning to our existence, humans can perceive the world in a multitude of ways utilizing all the senses plus our memory and imagination. Abstractions, generalizations, and numeric systems that coincide with technological development must be offset by value systems that are essentially human, spatial, temporal, and qualitative.

The geographical imagination, then, claims the necessity of bringing the detached mediated visions (supraterritorial) of globalization into a balanced relationship to attributes that are humane. The former is a technologically induced detachment, the latter focuses on embracing complexity and the nuanced connections of our world. How this is done successfully is a matter of how we place technology within the natural and cultural landscapes that it transforms in its spread. Heidegger frames this issue with a question: how do "we let technical devices enter our daily life, and at the same time leave them outside, that is, let them alone, as things which are nothing absolute but remain dependent upon something higher"?[36] In other words, how can the benefits of globalization and its technologies of mediation be encountered, so that the essential value of our surrounding landscapes is not lost and the attributes defining our essential humanity are not overrun?

The Modern Nomad: Navigating Space/Mediated Space in a Rapidly Globalizing World

The development of the ability to inhabit both the world of our immediate perceptual experiences and the technological visions that provide a detached and overarching view is not only possible but imperative. It is possible only if our value systems properly align our perceptions of "things" with our abstract paradigms, generalized descriptions, and singular agendas of development. In addition, these values must be flexible and continually forming with the attitudes they demand, not wielded timidly but with the conviction that emerges only after deeply circumspect evaluation. For the balance between our perceptual and mediated realities to be struck, a new type of geographical imagination must be forged. One not solely "rooted" in a particular landscape or space but has a rootedness nonetheless.

This connection is similar to the attribute formed by many traditional nomadic tribes. They were not tied to one locale but inherently connected to the entire system forming their surroundings. These individuals were in tune with seasonal changes, environmental rhythms, and natural variations and had a profound sense of their place in the overall schema of the cosmos through an abstracted, but sophisticated, understanding of its structure. Details such as rock formations and certain species of animals were studied to comprehend the relationships of things encountered in a hunt. One reason for the necessity of this understanding was immediate, for daily survival; the other was for the long-term progress of the tribe. There was a continued attempt to comprehend the meaningfulness of the whole as well as the meaning of the individual life contained within it at various scales. These "primitives" were acutely aware of both their immediate surroundings and its place within the temporal continuum of the cosmos. Though homeless in the sense of a particular locale, they were acutely "at home" within the landscapes that they inhabited.

Our modern geographical imagination must take on a similar form because of the inherent homelessness of our contemporary existence. As the mediated imagery of globalization forces its way into our psyches and its demands for mobility and change increase, modern individuals must adapt by cultivating the ability to inhabit simultaneous scalar realms. One realm is immediate, qualitative, and tactile, the other, abstract, detached, and highly mediated. This simultaneous inhabitation of these realms still demands a richness and diversity of detail so important to our humanity. A balance must be maintained for our drive toward material prosperity that recognizes the needs of the human spirit or the latter will succumb to the superficiality of the image. To maintain a healthy tension between these structures, change and temporality must be acknowledged as a fundamental attribute of space. If engaged forthrightly, there is no reason to fear the technological advancements of globalization, for a continuously adaptable value system can forge a unity between new and old. By this, the values traditionally grounding us can be recalled to serve as a guide to the empathetic assimilation of a technologically mediated future. One where our relationship to it is simple, relaxed, and spiritually fulfilling.

Endnotes

1. Paul Virilio, *Virilio Live*, ed. John Armitage (London: Sage Publications, 2001), 71.
2. See Rohit Chopra, "Introduction," this volume, 2.
3. Eugene Robinson, "The Moment for This Messenger?" *Washington Post*, March 13, 2007, http://www.washingtonpost.com/wp-dyn/content/article/2007/03/12/AR2007031200983.html; Chopra, "Introduction," 2.
4. Chopra, "Introduction," 2.
5. Jan Aart Scholte, *Globalization: A Critical Introduction* (New York, NY: St. Martin's Press, 2000), 46.
6. Rob Bartram, "Visuality, Dromology and Time Compression: Paul Virilio's New Ocularcentrism," *Time & Society* 13, no. 2–3 (2006): 292.
7. Ibid.
8. Mitchell Schwarzer, *Zoomscape: Architecture in Motion and Media* (New York, NY: Princeton Architectural Press, 2004), 16.
9. Scholte, *Globalization,* 46–8.
10. Doreen Massey and Pat Jess, "Introduction," in *The Shape of the World: Explorations in Human Geography*, Vol. 4, ed. Massey and Jess (Oxford: Oxford University Press, 1995), 1.
11. Paul Ricoeur, "Universal Civilization and National Cultures," in *History and Truth*, trans. Chas A. Kelbley (Evanston, IL: Northwestern University Press, 1965), 16.
12. Paul Virilio, *Open Sky*, trans. Julie Rose (New York, NY: Verso, 1997), 37.
13. David Harvey, "The Social and Geographical Imaginations," *The International Journal of Political and Cultural Sociology* 18 (2005): 212.
14. Doreen Massey and Pat Jess, "Introduction," in *The Shape of the World: Explorations in Human Geography*, Vol. 4, ed. Massey and Jess (Oxford: Oxford University Press, 1995), 46.
15. Christian Norberg-Shultz, *Genius Loci: Towards a Phenomenology of Architecture* (New York, NY: Rizzoli, 1979), 6.
16. Paul Virilio and Sylvère Lotringer, *Pure War* (New York, NY: Semiotext(e), 1997), 36.
17. Rob Bartram, "Visuality, Dromology and Time Compression," 295.
18. Ibid.
19. Norberg-Shultz, *Genius Loci*, 7.
20. Edward Relph, *Rational Landscapes and Humanistic Geography* (Totowa, NJ: Barnes and Noble Books, 1981), 14.
21. Ibid., 18.
22. Paul Virilio, *The Paul Virilio Reader*, ed. Steve Redhead (New York, NY: Columbia University Press, 2004), 136.
23. Virilio (*VR*), 86.
24. Ibid., 87.
25. Ibid.
26. Ibid., 89.
27. Ibid., 91.
28. Bartram, "Visuality, Dromology and Time Compression," 286.
29. Ibid., 291.

30. Ibid., 422.

31. Vincent Miller, "The Unmappable: Vagueness and Spatial Experience," *Space and Culture* 9, no. 4 (2006): 461.

32. John Ruskin, *The Modern Painters*, vol. IV (London: G. Allen, 1906), 28; Relph, *Rational Landscapes*, 181.

33. Harvey, "Geographical Imagination," 214.

34. Relph, *Rational Landscapes*, 177.

35. Ibid., 176.

36. Martin Heidegger, "Memorial Address," in *Discourse on Thinking* (New York, NY: Harper & Row, 1966), 54; Robert Mugerauer, *Interpretations on Behalf of Place: Environmental Displacements and Alternative Responses* (New York: State University of New York Press, 1994), 132.

CHAPTER 5

Overseas Print Capitalism and Chinese Nationalism in the Early Twentieth Century

DAVID KENLEY

Chapter Description

During the early twentieth century, overseas Chinese intellectuals argued about the cultural contours of the Chinese nation. As they were living abroad, their notions of the nation went beyond simply territory or even citizenship. Throughout this process, they relied heavily on newspapers and other serial publications to share their ideas and discredit the ideas of their opponents. Many of them saw themselves as living in the Chinese diaspora, and therefore, they felt entitled to participate in the construction of the nation. Nevertheless, their unique conditions also allowed them to shift their identities from nationalism, to regionalism, to transnationalism, as situations dictated. This chapter looks at the serial publications of Tokyo, Singapore, San Francisco, and Paris to investigate their role in the construction of Chinese national identity.

* * *

During the early twentieth century, Chinese intellectuals passionately debated one another regarding the cultural contours and future of the Chinese nation. Some chose to focus on the perceived Chinese "essence" in defining the nation. Others suggested discarding much of China's heritage in favor of greater Westernization, yet even they could not decide on which cultural elements to eliminate and which to keep. Throughout the process, newspapers served as the primary forum for discussing these issues.

Not surprisingly, overseas Chinese eventually entered this debate. Since the nation, as constructed in the meta-narratives of the day, emphasized territory, citizenship, and international boundaries, overseas individuals were forced to reinterpret nationalism and national identity according to their unique geographical situation. By portraying themselves as members of a Chinese diaspora, intellectuals claimed a participating role in the construction of a new nation. Furthermore, as with their contemporaries in China, overseas intellectuals also used newspapers and other serial publications to broadcast their views on nationalism and Chinese identity.

It is illuminating to study the convergence of these two trends—the growth of nationalism and the proliferation of newspapers—within the overseas Chinese communities. It has been nearly three decades since Benedict Anderson published his revolutionary work, *Imagined Communities*.[1] For those living beyond the geographic borders of the nation, this "imagined community" was certainly more ethereal. On the other hand, as Craig Calhoun points out, space-transcending media, such as newspapers, create powerful linkages across dispersed populations.[2] It should not surprise us, therefore, that overseas Chinese communities saw the simultaneous growth in nationalism and newspaper publications.

Newspapers (and the people who write them) do not simply highlight and publish underlying cultural codes, broadcasting the identity of nations. They also function as forums for the construction and deconstruction of collective identity. Newspapers allow political elites to nurture their own versions of nationalism while discrediting competing versions, and yet, newspapers are also frequently open to sub-elites, providing them with a public sphere to challenge and contest previously accepted national "borders." Discourse helps to define social reality, reinforce accepted identities, and replicate social structures. At the same time, discursive outlets also transform widely accepted realities, challenging cultural and social assumptions. In short, the malleability of newspapers allowed overseas Chinese to reconstruct the Chinese nation, creating space for their widely divergent communities within that nation.

This chapter looks at "China" from a broad geographic perspective, analyzing overseas Chinese communities in Tokyo, Singapore, San Francisco, and Paris during the early twentieth century. Each of these communities had an active publishing industry and each added to the ongoing dialogue on nationalism. Beyond these similarities, however, the individuals in each location had rather different experiences. By placing them side by side, this chapter demonstrates the powerful appeal of nationalism across spatial and experiential boundaries.

Serials in Tokyo

Between 1898 and 1907, approximately 30,000 Chinese students traveled to Japan to study. At this time, Chinese and Japanese leaders frequently spoke of Pan-Asian unity in the face of Western encroachment, and leaders of the two empires encouraged greater cooperation and cultural exchange, including an invitation from Tokyo for Chinese students to enroll in Japanese institutions. Soon, approximately 20,000 Chinese youth were studying in Japan.[3]

As the student population grew, so did the publishing industry. Japan's first Chinese-language serial was created by the followers of Kang Youwei in 1898. Kang, a leading intellectual of the period, advocated the establishment of Western-style schools, the development of more railways, and the formation of an export-oriented economy. However, the goal of these reforms, in his view, was to preserve the essence of traditional Chinese culture, including Qing Dynasty imperial rule, Confucian social structures, and defined gender roles. Kang found overseas Chinese communities particularly supportive of his ideas, and beginning in 1898, he traveled throughout the world, including Japan, promoting his limited reforms for China.

Established in Yokohama, *China Discussion* (*Qing Yi Bao*) served as a forum for discussing Kang's ideas. As recorded in the first edition, the journal sought to stimulate the spiritual strength of the people, increase knowledge, unite China and Japan in friendship, and preserve Asian learning.[4] As it was the first of its kind, *China Discussion* had a large impact on its readers. In its pages, Chinese students were introduced to the ideas of political revolution, biological evolution, and international law.[5]

Not everybody accepted the ideas of Kang Youwei. Others, namely Sun Yat-sen, believed Kang's programs would only delay the inevitable collapse of the government. Instead, Sun wanted a thoroughgoing revolution, with the establishment of a Western-style republic. In 1901, Sun's camp launched the *National Daily* (*Guo Min Bao*) in Japan. Quickly, *National Daily* became the leading rival of the reform-minded *China Discussion*. Deriding the reformists as backward counter-revolutionaries, *National Daily* steadily increased in popularity and circulation.[6] Predictably, imperial officials in Beijing hated the publication and repeatedly blocked its importation to China.[7]

Although *China Discussion* and *National Daily* were some of the earliest and most influential publications, they represent only a tiny fraction of the total. Between 1898 and 1911, at least 65 additional journals and newspapers emerged in Japan. Many of these were "provincial journals." On arriving in Japan, students most frequently associated with classmates from their home province. Eventually, students formed study groups based on provincial origins, and in turn, these study groups published newspapers and journals. At least 11 such provincial journals existed. Most focused on nationwide issues, openly calling for revolution and the overthrow of the Qing Dynasty. They also introduced a wide range of sociopolitical theories, ranging from democracy and equality to socialism, anarchism, and Russian nihilism.[8] Others, however, focused on provincial issues. Students from Guangdong province even went so far as to advocate independence from China.[9] Fearful that such fragmentation would become endemic, the provincial journal *Zhejiang Tide* (*Zhejiang Chao*) suggested that all local boundaries be dissolved and the Chinese state be administered as an undivided whole.[10] Other publications were less radical than those of either the Guangdong or the Zhejiang students. For instance, students from Hunan, Hubei, Shanxi, and Gansu all formed interprovincial organizations or published interprovincial serials.[11]

A scan of the remaining serial titles illuminates several other important trends. *Notes of Enlightenment, New People's Miscellany, Awakened Lion,* and *The Restoration* suggest a preoccupation with newness and rebirth. Other titles demonstrate a concern with nationalism and Chinese identity, including *China's Voice, The People, China New Daily, China's Flag,* and *Wind of China.* Still others reveal that the sociocultural contours of the Chinese nation were still being formed, such as *China New Women's World, Women's Soul, Essence of Learning of Chinese Youth,* and *New Knowledge of Constitutions.* Obviously, the students in Japan were a diverse group of individuals, united in their concern for self-definition.

In addition to publishing original essays, Japan's serials served as platforms for advertising and for distributing translated works in book form. The sponsoring student groups were often the same for both the serials as well as the translations. Some of the more notable translations included Katō Hiroyuki's *The Struggle for Existence,* Ōhashi Otowa's *The Precarious East,* and Takada Sanai's *A Theory of Politics.* Students also retranslated Western works already existing in Japanese form. Some of these titles included the following: Francis Lieber, *On Civil Liberty and Self-government*; John Stuart Mill, *On Liberty*; Samuel Smiles, *Self-help*; Alexis de Tocqueville, *De la démocratie en Amérique*; Karl Marx, *Manifesto of the Communist Party* and *Das Kapital*; and Frederick Engels, *Socialism: Utopian and Scientific.* Such works had an immense impact on the students' sense of national identity.

It is possible to make several conclusions regarding print capitalism and Chinese nationalism in the case of Japan. First, the overseas Chinese were conflicted between their national identity and their provincial identity. Although they organized along provincial lines, they more often focused

on national issues. It might be assumed that over time provincial segrega-
tion would give way to Chinese nationalism. However, at the highpoint of
the immigration movement, approximately 1906–1907, 10 new provincial
journals emerged. Even in a period of tremendous national change, provincial
identity remained strong.

Second, these publications introduced an entirely new worldview, as
they debated issues of language, politics, and sociology. In the process, editors discovered that the Chinese language did not contain the necessary
terminology to describe their newfound identities. Consequently, they borrowed Japanese terms to write about complex new ideas. Some of the
neologisms adopted in the Chinese–Japanese press included the following:
"counter-revolutionary," "liberty," "democracy," "communism," "religion,"
"feudalism," and "proletariat." It is difficult to fathom Chinese identity in
the twentieth century without these important terms.

Third, publishers in Japan experienced tension between their identity as
Chinese nationals and Pan-Asians. Initially, many of them were drawn to
Japan because of perceived similarities in race and culture. Several mas-
tered the Japanese language and some even took Japanese wives. However,
their publications reveal a startling lack of local Japan news, instead focusing on Chinese events and trends.

Finally, the serial industry demonstrates that Chinese students viewed
Japanese learning as a conduit to Western learning and not a goal in and
of itself. Even though they were translating Japanese-language texts, many
of these were retranslations of texts originally written in English, German, or
French. Consequently, China's initial knowledge of Marx, Tocqueville, and
Mill came through the prism of Japan.

It is difficult to overstate the importance of Japan's publishing industry
for Chinese identity. Future Chinese leaders including military generals
(Chiang Kai-shek), communist party secretaries (Li Dazhao and Chen
Duxiu), and literature greats (Lu Xun) all participated in the Japan study
movement and its accompanying publication industry. The overseas serials
in Japan provide a unique insight into the relationships between local identities, national identities, and transnational identities.

Serials in Singapore

In contrast to the students in Japan, the Chinese residents of Singapore
were often second- and third-generation immigrants. Furthermore, they
represented the majority culture. For these reasons, their "memory" of the
homeland and their diasporic experience differed from the tiny Chinese
minority living in Japan. Nevertheless, no other overseas city was more
actively involved in the newspaper industry than was Singapore.

Chinese newspapers have a long history in Southeast Asia. Under British colonial rule, the Malaya colony welcomed thousands of Chinese immigrants to its shores. The first Chinese-language paper to capitalize on this market was *The Straits Times* (*Le Bao* or *Lat Po*). First published in 1881, *The Straits Times* included imperial rescripts, reprints from other Chinese papers, local government announcements, advertisements, and short stories.[12] With head-lines such as "A Discussion on Ruling the Family," "On Teaching the Children," and "On Repaying with Kindness," *The Straits Times* perpetuated traditional morals and identities, helping the local population to maintain its political and cultural ties with China.[13]

Between 1890 and 1911, several new serials emerged in Singapore. These papers were increasingly partisan, with some representing Kang Youwei's reformist camp and others representing Sun Yat-sen's revolutionaries. The mouthpiece of the reformist camp was *The Singapore Times* (*Xing Bao*). It covered not only the political events of the mainland but also attempted to influence cultural debates. It warned of excessive "Westernization" and assimilation among the Singapore Chinese. An 1894 editorial cautioned,

> Many of the local-borns no longer understand and observe the tra-ditional five relationships; the men here listen to their wives more than to their parents; the women have abandoned their traditional virtues and are gradually Westernized. We must try to change their evil tendencies in Singapore.[14]

The mouthpiece of the revolutionary camp was *New Tiannan Times* (*Tiannan Xin Bao*). Rather than fearing Westernization, *New Tiannan Times* wanted to "give every facility for the expression of progressive ideas and the elucidation of the methods which have lifted up the European nations from the . . . follies of the past."[15] In covering mainland affairs, *New Tiannan Times* was generally critical of the Manchu Qing court.

This rivalry between the reformists and the revolutionaries became a moot point with the collapse of the Qing court in 1911. Sun Yat-sen and his followers quickly declared the founding of the Republic of China, though they never established firm control over the former Qing Dynasty territo-ries. Predictably, Singapore's newspaper industry changed because of the 1911 revolution. No longer serving as simply propaganda outlets for the reformists and revolutionaries, newspapers began catering to a more diverse readership. For example, business mogul Tan Kah-kee (Chen Jiageng) created a new paper for local businessmen.[16] Called the *South Seas Commercial News* (*Nanyang Shang Bao*), the paper was filled with adver-tisements for everything from the Asiatic Petroleum Company to Beka Phonographic Records to Bayer Aspirin. Newspapers also shifted attention away from solely mainland China news. *The Singapore Daily* (*Xing Zhou Ri Bao*) was divided into sections for "local news," "Malaya news," "Southeast Asian news," "Guangdong and Fujian news," "foreign news," and "news commentary." The special Sunday edition included sections on economics, women's affairs, international problems, exercise, and travel.

One of the more popular sections of the Singapore newspapers was the "literary supplement," which would publish poetry, short stories, and essays of local writers. Increasingly, editors called for "local color" within these works of literature. The editor of *The People's Daily* (*Guo Min Ri Bao*) explained that "[Southeast Asia] is rich and beautiful," making it an ideal location for literary inspiration.[17] Tin mines, coconut trees, and rickshaw pullers became the subject of various essays, and soon all the newspapers were competing to demonstrate their own local color. One writer suggested:

> The things I wish to discuss take Southeast Asia as the center. I immigrated to Southeast Asia as a child. Consequently, I think it is very loveable. For all intents and purposes, Southeast Asia is already like my second home . . . As for China, I actually am not terribly interested. We live in Southeast Asia and we should talk about the affairs of Southeast Asia.[18]

By the late 1920s, Singapore's Chinese writers began referring to their published literature not as "Chinese," but as "New Malay-Chinese literature" (*Mahua xin wenxue*). However, the authors continued to use Chinese ideographs while drawing heavily from traditional Chinese tropes, themes, and symbols to demonstrate local color.

By looking at the history of newspapers in Singapore, several important conclusions emerge. In their early years, 1880–1911, the newspapers focused almost exclusively on political events from the mainland. Especially during the waning years of the Qing Dynasty, Singapore's newspapers functioned as political organs for the Kang Youwei and Sun Yat-sen camps. By the 1920s, however, the tables had turned, as more and more local-born Chinese seized control of the newspapers—especially the literary sections— and used them to advocate local color. Throughout the process, there was a continuing intellectual tug-of-war between the homeland and the adopted country in determining what it meant to be Chinese.

Serials in San Francisco

As in the previous cases, the Chinese community in San Francisco was also deeply involved in the debate over Chinese national identity, and the newspapers of this community perpetuated the ongoing discussions. Because of violence and discrimination, San Francisco's "Chinatown" was isolated from the larger American population, forcing the Chinese immigrants to create their own organizations for government, education, and entertainment. Newspapers were part of this process. As explained in the San Francisco Chinese-language newspaper *Young China* (*Shaonian Zhongguo*):

> We Chinese trying to make a living abroad have suffered all kinds of discrimination . . . The United States has established special laws excluding Chinese laborers, which was a non-humanitarian act. Yet that was not enough. There have been increasing strict regulations and meticulous fault-finding practices, which intended to wipe all Chinese from the American continent . . . If we Chinese wish to defend ourselves against such discrimination, we must first of all restore our national independence. In order to restore our national independence, we must first restore the Chinese nation.[19]

In San Francisco, three newspapers played a major role in "restoring the Chinese nation." They were *Chinese World* (*Shijie Ribao* or *Sai Gai Yat Bo*), *Young China*, and *Chinese and Western Daily* (*Zhong Xi Ribao* or *Chung Sai Yat Po*). *Chinese World* was the official organ of Kang Youwei and his reform-minded followers. In the early years of the twentieth century, it was the most popular of the three papers. *Young China*, by contrast, was the paper of Sun Yat-sen's revolution advocates. Both before and after the 1911 revolution, this paper struggled to represent the mainstream voices in San Francisco. *Chinese and Western Daily*, self-proclaimed as "The leading Chinese Daily Paper Outside China," first circulated the streets of San Francisco in 1900. Founded by Wu Panzhao (Ng Poon Chew), a Christian convert, *Chinese and Western Daily* promoted cultural reform and adaptation for the Chinese immigrants in the United States. In many ways, it occupied the middle ground between the *Chinese World* and *Young China*. All three newspapers tackled the thorny identity issues of the day, including the perpetuation of Chinese tradition, republicanism, communism, and equality.

In defining the nation, all three serials had to come to terms with Chinese tradition, most notably Confucianism. What role would traditional Chinese practices play in the new nation? What should be maintained and what should be discarded? How much should China emulate the West and how much should it adopt? *Chinese World* was the most vocal in its support of Confucian tradition. Calling Confucius "China's Arch Bishop," the paper often wrote that Confucianism held the keys to stability, harmony, and national unity.[20] Indeed, it was "the fountainhead for Chinese civilization."[21] The paper's editors claimed Confucianism was completely compatible with a modern Chinese nation-state, as it required civilian participation in the political arena for the betterment of society as a whole. As such, they pointed out, Confucianism created a proto-democracy in China thousands of years before the United States existed.[22]

Young China typically disagreed with the editorial slant of *Chinese World.* Predictably, in 1919 it published an editorial titled "On the Conflict between the New and Old Schools of Thought in Beijing." Although *Chinese and Western Daily* was far from revolutionary, it too maintained a critical stance toward Confucianism and other elements of Chinese tradition. It pointed out that, in the eyes of the West, many of the rituals associated with Confucianism were ridiculous and therefore Chinese immigrants ought to reevaluate their usefulness.[23] Editorialists in *Chinese and Western Daily* called for Chinese on the mainland to abandon the lunar calendar, adopt a 7-day week, and reform "bad habits."[24] However, both *Young China* and *Chinese and Western Daily* offered relatively few attacks on tradition in general and Confucianism in particular. Unlike intellectuals in other overseas locales, the Chinese community in San Francisco did not see a stark contrast between Confucianism, Chinese tradition, and a new nationalist identity.

All three newspapers also discussed the role and scope of republicanism for China. Although *Chinese World* initially opposed the 1911 Revolution, by the end of that decade, all three papers supported a republican form of government. By creating a republic, *Young China* wrote, China had finally joined the family of great nations, and both *Young China* and *Chinese and Western Daily* wrote in defense of republicanism.[25] By contrast, *Chinese World* had a more nuanced view of republicanism. It claimed that constitutionalism was the most important element in any governing structure. As the 1911 revolution produced a constitutional republic, *Chinese World* wrote, it was foolhardy to abandon it for a nonconstitutional alternative.[26] Instead, *Chinese World* suggested maintaining a republican system modeled closely along the lines of the U.S. government.[27]

Just as all three papers generally supported republicanism for China, all three rejected communism as inappropriate for the Chinese nation. As early as 1919, 2 years before the Chinese Communist Party was formed, *Young China* referred to Bolshevism as "a plague" and *Chinese World* derided communism as destructive of individual rights and detrimental to civilization.[28] *Chinese and Western Daily*, generally a pro-business paper, also attacked communism. China needed economic development, the paper wrote, and communism would retard the progress China was making, as it would scare off foreign investors and limit individual initiative.[29] Instead of directly challenging communism on theoretical grounds, the papers typically covered national and international events from an anticommunist point of view. For instance, when China's political leaders made overtures toward Moscow, *Chinese World* accused them of political tomfoolery whereas *Chinese and Western Daily* warned of socialist imperialism.[30] Even though *Young China* defended the proposed alliance as politically necessary, it quickly pointed out the ideological differences between China's leaders and Soviet Russia.[31]

In the process of delineating national borders (real or figurative), some individuals inevitably are included within the nation, whereas others are excluded. All three papers discussed the issues of citizenship, fraternity, and equality for Chinese nationals. When the Manchu Qing court established *jus sanguinis* citizenship in 1909, the overseas Chinese in San Francisco rightfully claimed membership in the Chinese nation, and newspaper editors began discussing the rights, duties, and expectations of citizens. They forced their readers to ask themselves, does citizenship and fraternity necessitate equality? Should equality exist in the political arena, the economic arena, or both? Are women equal to men and what should be the proper role of women in the nation?

Shortly after the 1911 revolution, *Young China* published an article calling for greater equality, specifically economic equality, among Chinese citizens. The state, it wrote, had the responsibility for instituting a progressive tax structure, creating a nationalized banking system, and promoting key industries for the betterment of all.[32] By doing so, all citizens would feel a greater commitment to the maintenance of the nation. *Young China* further suggested that, in the realm of politics, all citizens were to be equal and that such terms as "your excellency" should no longer be used when addressing public officials.[33] On the other hand, *Chinese World* advocated a Confucian-based social order, complete with hierarchical differentiation. As the gentry class was better educated, the paper suggested, its members should have a larger voice in national affairs.[34] *Chinese and Western Daily* also warned against complete egalitarianism, arguing that strikes, protests, and other undesirable forms of social discord typically erupted with unrealistic promises of "equality."[35] In terms of gender equality, *Chinese World* was the most vocal of the three papers. It asserted that women should be excluded entirely from the political process.[36] The role of China's women was in the home, raising and educating children to serve the nation, and any attempt at political dialogue involving women was futile.[37]

As can be seen, newspapers in San Francisco highlight the changing nature of being Chinese. Unlike publications in Tokyo and Paris, the American papers were more conservative and traditional. Whether they were discussing Confucianism, republicanism, communism, or egalitarianism, the major publications drew heavily on Chinese tradition and remained hesitant to adopt radical change. When they did embrace reform, they were frequently motivated by a desire to protect their precarious situation in San Francisco.[38] In other words, they envisioned a "new China" through the lenses of their overseas experience.

Serials in Paris

The growth of the Chinese community in France proceeded in fits and starts. As early as 1902, Chinese students traveled to Paris for study. These early individuals were fervent admirers of French culture, politics, and history. In 1908, one of these students—Li Shizeng—opened a bean-curd factory in Colombes (a suburb of Paris) and staffed it with 30 workers whom he recruited from his home village. He decided to use these workers for a unique experiment in "diligent work and frugal study." Believing that a combination of hard work, structured living conditions, and formal study would produce disciplined, educated citizens, Li's model existed in one form or another for the next 13 years.[39]

With the onset of World War I, the work-study experiment was temporarily put on hold. Even so, the Chinese French community expanded rapidly. In desperate need of labor to sustain the war effort, the government in Paris encouraged thousands of Chinese to travel to France to work at munitions factories and construction sites. By the end of the war, 35,000 Chinese lived in France as laborers. Though most would return home after the war, many chose to stay in Europe.

Between 1919 and 1921, the two governments reinstituted a formal work-study program for Chinese already in France, as well as for new arrivals. During that 2-year period, approximately 1,500 students participated. As the immigrants became increasingly politically active, the French government became increasingly displeased with the program. For this and other reasons, the work-study program ended in 1921. Even so, many of the work-study students remained in France, helping to sustain a vibrant Chinese French community.

From the earliest years of the twentieth century, the Chinese living in France supported a publishing industry. Beginning in 1907, Li Shizeng and some of his associates published *New Century* (*Xin Shi Ji* or *Le Tempoj Novaj*). According to its own published guidelines, *New Century* was to pursue the principles of science and revolution, using the French Revolution of 1789 as a starting model, and pursuing on to an egalitarian socialist revolution similar to the Paris Commune of 1871.[40] In many ways, *New Century* was a much more cosmopolitan newspaper than those in Tokyo, Singapore, and San Francisco, as it advocated worldwide revolution and covered a range of global issues.

Though it was short-lived, *New Century* had a major impact on the political and linguistic debates of its time. From the beginning, *New Century* promoted the use of Esperanto (hence its Esperanto subtitle, *Le Tempoj Novaj*). Numerous contributors to the newspaper complained that Chinese characters were, by their very nature, elitist, because only those with higher levels of education could master them. Furthermore, writers claimed, it was impossible to translate the more advanced learning of the West into an archaic language such as Chinese. Evolution demanded that China surrender its cultural backwardness and adopt the trappings of the modern West (including phonetic alphabets, punctuation, and simple-to-use dictionaries). In short, the Chinese language was "barbaric." Only a truly international language such as Esperanto could save the Chinese from themselves.[41] Interestingly, throughout its existence, *New Century* remained a Chinese, not Esperanto, publication.

Ironically, *New Century*'s biggest critic was Zhang Binglin, the editor of *National Daily* (*Guo Min Bao*), an overseas serial published in Tokyo. Zhang pointed out that Western linguists developed Esperanto, and it was based on Western alphabets and vocabulary terms. Therefore, he claimed, it was a language "of the whites," and adopting it would result in linguistic imperialism and cultural suicide for China. In addition, Zhang took issue with *New Century*'s claims of China's cultural backwardness, accusing its editors of ignorance and self-hatred.[42]

Along with its fascination toward Esperanto, *New Century* introduced its readers to a wide variety of global leaders and issues. Its editors were staunch advocates of anarcho-communism and global revolution.[43] Throughout its publication history, *New Century* covered major strikes from around the world, repeatedly called for worker unity, and provided biographies of famous anarchists from Carlo Cafiero to Pierre Kropotkine. The journal also discussed the lives of other, more widely accepted government leaders, including Abraham Lincoln, Alexander II, and Queen Elizabeth.[44] Meanwhile, news items from China were also included, though typically not on the front page.

During later years, additional publications circulated among the Chinese French population. Shortly after the end of World War I, the General Association of Chinese Workers in France created the *Weekly Chinese Journal* (*Lü Ou Zhou Kan*, subtitled *Journal Chinois Hebdomadaire*). Designed to transcend geographic and dialectical differences segmenting the Chinese French community, the journal became the mouthpiece of the work-study advocates. Li Shizeng, one of the founders of *New Century*, was a frequent contributor to the *Weekly Chinese Journal*. Li was simultaneously a cosmopolitan anarchist and an unabashed Francophile. Writing in the pages of the journal, Li suggested that the Chinese were extravagant, unclean, and superstitious. Instead, they should model their own behavior on the French who were polite, humanistic, freedom-loving, and pacifistic (rather than the Germans, who were autocratic and militaristic).[45] They should also learn the principles of science and basic hygiene.[46]

The *Weekly Chinese Journal* frequently advocated *laodong zhuyi*, or "laborism." Students attending classes in the United States came from privileged backgrounds, the journal pointed out, and they were eagerly studying the tenets of capitalism. By contrast, the students in France came from modest backgrounds and were combining their in-class activities with invaluable out-of-class work. For this reason, they would return to China with a greater understanding of the needs of the laboring classes.[47] "Even if they do not study anything," one of the program's supporters wrote, "if at least they learn how to clean toilets it will be worth it."[48] The *Weekly Chinese Journal* wrote, "today's workers in the future can become students, while today's work-study students will soon become 'complete workers.'"[49]

Given the combination of anarcho-communism advocated in the pages of *New Century* and the laborism advocated in the pages of the *Weekly Chinese Journal*, it is not surprising the Chinese Communist Youth Party emerged from among the student community in France. Eventually, this group grew to include such future notables as Zhou Enlai, Deng Xiaoping, and Li Lisan. Fed with a constant print diet of anarchism and laborism, the Chinese community in France became increasingly belligerent. Between 1917 and 1925, at least seven protests rocked the Chinese French community, with more than 100 individuals deported as a result.

In summary, the publications in France appear to be far more cosmopolitan than those in either Japan or Southeast Asia. Chinese politics were much less conspicuous within their pages, and editors gave less coverage to Chinese events than their counterparts did in other overseas publications. At the same time, publishers in France were more ideologically motivated, as seen in the case of Esperanto, anarcho-communism, and laborism. Despite their relatively small numbers, the contributors to the serials in France demonstrate the powerful cultural influence of newspapers on Chinese national identity.

Conclusion

This chapter adds an important perspective to the study of overseas print capitalism and nationalism. In the cases of Tokyo, Singapore, San Francisco, and Paris, Chinese editors and writers confronted issues of diasporic, national, and transnational identity. Though their individual experiences differed, they asked and answered many of the same questions.

At first glance, it may appear that the overseas Chinese press was a product of diaspora consciousness. Typically, a diaspora consists of a group of people sharing a common point of origin but dispersed to at least two different areas. Diasporic individuals maintain a memory of the homeland and believe that assimilation is impossible in their adopted lands. For these reasons, they remain committed to the maintenance of the homeland and hope eventually to return.[50] In other words, the homeland is the defining ingredient in their identity. Indeed, the Chinese press did cover the seminal events of Chinese history, such as the 1911 revolution. This allowed overseas readers to maintain an emotional and intellectual tie with their homeland. However, these same publications introduced new concepts—ranging from republicanism to feminism—that redefined the Chinese nation for their readers. Newspapers became public spheres for the formation and reformation of the Chinese nation.

At the same time, newspaper and journal editors debated issues decoupled from, or antithetical to, the nation-state. Immigrants often segregated themselves according to their provincial origins, and their serial publications highlight such divisions. At the other end of the spectrum, writers deliberated global affairs, ranging from worldwide revolution to the spread of Esperanto. They searched for transnational solutions—including anarcho-communism, socialism, Pan-Asianism, and even Christianity—to local and global problems. Because of their cross-cultural experiences, they viewed themselves as global citizens searching for global answers.

It seems that, for the overseas Chinese, identity was multilayered and situational. Depending on the context, publishers could privilege regionalism, nationalism, or even transnationalism within the context of their pages. The space-transcending media of these overseas communities allowed them to imagine themselves as members of a "Greater China." Writers in Tokyo debated with writers in Paris. Editors in Singapore covered issues relating to readers in San Francisco. Students in Beijing read smuggled copies of revolutionary publications printed in Southeast Asia, North America, and Europe. If newspapers allow for an imagined community, then these overseas locales demonstrate just how large and diverse such a community may be.

Endnotes

1. Benedict Anderson, *Imagined Communities* (London: Verso, 1980).
2. Craig Calhoun, "Nationalism and Ethnicity," *Annual Review of Sociology* 19 (1993): 211–39.
3. Douglas R. Reynolds, "A Golden Decade Forgotten: Japan–China Relations, 1898–1907," *Transactions of the Asiatic Society of Japan*, 4th ser., 2 (1987): 114–15.
4. "Qing Yi Bao Xu Li," *Qing Yi Bao* 1 (1898): 1, as quoted in Huang Fu-ch'ing, *Chinese Students in Japan in the Late Ch'ing Period*, East Asian cultural studies series, no. 22 (Tokyo: The Centre for East Asian Cultural Studies, 1982), 161.
5. Huang, 163.
6. Ibid., 177.
7. Ibid., 150.
8. Ibid., 191.
9. Ibid., 177.
10. *Zhejiang Chao*, 3 (1903): 1–20, as quoted in Huang, 182.
11. Huang, appendix 4.

12. He Shumin, *Xinjiapo zui zao de huawen ribao—Le Bao (1881–1932)* (Singapore: Nanyang bianzesuo chuban, 1978), 15–16.
13. Ibid., 31.
14. *Xing Bao (Singapore Times)*, March 13, 1894, as quoted in Chen Mong Hock, *The Early Chinese Newspapers of Singapore, 1881–1912* (Singapore: University of Malaya Press, 1967), 60.
15. *Haixia huaren zazhi/Straits Chinese Magazine* 2 (1898): 77, as quoted in Chen Mong Hock, 68.
16. Cui Guiqiang, *Xinjiapo huawen baokan yü baoren* (Singapore: Huo hua wen xin wen ye ji jin can jü, 1993), 29.
17. Yan, "Nanyang yü wenyi," *Huang Dao*, April 1, 1927. Reprinted in Fang Xiu, comp. *Mahua xin wenxue da xi* (Xinjiapo: Xing zhou shi jie shu jü yu xian gong si, 1972), vol. 1, 119–21.
18. Lianqing, "Nanyang di weny piping" (A critique of Nanyang literature), *Ye Lin* (Coconut Grove), September 15–24, 1930. Reprinted in Fang Xiu, 1: 224.
19. Shehong Chen, *Being Chinese, Becoming Chinese American* (Champaign: University of Illinois Press, 2006), 17.
20. *Shijie Ribao*, 16 October 1911, 17 October 1911, 27 May 1912.
21. *Shijie Ribao*, 22 September 1916, trans. Shehong Chen, 119.
22. *Shijie Ribao*, 8 January 1919, 9 January 1919.
23. *Zhong Xi Ribao*, 14 January 1911.
24. *Zhong Xi Ribao*, 14 February 1912, 20 February 1912, 26 February 1912.
25. *Shaonian Zhongguo*, 30 October 1911, 29 July 1915, 11 November 1915; *Zhong Xi Ribao*, 4 September 1915, 27 January 1916, 27 March 1916, 5 April 1916.
26. *Shijie Ribao*, 29 February 1916, 3 March 1916.
27. *Shijie Ribao*, 29 June 1916, 30 June 1916.
28. *Shaonian Zhongguo*, 19 August 1919; *Shijie Ribao*, 15 March 1920.
29. *Zhong Xi Ribao*, 17 May 1922.
30. *Shijie Ribao*, 9 January 1923; *Zhong Xi Ribao*, 5 January 1923.
31. *Shaonian Zhongguo*, 2 February 1924, 3 February 1924.
32. *Shaonian Zhongguo*, 6 October 1912.
33. *Shaonian Zhongguo*, 7 April 1912, 20 April 1912.
34. *Shijie Ribao*, 27 May 1912.
35. *Zhong Xi Ribao*, 13 May 1913.
36. *Shijie Ribao*, 6 June 1912, 17 June 1912.
37. *Shijie Ribao*, 29 June 1920.
38. Shehong Chen, 17.
39. For more information on this generation of students, see Paul Bailey, "The Chinese Work-Study Movement in France," *The China Quarterly* 115 (September 1988): 454.
40. *Xin Shi Ji*, 22 June 1907.
41. *Xin Shi Ji*, 35: 4, 36: 1–2, 40: 3–4, 44: 2–3, 45: 2–3. See also Gotelind Müller and Gregor Benton, "Esperanto and Chinese Anarchism, 1907–1920," *Language Problems and Language Planning* 30, no. 1 (2006): 45–73.
42. *Minbao*, 17 (October 1907); *Minbao*, 21 (June 10, 1908). See also Müller and Benton, 50–2.
43. *Xin Shi Ji*, 29 June 1907, 20 July 1907, 3 August 1907.
44. *Xin Shi Ji*, 28 March 1908.
45. *Lü Ou Zhou Kan*, 22 November 1919, 29 November 1919. See also Bailey, 444, 448–9.
46. *Lü Ou Zhou Kan*, 15 November 1919.
47. *Lü Ou Zhou Kan*, 18 December 1920.
48. Wu Zhihui as quoted in Bailey, 447.
49. *Lü Ou Zhou Kan*, 28 February 1920, trans. Bailey, 454.
50. Khachig Tölölyan, "The Nation-State and Its Others," *Diaspora* 1 (Spring 1991): 3–7.

PART II

Entanglements of the Global, Regional, National, and Local

CHAPTER 6

Reading the i-pill Advertisement

The Pleasures and Pressures of Contemporary
Contraceptive Advertising in India

NAYANTARA SHEORAN

Chapter Description

Pharmaceutical advertising has drawn the interests of scholars in visual and media studies, as in the fields of medical anthropology and Science, Technology, and Medicine. This chapter bridges together these fields of knowledge, by reading advertisements for one particular emergency contraceptive—the i-pill—which was launched in India in 2007 accompanied by a savvy media campaign. By demystifying the contradictory messages carried within the advertisements, the chapter sheds light on the relationship between contemporary advertising for emergency contraceptives and society. With the reach of these advertisements into the deepest parts of India, the national population has been implicated in a family planning project that extends into the everyday. For women these conversations are particularly important—not only for reproductive health information but also as markers of their identities in contemporary India. The chapter analyzes the conflicting messages in pharmaceutical advertisements, as well as the vocabularies that the advertisements provide to women consumers.

* * *

Your daughter needs your morning cuddle to begin her day. Your office colleagues eagerly wait for your sunshine smile. But today, everyone has been disappointed. You are just not yourself. Is it because you are *Worried you might get pregnant after last night?* You can put your mind at ease now. There's i-pill from Cipla, an emergency contraceptive pill. It is created especially for times when you could be facing the risk of an unplanned pregnancy.

(i-pill advertisement, italics added)

The above is an excerpt from the opening lines of an advertisement for an emergency contraceptive pill, i-pill.[1] Television and print advertisements for emergency contraceptives such as i-pill and Unwanted-72, which are the two premier brands in the Indian market, have been becoming part of the everyday vocabulary of both men and women in India since 2007. Contrary to popular belief, India has an interesting and long history of birth control from institutionalized state-sponsored family planning programs to informal cultural practices. The government of India acknowledges that population growth is one of the greatest challenges facing the country, thus making it an important policy issue. However, it is within the public sphere that these conversations materialize as family planning and birth control have historically consumed the imagination and governed the discourse of the Indian population at large.

From public service announcements on national television to sterilization camps during the term of the Indira Gandhi government in the 1970s, the population has participated in the discourse of family planning and birth control. The sensationalistic condom advertising for Kama Sutra in the 1990s marked the new era of birth control, where prophylactics became consumer products with attachments to lifestyles and choice.[2] With the growth and reach of television advertisements into the deepest part of India, the population has been implicated in a family planning project that extends into the everyday. Particularly for women, these conversations are important not only for reproductive health information but also as markers of their identities in contemporary India. Given that women are seeing these advertisements and sales for emergency contraceptives are increasing, I want to identify the vocabulary these advertisements are capable of espousing among women while also examining the conflicting messages carried within them.

Reading the advertisements for one particular emergency contraceptive, i-pill, allows me to interrogate the meaning-making processes undertaken by Indian women. Emergency contraceptives as pharmaceutical products provide a glimpse into the larger impact of science, technology, and medicine on subject formation in globalized societies. "As medical technology, pharmaceuticals are not only products of human culture, but producers of it."[3] Moreover, the promotions and advertisements for these pharmaceutical products afford us the opportunity to examine the link between science, technology, and medicine and resultant shifts in cultural identities. The regulated yet ubiquitous nature of pharmaceutical advertisements provide a lens into the medicalized subjectivity that is quickly becoming part of globalized communities in locations such as India.

Pharmaceutical advertising has come to the forefront of academic research in recent years. In a seminal text, Sjaak van der Geest et al. have identified the life cycle of the pharmaceutical commodity and the corresponding research project.[4] Identifying more than 200 texts, they trace projects that have examined the various stages of pharmaceuticals, from development to consumption and efficacy. However, they identify one area where additional work is required—the relationship between pharmaceuticals as symbolic artifacts and how this information flows or transfers in the popular sector.[5] There has been some research into decoding pharmaceutical advertising. Goldman and Montagne's work, for instance, unpacks the meanings of antidepressant advertisements.[6] They found, for the most part, that the advertisements were encoded in a particular manner to enable social effects where depression and its symptoms were reified. In closely reading the text of the pharmaceutical advertisements, Joseph Dumit proposes that the "average patient" is provided a vocabulary by which to explore his or her own body and understandings of health risks and health.[7] This vocabulary is provided by marketers and circulated through promotions and advertising campaigns.

If advertising is the "art of our times,"[8] the apparatus for mass deception,[9] and a reflection of our cultural values and aspirations,[10] then emergency contraceptive advertising is an example of artistic deception/depiction of women's life and contraceptive choices. Adriana Petryna and Arthur Kleinman have proposed that drug and pharmaceutical advertisements support a consumption-oriented logic where "well-being is re-cast as a commodity."[11] Andrea Tone, while tracing the history of all contraceptives in American history, writes that "Aggressive advertising was instrumental to the industry's success."[12] Contraceptives as pharmaceutical products have historically been connected to markets and profits. Furthermore, she notes that "Having divulged the ugly and myriad hazards of unwanted pregnancies while saddling women with the burden of its prevention, advertisements emphasized that peace of mind and marital happiness were conditions only the market could bestow."[13] Advertisements for contraceptives have promoted various subliminal connections to choice, life, and health.

It is these connections that need unpacking and stress the case for an examination of advertisements for emergency contraceptives within the context of India. Pharmaceutical companies have typically targeted their audiences through doctors and pharmacists; however, direct-to-consumer advertising (DTCA) is a newer trend that is still being debated, particularly in the United States. Gagnon and Lexchin found that, in 2004, the U.S. pharmaceutical industry spent 24.4% of its sales dollars on promotion, versus 13.4% for research and development.[14] In the United States, the jury on DTCA's benefits versus problems is still out, thus providing a pedagogical moment where the implications for such advertisements can be examined.[15]

The Indian Pharmaceutical Nexus

Comparisons of pharmaceutical markets between the United States and India are limited because of the different levels of purchasing power of the customers. However, since the 1990s, the "opening up" of Indian markets as a result of the economic liberalization policies adopted by the government of India allows for economic aspirations on part of the "new" India that are very similar to the United States. Globalization and overwhelming growth in some economic sectors allows particular industries to flourish. One of the industries that has experienced dramatic change is the pharmaceutical industry.[16] Since 2005, India has complied with the World Trade Organization's Agreement on Trade-Related Aspects of Intellectual Property Rights (TRIPS), which has mandated changes such as adherence to international patent laws and a nonprotectionist environment for Indian pharmaceutical companies. Although this has enabled multinational pharmaceutical companies to enter and operate in India more efficiently than in the past, the Indian pharmaceutical companies—both large and small—continue to maintain a trade monopoly within the country drawing on their previous positions in the market. Additionally, the multinationals that have started operating in India are marketing their pharmaceutical products to a limited population that is concentrated in urban-rich and middle-class areas.[17] This leaves the market open to Indian pharmaceutical companies that promote their products to the larger population segment at an exponential growth rate.[18] This growth rate can be attributed to a number of things—rising demand for "modern medicines," population growth, but above all awareness and availability of pharmaceutical products.

Although emergency contraceptives have been available in India since the late 1980s on a prescription-only basis, they were not advertised, as advertising prescription drugs in India is prohibited. However, in 2005, the regulations for emergency contraceptives were changed. The pills were made over-the-counter and hence permitted to be advertised directly to customers.[19] Two years after the legislative change, Cipla became one of the first companies to nationally launch a one-dose emergency contraceptive pill (the i-pill) accompanied with a visually savvy advertising campaign. Cipla has spent Rs. 10 crore (a hundred million rupees or about US$ 2 million) on the advertising campaign in its initial phase in 2007. However, it expects i-pill to bring in sales of Rs. 1 crore (10 million rupees) per month.[20] The i-pill, a new product in the market, did have prior competition in the emergency contraceptive market. Unwanted-72, a two-dose emergency contraceptive, was available with a prescription at pharmacists and doctors. Soon after Cipla's successful launch of the i-pill, Mankind Pharma relaunched Unwanted-72—this time as a one-dose pill. This is indicative of the growth and the sustained efforts of newer companies to target the growing market.

Reading the Advertisement

The relationships between growing markets and the marketing promotions that stimulate this growth have an impact beyond the immediate decision to purchase a particular product—in this case the i-pill. There is a long and rich history of the scholarly analysis of visual content of commercial images. From content analysis to semiotics, advertising and the meanings it conveys have afforded academics opportunities to propose the potentialities of the messages and meanings that are intended as part of an advertisement. A peeling off with an attempt to understand the "meaning-making process" of the i-pill advertisements is undertaken below (Figure 6.1).

Figure 6.1 i-pill Advertisement, "Mother and Daughter Sitting on the Floor"

Source: Reproduced with permission from Network Advertising, Mumbai, India.

For the purposes of this chapter, I will concentrate on three of the double-page spread print advertisements that were in English and generally appeared in women's magazines targeted at the urban consumer.[21] The advertisements all have a white background, with black and pink text. Most of the space is taken up by text; however, it is not cluttered. The advertisements all have one image, that of a woman sitting. In one of the spreads, the woman is accompanied by her daughter, who has her arms around the mother's shoulders. The image and conversational text (a part of which is identified in the opening section of this chapter) are on the left page of the double spread and the right page is information about the scientific facts of the i-pill and its usage. The right side of the page at the bottom right corner has an image of the actual box of the product with its logo. The logo itself is an abstract silhouette of a woman, with her hands up in the air. She has no breasts, only hips. She is marked out in shades of pink and orange. Next to the box the tag line reads, "Get back to life." My analysis here centers on four components that are either identical or similar in all three advertisements: the logo, the photographic images of the models, the two major tag lines shared by all i-pill advertisements, and finally the informational/educational section on the facing page.

The logo for the i-pill is the abstract representation of a silhouette of a dancing woman in shades of red and pink; however, if examined closely, the top half of the logo is also an inverted triangle. The inverted triangle was used during the late 1970s and 1980s as the government-sponsored logo for all birth control measures in India. With the two top corners of the triangle symbolizing a man and a woman, the bottom corner stood for the single child that should be the result of that union. The i-pill logo itself makes two obvious discourses available. In the first instance, the contemporary consumer is asked to make a shift from the government-dictated birth control project to a more consumer-oriented personal birth control option. From a simplistic red colored inverted triangle (which spoke to the stark socialist undertones of India's public sector) to a more contemporary, fluid, individualistic, and cosmopolitan image. Second, the logo in its feminine representation places women as primary decision makers in terms of birth control. However, it is also essential to note that the logo, despite its contemporary feel, continues to advance a governmental/nationalistic agenda. The Indian media, to assuage its consumerist existence, has always been eager to contribute to a "modernizing" project for India visually through the media, and this seems to be such an effort.[22]

The family planning project creates a co-dependent relationship between the Indian government and the contemporary advertising agency as summarized by Mazzarella, when writing about the advertising campaign for

Kama Sutra condoms—a brand of self-proclaimed "premier" condom launched in India in 1997. As Mazzarella puts it:

> Family planning was a strategically attractive area of intervention for the advertising industry for three reasons: first, it offered social legitimization for an industry often accused of encouraging dubious desires; second, it provided a large-scale opportunity for the radical efficacy of marketing and advertising; and third, it held up the prospect of vast billings. But from the very beginning, it also shaped up as a terrain of bitter confrontation between government and private sector interests.[23]

In forwarding the nationalistic aspiration of population control in an overpopulated nation, contemporary advertisements rhetorically profess allegiance to goals of contemporarizing India rather than making India a nation of consumers. There seems to be an acknowledgment that values based on pure consumerism are contradictory to the "traditional" Indian values of thrift and community. However, clearly, the i-pill advertising campaign goes beyond previous birth control and prophylactic advertising (like the Kama Sutra advertising campaign) in that it takes on the dual project of education and consumerism while still drawing on the moral framework provided by the government. This particular campaign then negates the "bitter confrontation" mentioned earlier.

Keeping in mind that the state has targeted women in the past with free distribution of contraceptive pills, the logo may be read as suggesting a shift in the responsibility of this birth control project largely from men and the government to women and the private sector.[24] In those cases, women were *given* the pill; however, now they are asked to *choose* the pill. Combining this history with a semiotic reading, the signifier here is the curvaceous fluid, and abstract representation of a woman and the signified is the "modern" Indian woman responsible for her own health decisions. This sign of the autonomous and modern Indian woman in turn invites viewers to invest themselves in the nation's larger modernizing project. This additionally ties into the expected emotional labor the woman is constantly asked to perform in every single one of these advertisements, from being available to "colleagues," "daughters," and even pets to the unspoken contribution to the nationalistic agenda of population control. Just as the advertisement with its embedded logo puts forward an emancipatory discourse for women as being responsible for their own sexual decisions, it immediately curtails this project by highlighting the affective labor they are currently *not* performing due to their "worry" about being pregnant. A worry, combined with nonperformed labor, is a problematic project for women—particularly those charged with a responsibility as large as birth control in a nation such as India. Just as the women are offered autonomy and independence on one hand (they are responsible for their own decisions, etc.), this autonomy is circumscribed by the accompanying text. They are not performing their womanly duties to always be available and kind to others because they are worried that they have failed their responsibility to manage their reproductive lives. This is the tension between the expectations of modernity (i.e., you are on your own now) and the still powerful pull of traditional gender roles (i.e., you must live to please others). However, the i-pill is provided as the magical solution to this tension, where the discourse suggests that consuming the pill allows you to stop worrying, perform your labor, participate in the modernizing project, and still maintain your traditional gender roles! A similar dialectic is present in the photographic aspects of the advertisements.

In all three advertisements, the photographic images that accompany the text have models sitting in the bottom right corners of each page. Notice that each of these women is *sitting* at the *bottom* of the page. In one of the images, there is a young daughter with her arms wrapped loosely around her mother's neck (see Figure 6.1). In another advertisement, the woman is sitting on a floor cushion with a cup of coffee next to her on the floor. In a third, the woman is sitting on the floor with an alarm clock right next to her. If, indeed, the i-pill wished to provide a space and a product that allowed women a rightful place in their sexual health decisions, the models would have been standing up and in more central locations on the page. Again, the dialectic between emancipation and subjugation begs the question as to what the campaign is trying to achieve here. Additionally, the images show women who appear disconnected from all reality that is Indian. The settings, either a throw pillow or a rug on the ground, are floating on a white background—detached, sanitized, and unrealistic. For a product that is entrenched in a social project that dates back to colonial India, the advertising image goes to great length to negate all markers of that history and of the women asked to participate in becoming modern consumers with the choice of birth control in their hands. Although I do not wish to allude to an essentialist reading of what an "Indian woman" ought to look like, I am also wary of images that explicitly remove markers of "India" from the Indian "modern woman." Not because I seek an attachment to Indian femininity (as that is a problematic project in and of itself), but because we run the risk of making Indian women "empty" and alienated bodies possibly subject to symbolic violence.

In *Gender Advertisements*, Erving Goffman posits that social behaviors and interactions between men and women are exemplified, where the identity of the self is created and determined externally. His main argument is that advertisements depict not our natural behavior but what we, the audiences, assume natural behavior between men and women should look like. Goffman proposes, controversially, that these depictions have the ability to convince us that we *want* to inculcate the behaviors of dominated/ dominator between women and men, in addition to thinking that this is how it *is* universally. This universal acceptance of how relationships should, could, would, and do exist was what Goffman called *normalization* of the social behaviors based on advertising images. We act into systems that we believe are the way things are, and thus reproduce those same systems. Goffman proposes that humans in societies learn social behavior by social institutions. I would suggest that there is no social institution more pervasive than advertising.

In the case of the i-pill advertisements, the relationship between the viewers and the models is being established—where the submissive placement of the female models in the advertisements is also the process of "normalization" of women's space. In any advertising design class, the first lesson taught is that the eye of the viewer moves from the top left to the bottom right. As students, you are asked to place the *important* aspects of your design in the top left or bottom right corner. The secondary aspects of the design get the bottom left and top right corners. The text which then directly addresses women as the consumer of its product by its placement also dictates that women need to be relegated to certain spaces. Women, though asked to embrace the modernist project of birth control as per the state's wishes, are not afforded a voice in the discourse. However, it is interesting to note that the text does profess one solution to this problematic placement—the i-pill. To get back to life and the project of empowerment, the i-pill is purchasable at a local pharmacist. The subjected position afforded women can be overcome, and the i-pill is what offers this possibility.

Next, the components of the copy that warrant attention are the tag lines—"Get back to life" and the paternalistic concerned voice within the copy "Worried you might get pregnant after last night?" Both these lines, conversational for the most part, suggest to the reader that the pill will provide a solution and get the reader back to "life." This is a trope used in most advertising campaigns, where a "lack" is identified and then a tailor-made solution is provided. However, it also makes visible a conversation that might have posed as problematic prior to the i-pill and its investment in the advancement of the national family planning project. The i-pill then is a commodity that delivers, by implication, sex and life. The first two little stories (your kid needs a hug, your officemates need your "sunny smile") in each of the advertisements treat a woman's life as essentially serving others. The third text (morning coffee) is slightly different. It makes no mention of kids or husbands (only a pet dog!), and the lack here is not serving others but of not being able to appreciate a commanding view of the city. Here life seems indeed about appreciating what you have, that is, your position in life and your ability to consume, which a child (by implication) would threaten. The pill goes beyond its pure medical value and symbolically attaches itself to consumer logic behind life and "sex"—both now purchasable middle-class commodities.

Mazzarella, when talking about the Kama Sutra advertising campaign, proposed that the campaign raised quite a commotion socially and politically, not necessarily because of "selling of erotica rather [with the] eroticization of selling in a wider sense."[25] In a similar vein, it can be argued that the i-pill advertisements do not aim to sell the emergency contraceptive pill but rather have the pill be symbolic of access to a life and sex that are viewed as global middle-class commodities. These advertisements attempt to commodify life and sex by pulling them into the service of selling a commodity—the i-pill. Here, noncommodified desires are pulled into the service of commodity production and distribution. However, the i-pill advertising campaign is considered less problematic than the Kama Sutra ads because the ads are packaged under the nationalistic goal of birth control and family planning with a very visually conservative advertising campaign.

Finally, an examination of the text-heavy informational side of the advertisement campaign is important because the advertisers devote half of the advertising space to this educational information. These three advertisements are divided into two sections—the promotional side with images and conversational text and the "informative"[26] side that purports to support the claims of the advertisement with scientific facts. Therefore, the i-pill not only professes to provide birth control to a population where population control is a major concern but also aims to educate and inform the consuming (and also English-speaking) middle-class consumers on the scientific facts of emergency contraceptives. The overall project of education cannot be faulted, and there are two things that merit critical attention. First, the scientific discourse attached to the advertisements is "Western" for the most part. The first paragraph on the scientific side simplistically explains how the i-pill works and ends with the line "It is therefore not an abortion pill." In a nation where an estimated 79% of pregnancies are unplanned and where 30% of the about 50 million conceptions end up in abortions, the need to sell the pill as not being an "abortion" pill seems tinged with Western sensibilities.[27] Abortion in the United States has been viewed as a religious and political problem, but this is not the case in India. It is not my intention to make light of the moral platforms the religious and political leaders in India regularly use; however, I do wish to make clear the reality of a nation that acknowledges abortion as a necessary aspect of family planning and reproductive health in India. India was one of the few countries in the world to legalize abortion in the early 1970s.[28]

Second, the discourse on the informational side of the advertisement offers the consuming middle class a vocabulary that privileges scientific knowledge over other understandings of reproductive health. Is this a giant step or a small leap toward medicalization of society? It would seem that the product, combined with its promissory (also read illusionary) access to life, sex, and education, also contributes to an ideological project where reproductive health and choice is (re)configured in sanitized, commodified, and medical terms. Just as the edu-information project is inclusive in sharing this medicalized discourse with the larger population, it is exclusionary in what it omits or negates. In particular, the historical materiality of the family planning project in India is excluded in this new privatized gloss on birth control.

In a lecture, Foucault proposed that discourse should be viewed as a system of representation.[29] He posited that academic inquiry should focus on the rules and practices that produce meaningful statements and how these rules regulate the discourse that becomes part of the everyday. For him, discourse typically was a collection of statements that contributed to a vocabulary that enables a conversation about a particular topic at any particular moment in history. Foucault put forward that discourse helps in shaping the topic and our knowledge and understanding of the topic. Discourse, then, "governs" the way a topic is voiced and reasoned about in public spaces. Using this framework, I wish to propose that the i-pill advertising campaign makes available a particular discourse for the consuming middle class in India. It makes contraceptive choice a commodity, in that it is viewed and imagined in terms of sanitized and Western notions and is also purchasable at the local pharmacist now without a prescription. A scientific approach to sexual health within the advertisement makes available the vocabulary to the masses, where they themselves can partake in this medicalization project. This discourse *governs* our understanding of pharmaceutically negotiated health and makes consumers who not only "buy into" commodified family planning but also consumerism as the emancipatory revolution enabled by the advertisement campaign as a whole.

Furthermore, the discourse provided and privileged in the i-pill advertising campaign is a rationalized and dehistoricized project that ignores or negates the history of birth control in India. Questions of health, sexually transmitted disease, HIV-AIDS, and the actual usage practices of these pills make an appearance in these pages in very small print and outside the margins of the advertisements. In making these images of Indian women appear in the service of a product that promises an illusionary emancipation (choice and freedom have been called as such), the potential of the current modern moment is circumscribed.

Conclusion

In conclusion, I would like to suggest that this reading of the advertising campaign is not an attempt to suggest an overt move by the government, the pharmaceutical company, or even the advertisers to provide images and texts that subjugate women. Rather, my aim has been to highlight the tropes that unintentionally get used in the larger ideological motivations of contemporary capitalism. As Catherine Lutz and Jane Collins illustrate in their ethnographic study of *The National Geographic* magazine, the producers of the magazine do not willingly participate in the project of making the "exotic other."[30] Rather the authors highlight how hegemony operates and how the producers of the texts participate in the reification of the American middle class to provide a favorable view of the world to that demographic. In a similar vein, the value of the i-pill and its accompanying advertisements is essential in a nation that strives to manage limited resources and a growing population. Furthermore, the advertisements do partake in this project, first of course as providers of information and then also as arbiters of articulations of the new modern Indian woman. In addition, the campaign has been successful in fashioning a discourse that appeals to the growing middle class, where the class itself partakes in this modernizing project. Urban, middle-class life has become symbolically attached to markers such as sex, life, and health and in turn products such as i-pill.

I do wish to once again briefly discuss Foucault's notion of discourse and how it may be a helpful tool in understanding the discourse within these advertisements. As mentioned earlier, the rationalized, scientific, medical discourse is an integral part of the i-pill advertising campaign. In *The Birth of the Clinic*, Foucault proposed that the medical profession saw a shift to empiricism and precision—not because the science became more pure or developed, but because the medical profession was entrenched in social and political movements.[31] These movements—including government-sanctioned and mandated movements—that aimed to categorize and privilege certain forms of knowledge were the driving force behind the new clinic. Although a direct comparison cannot be made between the medical profession and the medicalization of Western society to that of the i-pill advertising campaign and commodified health in India, it should be acknowledged that both offered this scientific discourse as their first step to social legitimization.

After liberalization, India has a burgeoning middle class, which wishes to privilege itself by partaking in this particularistic discourse. This scientific discourse, accompanied by sanitized and regulated images, allows the middle class access to another global commodity—the morning after pill. The i-pill advertising campaign, under the garb of family planning and in implicitly forwarding the nationalistic family planning agenda, does in fact forward a consumerist agenda. Sanctioned and approved, it also makes interesting contradictory symbolic connections in first offering empowerment and control and then immediately circumscribing this control by reinforcing notions of femininity as service to others. Additionally, these advertisements and the surrounding discourses suggest that social concerns such as birth control can be transferred from previous disastrous governmental projects to savvy and sanitized consumerist products. The discourse in the above-mentioned advertisements encourages us to imagine ourselves emancipated from concerns where we are asked to stop worrying and get back to life. However, here, life is always attached to a commodity. These commodified health concerns are first created and then perpetuated through marketing and advertising.

Finally, not to be part of the family planning project in India is tantamount to being unpatriotic in some middle-class progressive settings. The i-pill then makes pharmaceutical citizenship to extend beyond the action of ingesting a pill. As Mankekar suggests, identities are configured in response to television viewing, thus locating women within family, state, community, nation, and class boundaries.[32] In this chapter, I have identified one particular advertising campaign to examine the dialectical in the advertisements themselves and how this contributes to reimagining of identities of the new modern Indian woman. The woman is not only a subject in these advertisements but also an object. A subject of the state and object of the gaze; her new identity requires that she be the "mother India" that takes responsibility for the birth control project, but within the strictures sanctioned by the patriarchal state.

Endnotes

1. See http://www.ipillwoman.piramal.com/pdf/advertorial_mother_daughter.pdf (accessed January 14, 2009). The advertisement or advertorial does not have a title but may be termed "Mother and daughter sitting on the floor."
2. William Mazzarella, *Shoveling Smoke: Advertising and Globalization in Contemporary India* (Durham: Duke University Press, 2003).
3. Sjaak van der Geest, Susan Reynolds Whyte, and Anita Hardon, "The Anthropology of Pharmaceuticals: A Biographical Approach," *Annual Review of Anthropology* 25, no. 1 (October 1996): 156.
4. Ibid.
5. Ibid., 156–7.
6. Robert Goldman and Michael Montagne, "Marketing 'Mind Mechanics': Decoding Antidepressant Drug Advertisements," *Social Science and Medicine* 22, no. 10 (1986): 1047–58.

7. Joseph Dumit, "Pharmaceutical Witnessing: Drugs for Life in an Era of Direct-to-Consumer Advertising" (unpublished essay).

8. Raymond Williams, "Advertising: The Magic System," in *The Cultural Studies Reader*, ed. Simon During (London: Routledge, 1993), 421.

9. Max Horkheimer and Theodor W. Adorno, "The Culture Industry: Enlightenment as Mass Deception," in *Dialectic of Enlightenment*, trans. John Cumming (New York: Continuum, 1997), 120–67.

10. Erving Goffman, *Gender Advertisements*, 1st ed. (New York: Harper & Row, 1979); Judith Williamson, *Decoding Advertisements: Ideology and Meaning in Advertising* (New York: Boyars, 1984).

11. Adriana Petryna and Arthur Kleinman, "The Pharmaceutical Nexus," in *Global Pharmaceuticals: Ethics, Markets, Practices*, ed. Adriana Petryna, Andrew Lakoff, and Arthur Kleinman (Durham: Duke University Press, 2006), 3.

12. Andrea Tone, *Devices and Desires: A History of Contraceptives in America*, 1st ed. (New York: Hill and Wang, 2001), 157.

13. Tone, *Devices and Desires*, 9.

14. Marc-André Gagnon and Joel Lexchin, "The Cost of Pushing Pills: A New Estimate of Pharmaceutical Promotion Expenditures in the United States," *Public Library of Science (Medicine)* 5, no. 1 (2008): 29–33.

15. U.S. Congress. House of Representatives. The House Committee on Energy and Commerce Democrats: The Public Record: Detail Page. "The House Committee on Energy and Commerce: The Public Record: Subcommittee on Oversight and Investigations Hearing Entitled, 'Direct-To-Consumer Advertising: Marketing, Education Or Deception?'" Text (May 28, 2008), http://archives.energycommerce.house.gov/cmte_mtgs/11-oi-hrg.050808.DTC.shtml (accessed January 18, 2011).

16. Kaushik Sunder Rajan, *Biocapital: The Constitution of Postgenomic Life* (Durham: Duke University Press, 2006).

17. C. H. Unnikrishnan, "Patents Carve up Drug Market," *Business Standard*, July 29, 2005, http://www.business-standard.com/india/news/patents-carvedrug-market/217607/ (accessed January 14, 2009).

18. Uwe Perlitz, "India's Pharmaceutical Industry Goes Global (Deutsche Bank Research)," May 6, 2008, http://www.euractiv.com/en/health/india-pharmaceutical-industry-goes-global/article-172137# (accessed January 14, 2009).

19. Vishakha Talreja, "Morning After, Men Try to Find What's i-pill," *Economic Times*, September 29, 2007, http://economictimes.indiatimes.com/Morning_after_men_try_to_find_whats_i-pill/articleshow/2413553.cms (accessed January 14, 2009).

20. Bureau Report, Hindu Business Line, "Mankind Pharma Mulls New Wing," *The Hindu—Business Line*, March 30, 2007, epaper edition, http://www.thehindubusinessline.com/2007/03/30/stories/2007033005240300.htm (accessed January 14, 2009).

21. "Mother and daughter sitting on the floor" cited earlier is one of these advertisements. The other two may be termed, "Woman sitting on the floor with an alarm clock," http://www.ipillwoman.piramal.com/pdf/advertorial_english01.pdf (accessed January 14, 2009); and "Woman sitting on a floor pillow with a cup of coffee," http://www.ipillwoman.piramal.com/pdf/advertorial03.pdf (accessed January 14, 2009).

22. Purnima Mankekar, "Dangerous Desires: Television and Erotics in Late Twentieth-Century India," *The Journal of Asian Studies* 63, no. 2 (2004): 403–31; William Mazzarella, "'Very Bombay': Contending with the Global in an Indian Advertising Agency," *Cultural Anthropology* 18, no. 1 (February 2003): 33–71; Mazzarella, *Shoveling Smoke*.

23. Mazzarella, *Shoveling Smoke*, 80.

24. Sarah Hodges, *Reproductive Health in India: History, Politics, Controversies* (New Delhi: Orient Longman, 2006); Sarah Hodges, *Contraception, Colonialism and Commerce: Birth Control in South India, 1920–1940* (Aldershot, England: Ashgate, 2008).

25. Mazzarella, *Shoveling Smoke*, 65.
26. The informational page is divided into two columns, with six major questions in deep pink. The answers are all in blacktype face. The font for the writing is clean and crisp and not cluttered. The first question is "How does the i-pill work?" and the answer is

> i-pill can work in any of the three different ways depending on where you may be in your menstrual cycle: It may stop the egg being released from the ovary[;] If an egg has already been released, i-pill may prevent the sperm from fertilizing it[;] If the egg is already fertilized, it may prevent it from attaching itself to the lining of the womb. I-pill is ineffective if the pregnancy is established (i.e. the fertilized egg has not attached itself to the womb). It is therefore not an abortion pill.
> (Quoted from the i-pill advertisement printed above)

27. B. Harish, "Marketing Practice: i-pill: Get Back to Life," e-blogger, *Marketing Practice*, August 17, 2007, http://marketingpractice.blogspot.com/2007/08/i-pill-get-back-to-life.html (accessed January 14, 2009).
28. Veena Soni, "Thirty Years of the Indian Family Planning Program: Past Performance, Future Prospects," *International Family Planning Perspectives* 9, no. 2 (June 1983): 35–45.
29. Michel Foucault, "The Order of Discourse. Inaugural Lecture at the Collège de France, Given 2 December 1970," in *Untying the Text: A Post-Structuralist Reader*, ed. Robert Young (Boston: Routledge & Kegan Paul, 1981), 48–78.
30. Catherine Lutz and Jane Lou Collins, *Reading National Geographic* (Chicago: University of Chicago Press, 1993).
31. Michel Foucault, *The Birth of the Clinic: An Archaeology of Medical Perception* (New York: Vintage Books, 1975).
32. Purnima Mankekar, *Screening Culture, Viewing Politics: An Ethnography of Television, Womanhood, and Nation in Postcolonial India* (Durham: Duke University Press, 1999), 16.

CHAPTER 7

The Fetishistic Challenge
Things in Nineteenth-Century Danish Literature as Mediators of Identity

FREDERIKE FELCHT*

Chapter Description

This chapter analyzes the role of things in the nineteenth-century Danish literature of Hans Christian Andersen and Adam Oehlenschläger. As literature became part of a global market in the nineteenth century to early twentieth century, it also played a central role in the formation of emergent national identities. The idea of the global was involved in these contestations, taking shape in the world of things. Things are centrally involved in the formation of global networks and in the construction of identities that mediate local, national, regional, and global attachments. This chapter demonstrates how literary texts recognize these functions, whereas scientific theories tend to neglect the participation of things in the formation of the social.

* * *

It was as if the shoes controlled her.

(Hans Christian Andersen, *The Red Shoes*)

Things have an increasing influence on the construction of identities in capitalistic societies and are centrally involved in the formation of global

*I would like to thank Rohit Chopra, Gabriel Cooper, and Christina Gehrlein for their critical reading of the chapter and inspiring advice.

networks. Although Western scientific discourse tried to marginalize the role of things in society, literature was often aware of the power of things.[1] This chapter demonstrates consequences of this insight for concepts of identity in a globalizing world with texts by the Danish authors Adam Oehlenschläger (1779–1850) and Hans Christian Andersen (1805–1875). These texts acknowledge the hybrid character of actions, granting both human beings and things agency. On the one hand, constructions of Western identity are questioned from within; concepts such as the autonomous subject dissolve, given the integral role of things in human actions. On the other hand, things mediate between different countries and their imagination, and literature participates in these processes.

Oehlenschläger and Andersen wrote in a period of nationalization *and* transnational integration. Literature was an important field of identity negotiation in Denmark. Processes of identification proceeded between transnationalism and regionalism (e.g., in the form of Scandinavism), nationalism, and local ties (with landscapes or cities). In the economic and literary sense, Denmark was part of the semi-periphery:[2] Its European neighbors put it under political and economic pressure, but Denmark also acted as a colonial power itself. This situation had a significant impact on its imaginative geographies, where self-other and center-periphery binaries were slippery.[3]

Oehlenschläger's texts had great influence on Danish identity formation. Andersen's fairy tales were even more extensive: He is one of the most translated authors worldwide. Both authors tried to cross cultural and linguistic borders. Aimed at transnational audiences, their work was connected to the early dynamics of globalization. Oehlenschläger was bound to increasing literary exchanges through translations and personal contacts. Andersen's transnational success occurred in a tightly woven network of literary markets. Historians cite the period from 1840 to 1914 as one of the most dynamic phases in the history of globalization because of its economic and cultural changes,[4] and literature is deeply involved in these changes. During the nineteenth century, literary media reached more and more people. The expansion, densification, and acceleration of worldwide relationships changed the book trade and its strategies as well as the contents of books; literature became part of a global market. This process had a material dimension; it was made possible by changes in the modes of production and consumption. At the same time, national literatures emerged, and literature played an important role in the formation of national identities.

Today, globalization is often understood as the opposite of nationalization,[5] but historical works emphasize the stabilizing functions of nation-states in the development of global systems.[6] In the field of literature, continuities exist between national and global structures and the imaginations of communities connected with these structures. According to Benedict Anderson, capitalistic print media greatly facilitated the modern imagination of national communities. These media were positioned in a transnational context of competition and exchange. The imagination of a nation was shaped by its imagination of other nations. This system of imaginations consisted of translations and their critique, personal exchange, and the adoption of media models and ideas.[7] It was supplemented with local and regional attachments and cosmopolitan concepts such as "Weltliteratur," a term introduced by Goethe. Literature facilitates transnational connections and shapes identities in the nineteenth century in a way comparable with global media such as the Internet or television today; albeit less extensive, it produced similar effects. In contrast to Arjun Appadurai's emphasis on the differences between former and actual media,[8] I would like to stress the continuities between their functions.

The first part of this chapter shows how Andersen's texts offer alternative constructions of identity by challenging the divide between human beings and things. These texts display radically the possibilities of what I call a "connected identity." Following that, I will focus on processes of national and transnational identification mediated by things in Oehlenschläger's texts.

The global dimension of nineteenth-century literature is not only characterized by exotic scenes or images of non-European characters. These elements are mostly motivated by commercial purposes, trying to pique the audience's interest and thus participating in an affirmative form of hybridization closely connected to the development of a commodified global culture.[9] In the world of things in literature, however, modernity composes its counternarratives in a material constellation, and a superimposition of different layers of time and space takes place.[10] Hybridity crossing the human–nonhuman border has a critical potential in this realm.[11]

As Hartmut Böhme, Michel Foucault, and Bruno Latour have shown, the theoretical separation of human beings and things is a foundational principle of identity in modern Western society.[12] This separation included the construction of the autonomous subject and had its counterpart in the devaluation of the power of things.[13] Actions were exclusively attributed to human beings. In contrast, Actor-Network-Theory today understands agency as a trait that is not exclusively human and emphasizes the importance of hybrid techniques in the construction of the social.[14]

The power of things was devalued in the nineteenth century, even though things played an increasingly important role in life. Industrialization arrived with machines that called into question humans' dominance; more and more things were produced and changed everyday life; new technologies influenced humans' perception of the world. Things continue to contribute to global connectivity and are centrally involved in the construction of the social. Although the scientific definition of the social widely neglected this material dimension, literature turned out to be sensitive to it.

Using concepts such as fetishism, science ascribed the confusion of man and things to "primitive" cultures, and thus, the world was divided. The mechanisms of this separation are similar to the construction of the Orient that Edward Said has described.[15] The fetishistic character of the Western world was denied or, where it was conceded (e.g., by Karl Marx),[16] it was answered with the gesture of revelation.[17] The social power of things was conceived as the result of an act of projection based on self-delusion.[18] However, Böhme argues that fetishistic mechanisms are essential for the construction of modern societies. Hence, we should free fetishism from its status as social pathology.[19] Powerful things that have a (hi)story—which could be a minimal definition of fetishistic objects—create connected identities. These things leave a visible trace in nineteenth-century literature. Questioning the theoretical separation of men and things and acknowledging the hybrid character of actions, literature challenges the separation of the world into primitive and "modern" societies. Literature gives rise to a global consciousness by revealing the link between human beings and things, a link that reflects global circuits of production and consumption and constitutes local attachments.

To understand the global dimension of nineteenth-century literature, it is useful to distinguish between globalization as a perspective and globalization as a historical process.[20] Both aspects are found in literary texts. The latter includes the formation of transnational networks, a long historical process, closely connected to technological developments and commodification.[21] Literature both reflects and contributes to globalization as a historical process. It thematizes commodification and technologies that enable transnational exchange; at the same time, literature itself is a commodity made possible by technological developments. The former is a consciousness of the relativity of positions and a rethinking of dominant Western ideas such as progress and rationality against the background of deviant experiences resulting from encounters with non-European ideas as well as Western archaism, irrationality, and fetishism. Literature can take a position on globalization. In the following literary examples, the fetishistic mechanisms of Western societies are perceived in their fundamental function for the integration of communities, and the discrimination of primitive societies is questioned by inscribing fetishistic relationships in the heart of modernity.

In Andersen's fairy tale "De røde Skoe" (The Red Shoes) (1845), things have great power. Little Karen transgresses social norms to wear the forbidden shoes, and the shoes preoccupy her so much that she loses control of her thoughts and then her legs. She must dance until the hangman cuts off her feet. Having converted and having led a modest life, she dies during a mass and is granted forgiveness.

At first glance, the fairy tale seems timeless, but a closer look at its objects reveals a specific historical situation. The shoes are presented in a glass cabinet; they were fashioned for an earl's child, but having been rejected, they enter the market as a commodity. Karen wears them in church and at a ball—locations that point to a bourgeois European setting—although she is forbidden to do so.[22] Made from morocco leather, an uncommon material in Northern Europe until the 1770s,[23] the shoes embody not only Karen's dangerous passage from child to woman and her desire for social advancement but also a change in the modes of production and sales in the late eighteenth century. They are tied to the expansion of capitalistic networks.

The mobilizing potential of the red shoes is multilayered. As shoes, they enable personal mobility. Furthermore, they participate in the diffusion of luxury fashion products that increasingly reached nonaristocrats such as Karen, having its counterpart in the ascetic ideologies of her bourgeois environment. Thus, the shoes signify social advancement and its restriction. As part of a commodity chain, they embody and further transnational exchange. Arjun Appadurai has shown that the control and expansion of the movement of things structures society.[24] I would like to stress the agency of things in this process: The red shoes are not passive elements in a power struggle between humans; they are part of a struggle between humans as well as between humans and things. Erin Mackie writes that "the censure of Karen's fetishism itself works through fetish supernaturalism":[25] Karen *and* her environment are fixated on the red shoes.

Peer Sørensen's[26] interpretation evaluates the fairy tale as a regular, pietistically biased conversion story: In the end, Karen has to give up her desire to wear the red shoes. But a focus on the shoes and their loss also allows a very different interpretation: The required abandonment of material satisfaction through the desired shoes is an amputation; the autonomous subject that subordinates its sensuousness to duty becomes an invalid. The longing for the shoes is simultaneously produced and denied by nineteenth-century Western society. Karen cannot escape from it until she is dead; only in heaven no one asks her about the red shoes.[27] The rationalistic ideology of the autonomous subject freed of the power of things is in its brutal consequences no less irrational than the fetishistic obsession.

To be cut off from material objects as Karen is from her shoes also means exclusion from commodity flows. Today, one important form of exclusion is being cut off from global communication systems. Focusing solely on humans' interactions or the technical possibilities of a medium such as the

Internet, the importance of mere material connectedness and its control is often neglected in theories of globalization. In contrast, Andersen's "Den store Søslange" (The Great Sea-Serpent) (1872) emphasizes the materiality of processes of cultural exchange and communication and their structuring through power relationships. The protagonist of "Den store Søslange" is a transatlantic cable. The story stages the dialectics of connection and (violent) intrusion by way of an alienation effect: The laying of the cable is described from the perspective of fish. Some fish are beaten to death by the cable, whereas the survivors try to figure out what has happened to their habitat. The fish presume the cable to be alive, but they fail to identify its species. At the end of the story, the narrator's commentary on the transatlantic cable oscillates metaphorically between its man-made condition and its autonomous "life" and power, with both poles presenting good and bad potentialities:

> The great sea serpent . . . was conceived and born by man's ingenuity and laid on the bottom of the ocean, stretching from the eastern to the western lands, and carrying messages as swiftly as light flashes from the sun to our earth. It grows, grows in power and length, grows year after year, through all oceans, around the world . . .
>
> . . . Fishes and other sea creatures clash with it; they do not understand that thing from above. People's thoughts rush noiselessly, in all languages, through the serpent of science, for both good and evil; the most wondrous of the ocean's wonders is our time's.[28]

Technological progress and its global expansion are thus reflected in their complementary structure of human decisions and unforeseen effects, creation and destruction, and connection and oppression.

"Dryaden" (The Dryad) (1868) also demonstrates the dialectics of technology. Set in 1867 at the Paris World's Fair where the "world" is represented through commodities, "Dryaden" paints a compact portrait of material self-imaginations of the nineteenth century. At the World's Fair, conceptions of globality come to the fore explicitly in their materiality. The exhibition is depicted as a place where the overwhelming power of things undermines the intended representation of the world as a rational product of human work. Although the planners of the exhibition aspired to present a world order of progress headed by Europe,[29] "Dryaden" associates the desire to have the world at one's disposal with a child's Christmas wish, a naive perspective:

> The overwhelmingly great, colorful show should have been reproduced in miniature and squeezed into the dimensions of a toy, to be seen and appreciated in its entirety.

> There on the Champ de Mars stood, as on a huge Christmas table, Alladin's castle of art and industry, and around it were knickknacks of greatness from every country; every nation found a memory of its home.[30]

The childish fascination with things usually ascribed to primitive people is thus discovered by European adults. At the exhibition, things have *people* at their disposal. Things influence the behavior of the crowd, which undergoes a libidinous fusion with fashion, alcohol, and music. The crowd becomes reified through mechanized transport and production that dictate the rhythm of human movements. The fetishistic belief in the power of things and the European idea of progress turn out to be the same; humans are not omnipotent beings. The fetishistic other is situated in the heart of modernity.

These critical reflections on the ideas of progress, development, and the rationality of human actions are a key to global dimensions in identity concepts in nineteenth-century literature. Dipesh Chakrabarty has shown that progress and development are Eurocentric ideas, based on an understanding of historical time as godless, continuous, empty, and homogeneous.[31] Andersen's texts contain a different notion of time: Time is sensitive to contexts, contradictory, and multilayered. These stories demonstrate the magic character of modernity.

From National to Global: Things in Processes of Identification

Fetishistic mechanisms were the basis of processes of national and global identification in Danish literature. From the outset of the nineteenth century, things played an important role in the imaginative geographies of Denmark. Around 1800, inspired by German Romanticism, Nordic myths and folk literature were (re)discovered and national landscapes were invented.[32] The breakthrough of Romanticism in Scandinavia is associated with Oehlenschläger's poem "Guldhornene" (The Golden Horns) (1803). The poem consists of twenty stanzas, varying from one to twenty-six verses.[33] The poem laments the loss of the two Golden Horns of Gallehus. These horns from the fifth century were rediscovered in 1639 and 1734 but stolen from the Kunstkammer in Copenhagen and melted down in 1802.[34] The poem associates their story with an interpretation of Nordic history.

In "Guldhornene," the Golden Horns are mediators of a glorious mythological past, a gift of the gods. In spite of scholars' efforts to search for them systematically {"De higer og søger / I gamle Bøger / I oplukte Høie / Med speidende Øie"[35] [They quest and search / In ancient Books / In opened

Mounds / With prying Eyes (my literal translation, F. F.)]}, the horns are found by chance in the ground by a virgin and a young farmer.[36] Both the mythological objects and their finders are harmoniously embedded in their environment. This image depicts a coalescence of things, humans, and nature. But as the loss of the Golden Horns at the end of the poem shows, this premodern harmony has been disrupted. The impious presentation of the horns to curious eyes is punished with the disappearance of the holy objects.[37]

The poem can be read as an opposing standpoint to the rationalism of the Enlightenment, with its systematic research and the construction of objectivity through scientific representation. It is particularly the scientific notion of objectivity that separates humans from nonhumans, as Bruno Latour argues.[38] In contrast, the poem advocates the ideal unity between humans and nonhumans.

The history of the Golden Horns is multilayered: as objects from the fifth century, they change the people's relationship to the past when they appear and disappear. Thus, they are anchored in different temporalities.[39] In the poem, the Golden Horns gain relevance through processes of identification. "Guldhornene" seeks to establish a Nordic identity through the Golden Horns, presented as a lost identity and given a primordial value to be restored. The treasure is situated in the ground; its embeddedness entails an exclusion of other places. Denmark and Norway are named in the poem, suggesting that the North signifies primarily the Danish state (which included Norway in 1803). "Guldhornene" aims at a consciousness of belonging strengthened by historical objects. This politics of identification is based on a fetishistic mechanism: the Golden Horns will establish regional bonds; they are conceived as sacral objects. The poem conserves or even increases the socially integrating function of the stolen material objects by telling their story. The Golden Horns are powerful things that have a (hi)story, and they create connected identities. However, their range is limited to the regional level.

The poem suggests a concept of identity in the sense of a connected identity that is not based on the idea of an autonomous subject but rather conceives of humanity in terms of material embeddedness. Things integrate social communities. This material social integration gains global character increasingly during the nineteenth century. Networks of transportation and communication expedited national as well as transnational connectedness.

Oehlenschläger's influential drama *Aladdin* (1805) exemplifies the existence of a national as well as a global dimension in his antirationalistic concept of identity. Despite its Oriental setting, *Aladdin* continually refers to Denmark. Especially, objects such as Oriental "Æbleskivepander,"[40] pans that are used for a typical Danish pastry, crossfade the two worlds.

Georg Brandes, one of the most influential Danish literary critics, wrote in 1886: "*Aladdin* is the point of departure for contemporary Danish culture, the foundation stone upon which the building that constitutes Danish literature in the first half of the century is erected."[41] This diagnosis is astonishing, since Oehlenschläger took a Danish translation of Antoine Galland's *Mille et une Nuits* as the basis for his drama,[42] thus inscribing himself in a long tradition of telling *Thousand and One Nights* that Jorge Luis Borges has reconstructed and associated with the discovery of the Orient by the Occident.[43] Brandes documents Oehlenschläger's changes in the material and thus shows how Oehlenschläger constructs the figure of the lucky genius in the drama. This naive genius benefits from the Magical Lamp that is embedded in nature, such as the Golden Horns. The Magical Lamp is not attributed to a specific region but rather crossfades Nordic and Oriental motives.

The discovery of the magical object is prepared by the African wizard Noureddin, a Faustian figure, who shows Aladdin the way to the lamp. Noureddin, the anti-hero of the play, has been unable to obtain the lamp. In Brandes' view, this constellation is symptomatic of the Danish self-image: Danish artists and even scientists are considered to be naive geniuses such as Aladdin, whose strokes of genius are lucky moments, rather than the result of continuous work. Brandes is critical of the childish character of Danish great minds and their neglect of scientific Faustian striving. These result in incapability to profit theoretically or practically from their discoveries. Brandes generalizes this diagnosis and compares the Danish nation with a dreamy Aladdin who ignores political problems and ends up losing two wars.[44]

Following Elisabeth Oxfeldt's insightful interpretation of *Aladdin* and its reception, I argue that Oehlenschläger and Brandes' different conceptions of the relationship between humans and things separate them. Oxfeldt illustrates how relationships between Denmark and the Orient and Denmark and Germany changed during the nineteenth century. In his drama, Oehlenschläger presents a "merry mix of the Orient and the North."[45] In the prologue, he returns to the mythological connection between the North and Asia that had already been established in the *Edda*, a collection of poems and Old Norse myths. Aladdin is described as "Lovely red and white,"[46] sharing Denmark's national colors.

Oehlenschläger's humor consisted of dressing Copenhageners up as Persians who, nevertheless, remain entirely unfazed by the apparently incongruent elements of Orient and home, fantasy and reality ... The North is ultimately defined not through self-sufficiency but through its ability to connect with the rest of the world—even the exotic Orient—while remaining Danish at heart.[47]

According to Oxfeldt, it is Oehlenschläger's "absolute faith in a unique national core identity established through a particular Nordic landscape and language"[48] that allows the merry mix of Copenhagen and the Orient. But is it a national core identity that is presented in *Aladdin*? And what does it mean to remain Danish at heart while being connected with the rest of the world? The formation of a Danish national identity in the nineteenth century oscillated between inclusive tendencies, for example in Scandinavism, or in the adoption of Oriental cultural practices that Martin Zerlang describes,[49] and exclusive tendencies. Around 1800, Denmark was a multiethnic and multilingual state, its concept of nationality intrinsically hybrid. The concept of identity in *Aladdin* belongs to a period of extensive maritime trade and cosmopolitan ideals, whereas Brandes' critique occurred during a period of political disconnection and cultural nationalization. Between Germans and Danes, relationships became especially hostile. Modernity and democracy changed the Danish culture and politics, boundaries became precarious, and borders insecure. At the same time, pure concepts of identity substituted the hybrid concept of a multiethnic Denmark, held together by its monarch. Oxfeldt suggests that the Romantic fascination with boundlessness gave Brandes reason to attack *Aladdin*.[50]

The hybrid idea of identity in *Aladdin* that Brandes criticizes also has a fetishistic dimension if the focus is shifted from a human self–other relationship to a human–nonhuman relationship: objects dissolve the boundaries of human beings and vice versa. Gulnare, Aladdin's beloved princess, is imagined as a living jewel, and Aladdin is the *object* of luck,[51] one of his most important attributes. Only at the end of the play does he become an autonomous subject capable of taking decision-based action. He kills his last enemy, Noureddin's brother Hindbad, in a fight without the aid of magic, elevating it to a battle between truth and falsehood, good and evil.[52] Brandes disapproves of the moral-theological enthusiasm of this scene.[53] However, it is not only the sudden moralizing that irritates but also an unconvincing break in the conception of the hero. In *Aladdin*, agency is generally shared between the hero and magical objects, whereas in the fighting scene, Aladdin is suddenly driven by the idea of autonomous action—undermining the characterization of Aladdin as the lucky and passive genius that contributed to the drama's success. The predominant idea of shared agency in *Aladdin* suggests the aforementioned concept of agency that has been developed (or rediscovered?) by Actor-Network-Theory. In *Aladdin*, the relationship between magical objects and human beings activates their common force, and it is the history of the Magical Lamp that makes it valuable—and powerful.[54] Thus, the concept of agency in *Aladdin* acknowledges the embeddedness of human beings in networks of objects and vice versa. Objects in *Aladdin* are often "quasi-objects" or "quasi-subjects" in the sense of Michel Serres: Quasi-objects define the status of the subject. This status changes when the quasi-object moves; for example, in a ball game, the status of the subject changes with its distance to the ball.[55]

There are two magical objects in *Aladdin*: the lamp and a ring that brings its bearer to every place he or she wishes to go and lets him or her know everything that happened in the past or happens in the present. These attributes define quite precisely the abilities of new transportation systems, telecommunication, and modern media. Brandes claims that these magical objects "should be neutral powers like electricity or steam, indifferent tools for the human will."[56] Clearly, the objects do not correspond to Brandes' conception of things. There is no neutral power; human beings do not exert power that is situated inside them into an empty outside. Aladdin and the spirits always move within a field of relationships that structure the actions. For example, the building materials for Aladdin's palace are not magically produced but collected from all over the world. In *Aladdin,* there is no production outside social networks consisting of humans, spirits, animals, and things. These networks reflect existing networks in the nineteenth century: the rapid construction of huge buildings such as Aladdin's palace, the acceleration of traveling, and international trade with luxury goods[57] were bound in global structures. The aforementioned idea of a connected identity is called into question by the fighting scene that includes the idea of the autonomously acting subject. But the central idea of *Aladdin* is the openness of the characters that grants them access to luck. This openness crossfades Orient and Occident and combines the agency of human beings and things.

Oehlenschläger and Andersen's texts show the illusoriness of autonomously acting subjects. The hybrid concept of a connected identity has its global dimension in the consciousness of transnational integration. The separation of humans and things is challenged in the chosen texts and opens up perspectives on nonhostile, impure identities that allow the combination of national and global aspects in self-images. Things must be taken into account, because they participate in the construction of social life and its globalization. Without our red shoes, we cannot walk toward each other—be it things or human beings.

Endnotes

1. Cf. Uwe Steiner, "Widerstand im Gegenstand. Das literarische Wissen vom Ding am Beispiel Franz Kafkas," in *Literatur, Wissenschaft und Wissen seit der Epochenschwelle um 1800*, ed. Thomas Klinkert and Monika Neuhofer (Berlin: de Gruyter, 2008), 237–8.
2. For the core-semi-periphery-periphery model in world-systems analysis, see Immanuel Wallerstein, *The Modern World-System*, vol. 1, *Capitalist Agriculture and the Origins of the European World-Economy in the Sixteenth Century* (New York, NY: Academic Press,

1974), 63–129. Pascale Casanova developed a similar concept for literature. See Pascale Casanova, *The World Republic of Letters* (Cambridge, MA: Harvard University Press, 2004); cf. Christopher Prendergast, ed.,"The World Republic of Letters," in *Debating World Literature* (London: Verso, 2004), 1–25.

3. See Elisabeth Oxfeldt, *Nordic Orientalism: Paris and the Cosmopolitan Imagination 1800-1900* (Copenhagen: Museum Tusculanum Press, 2005), 13, 17–18. For the concept of an "imaginative geography" see Edward W. Said, *Orientalism* (New York, NY: Vintage Books, 2004), 49–73.

4. See Peter Fäßler, *Globalisierung: Ein historisches Kompendium* (Köln: Böhlau, 2007), 32, 74–97; Wolfram Fischer, *Expansion, Integration, Globalisierung: Studien zur Geschichte der Weltwirtschaft* (Göttingen: Vandenhoeck & Ruprecht, 1998), 36–48.

5. See Ulrich Beck, *Was ist Globalisierung? Irrtümer des Globalismus—Antworten auf die Globalisierung* (Frankfurt/Main: Suhrkamp, 1997), 34.

6. See Etienne Balibar and Immanuel Wallerstein, *Rasse Klasse Nation: Ambivalente Identitäten* (Hamburg: Argument, 1992), 87–130; Saskia Sassen, *Das Paradox des Nationalen: Territorium, Autorität und Rechte im globalen Zeitalter* (Frankfurt/Main: Suhrkamp, 2008), 7, 49.

7. See Benedict Anderson, *Imagined Communities: Reflections on the Origin and Spread of Nationalism* (London: Verso, 1983), 28–49, 66–79; cf. Casanova, *The World Republic of Letters.*

8. See Arjun Appadurai, "Disjuncture and Difference in the Global Cultural Economy," in *Global Cultures: Nationalism, Globalization and Modernity*, ed. Mike Featherstone (London: Sage Publications, 1990), 301.

9. See Marwan M. Kraidy, *Hybridity, or the Cultural Logic of Globalization* (Philadelphia, PA: Temple University Press, 2005), 9.

10. See Bruno Latour, *Wir sind nie modern gewesen: Versuch einer symmetrischen Anthropologie* (Berlin: Akademie, 1995), 98–104.

11. Cf. Kraidy, *Hybridity,* vii–viii, 1, 9.

12. See Hartmut Böhme, *Fetischismus und Kultur: Eine andere Theorie der Moderne* (Reinbek: Rowohlt, 2006); Michel Foucault, *Les mots et les choses: Une archéologie des sciences humaines* (Paris: Éditions Gallimard, 1966); Latour, *Wir sind nie modern.*

13. See Böhme, *Fetischismus und Kultur,* 17–20.

14. See Böhme, *Fetischismus und Kultur,* 72–94; Latour, *Wir sind nie modern,* 7–9, 145, 156; Bruno Latour, *Eine neue Soziologie für eine neue Gesellschaft: Einführung in die Akteur-Netzwerk-Theorie* (Frankfurt/Main: Suhrkamp, 2007), 25, 76–88, 109–49.

15. See Edward W. Said, *Orientalism,* 39–40.

16. See Karl Marx, *Das Kapital,* vol. 1, *Kritik der politischen Ökonomie* (Berlin: Dietz, 1962), 85–98.

17. See Böhme, *Fetischismus und Kultur,* 309–10, 327–30.

18. Ibid., 17.

19. Ibid., 25. Cf. Mackie's positive conception of fetishism referring to Michael Taussig in Erin Mackie, "Red Shoes and Bloody Stumps," in *Footnotes: On Shoes,* ed. Shari Benstock and Suzanne Ferriss (New Brunswick, NJ: Rutgers University Press, 1994), 234–5. Less radical than Böhme, Arjun Appadurai emphasizes the inevitability of "methodological fetishism." See Arjun Appadurai, ed., "Introduction: Commodities and the Politics of Value," in *The Social Life of Things: Commodities in Cultural Perspective* (Cambridge: Cambridge University Press, 1986), 5.

20. See Sebastian Conrad and Andreas Eckert, "Globalgeschichte, Globalisierung, Multiple Modernen," in *Globalgeschichte: Theorien, Ansätze, Themen,* ed. Sebastian Conrad, Andreas Eckert, and Ulrike Freitag (Frankfurt/Main: Campus, 2007), 20–2.

21. Appadurai ties the definition of the commodity closely to its exchange. See Arjun Appadurai, "Introduction," 3–16.

22. See Hans C. Andersen, *Eventyr og Historier*, ed. Det Danske Sprog- og Litteraturselskab (Copenhagen: Gyldendal, 2003), 1: 349–51.
23. See Jørn Lund, ed., *Den Store Danske Encyclopædi*, vol. 16, *Ranunkel-Schroeder* (Copenhagen: Gyldendal, 2000), 486.
24. See Arjun Appadurai, "Introduction," 16–29.
25. Mackie, "Red Shoes," 234.
26. See Peer E. Sørensen, *H. C. Andersen & Herskabet: Studier i borgerlig krisebevidsthed* (Grenaa: GMT, 1973), 195. Cf. Eigil Nyborg, *Den indre linie i H.C. Andersens eventyr: En psykologisk studie* (Copenhagen: Gyldendal, 1962), 167–8; Gerda Thastum Leffers, *Kunstnerproblematikken hos H. C. Andersen belyst gennem eventyrene* (Copenhagen: C. A. Reitzel, 1994), 62–70.
27. See Hans C. Andersen, *Eventyr og Historier*, 1: 353; Mackie, "Red Shoes," 241–2.
28. Hans C. Andersen, "The Great Sea Serpent," in *The Complete Andersen*, ed. Jean Hersholt (New York, NY: The Limited Editions Club, 1949), http://www.andersen.sdu.dk/vaerk/hersholt/TheGreatSeaSerpent_e.html, paragraphs 64–5 (accessed April 26, 2010); see Andersen, *Eventyr og Historier*, 3: 295.
29. See Volker Barth, *Mensch versus Welt: Die Pariser Weltausstellung von 1867* (Darmstadt: Wissenschaftliche Buchgesellschaft, 2007); Winfried Kretschmer, *Geschichte der Weltausstellungen* (Frankfurt/Main: Campus, 1999), 78–87.
30. Hans C. Andersen, "The Dryad," in *The Complete Andersen*, http://www.andersen.sdu.dk/vaerk/hersholt/TheDryad_e.html, paragraphs 28–9 (accessed April 26, 2010); see Andersen, *Eventyr og Historier*, 2: 200.
31. See Dipesh Chakrabarty, *Provincializing Europe: Postcolonial Thought and Historical Difference* (Princeton, NJ: Princeton University Press, 2008), 3–23, 73–7.
32. See Klaus Müller-Wille, "Romantik-Biedermeier-Realismus (1800–1870)," in *Skandinavische Literaturgeschichte*, ed. Jürg Glauser (Stuttgart: Metzler, 2006), 173–9.
33. See Thomas Bredsdorff, "Oehlenschläger's Aesthetics: Allegory and Symbolism in 'The Golden Horns' and a Note on 20th Century Eulogy of the Allegory," *Edda* 3 (1999): 212.
34. See Fritz Paul, ed., "Romantik und Poetischer Realismus," in *Grundzüge der neueren skandinavischen Literaturen* (Darmstadt: Wissenschaftliche Buchgesellschaft, 1991), 90; Sven H. Rossel, ed., "From Romanticism to Realism," in *A History of Danish Literature* (Lincoln: University of Nebraska Press, 1992), 178–9.
35. Adam G. Oehlenschläger, "Guldhornene," in *Oehlenschlæger Poetiske Skrifter*, ed. Helge Topsøe-Jensen, vol. 1 (Copenhagen: J. Jørgensen & Co., 1926), 19.
36. See Oehlenschläger, "Guldhornene," 21–3.
37. Ibid., 25.
38. See Latour, *Wir sind nie modern*, 40–1.
39. Cf. Kraidy, *Hybridity*, 62–3.
40. Adam G. Oehlenschläger, *Aladdin, eller den forunderlige Lampe: Et Lystspil*, in *Oehlenschlæger Poetiske Skrifter*, ed. Helge Topsøe-Jensen, vol. 2 (Copenhagen: J. Jørgensen & Co., 1927), 226.
41. Oxfeldt, *Nordic Orientalism*, 21; see Georg Brandes, "Adam Oehlenschläger," in *Samlede Skrifter*, vol. 1 (Copenhagen: Gyldendalske Boghandels Forlag, 1899), 215.
42. See Brandes, "Adam Oehlenschläger," 215–17, 231; Oxfeldt, *Nordic Orientalism*, 45.
43. See Jorge L. Borges, "Tausendundeine Nacht," in Jorge Luis Borges, *Die letzte Reise des Odysseus: Vorträge und Essays 1978–1982*, ed. Gisbert Haefs (Frankfurt/Main: Fischer, 2001), 116–31.
44. See Brandes, "Adam Oehlenschläger," 238–40.
45. Oxfeldt, *Nordic Orientalism*, 25.
46. Ibid., 24; see Oehlenschläger, *Aladdin*, 87, 150.
47. Oxfeldt, *Nordic Orientalism*, 25.
48. Ibid.

49. See Martin Zerlang, "Orientalism and Modernity: Tivoli in Copenhagen," *Nineteenth-Century Contexts* 20, no. 1 (1997): 81–110.

50. See Oxfeldt, *Nordic Orientalism*, 27–32.

51. See Oehlenschläger, *Aladdin*, 74–6, 79–80, 155–6.

52. Ibid., 372.

53. See Brandes, "Adam Oehlenschläger," 236.

54. See Oxfeldt, *Nordic Orientalism*, 48.

55. See Michel Serres, *Der Parasit* (Frankfurt/Main: Suhrkamp, 2007), 344–60.

56. Brandes, "Adam Oehlenschläger," 235; my translation.

57. Cf. Oehlenschläger, *Aladdin*, 76, 87–8, 199–204, 277–9.

CHAPTER **8**

How Far to the Global?
Producing Television at the Margins as Lived Experiences

IVAN KWEK

Chapter Description

How is the global in global media experienced from the margins? What do the subject positions of media producers working at the edges of an otherwise interconnected global media market render visible about the nature of the globalized and globalizing flows of media forms, images, and capital? This chapter, based on ethnographic fieldwork at a television channel in Singapore, considers how the global and regional are intertwined with the cultural politics behind the establishment and production of a minority-language channel. It demonstrates how a project that began as an attempt to produce a distinctive Singapore Malay identity and culture—different from other Malays in the region, at home in some bigger world, but firmly defined within the nation-state—became a site for their contestations. Competing versions of the global are produced, imagined, and experienced; sometimes as empowering, other times as disempowering, but always as complex and shifty. The ethnographic evidence presented here demonstrates a multiplicity of meanings of the global in global media by attending to the lived experiences of producers engaged in the production of otherwise "invisible" and "unprofitable cultural expressions." The definition of the global it concludes is not the exclusive domain of only those firmly seated in its "center."

* * *

With the often enthusiastic embrace of globalization as one of the key defining features of the contemporary world, it is easy to forget how distant the global may sometimes seem to those who are not already "there." What does the global mean and look like when viewed from its "margins"?[1] This seemingly rhetorical question arose out of a conversation I had with a television executive at Suria, a minority, Malay-language television channel in Singapore. The executive, Muhammad Fuadi, had just been moved to a newly setup unit in charge of marketing its programs overseas. At his desk, he had prominently pinned up a scrap of paper with "US$ 1,000,000" (about US$ 680,000) scribbled on it. It was his sales target. Until then, I had known the channel he worked at as little more than a community channel, targeted at the 460,000 Malays who made up about 14% of Singapore's population.

Although the ambition of going regional was ever present, it was usually limited to the occasional joint production with broadcasting stations or production houses in Malaysia, Brunei, or Indonesia, where most speakers of Malay (or some variety of it) are found. Half jokingly, I commented that the channel was entering the global media market. Fuadi was quick to temper any excitement I might have betrayed:

> There is no way we can compete, and even harder to try to sell to the Malaysian or Indonesian markets. They produce so many more programs of their own. They have big stars and big budgets. They don't need our productions. It will be like selling ice to the Eskimos.

Later, referring to the Malay diaspora elsewhere in the world, he added, "We have also many Malays living in the Arab world. But then, they won't want to watch Malay programs when they are there. They rather watch Arabic. To them, Malay is like lower class." Fuadi's dismal assessment underscores the point that beneath the celebrations of television as a global medium, and of transnational flows of images, money, technologies, ideas, and people,[2] lie spaces where "local" media and cultural productions remain sidelined amidst the headiness of the "global," however imagined.

Minding the Gaps

It is a well-worn mantra that globalization of media has been a highly uneven process and experience. A dominant narrative concerns itself with the concentration of media power and capital and how it has given rise to ever more interconnected media networks. Threats to national and cultural identities and formations have been experienced as real for some, overstated for many, and welcomed by yet others. With hindsight, we have come to understand how the vision of a largely Western hegemony weighing on the rest of the world has been rather naïve;[3] equally naive, however, are those premature celebrations of the "decentralizing multiplicity of global flows today."[4] Following Koichi Iwabuchi, we need to question the extent to which these decentralizations are in fact a reconfiguration of the old asymmetries such that existing corporate and cultural powers, concentrated in a handful of developed countries, consolidate themselves through complex webs of alliances and projects.

Driven by a logic of market and capital, it is often those already in positions to exploit and participate in the new configurations who will benefit the most. This intensifies the disparity between them and the ones left behind, those limited in their capacity to extend beyond the confines of a national or local framework. The new connections, Iwabuchi concluded, had tended to reaffirm existing patterns of inclusions and exclusions, leaving out "a tremendous number of people and their unprofitable cultural expressions and concerns in terms of gender, sexuality, race, ethnicity, class, age, region, etc."[5] Often deemed "unmarketable," these cultural productions are barely discernible on a global, regional, or even national scale when measured quantitatively in terms of production output, trade figures, market shares, and audience numbers, or simply their ability to travel beyond their original target audience. This essay is concerned precisely with such "unprofitable cultural expressions" within the context of the global.

To be sure, we can no longer take the notions of the global, as well as the local and regional, and the distinctions between them, as unproblematic.[6] As spatial metaphors, the various notions seem to imply a degree of distinctiveness from each other as if it were possible to leave one for the other. Against this view, this essay assumes that no matter how cosmopolitan we may seem, we are always embedded in the local and that what makes our lives and experiences global is partly our capacity to imagine and make connections to an expandable field.[7] What we call the global—and, by the same token, the regional and local—are not concrete spaces out there to be explored but tentatively produced through those articulatory practices,[8] both material and discursive, of making linkages of scale, movements, and continuities—and discontinuities—across otherwise disparate contexts of social action and experience. In arguing that the global (and for that matter, the local) are the effects of articulatory practices underscores the dual aspects of describing some connections as global while constituting them as such. Considered from the margins, how is the global imagined, experienced, or challenged? What does the global in global media look like from the standpoint of the producers[9] who operate here? How are notions of identities and cultures implicated, mobilized, or transformed in the processes of constituting the global?

These questions will be considered in the light of ethnographic encounters from my fieldwork at Suria, intensively for a year from late 2000 to 2001, and then periodically, for shorter stints, every year until 2007. Much of the fieldwork involved attempts at making myself useful at Suria, attending script sessions, reviewing programs, and participating in commissioning exercises, but mostly, it was just attending meetings and hanging around the producers as they went about their work and asking questions at opportune times.

Suria has been variously described as an ethnic, community, minority, and niche channel. It considers its audience to be "the Malay community" and brands itself as a channel for the "new Singapore Malay." Partly commercial, and partly funded by the state, the channel offers the only Malay-language, free-to-air television service in Singapore. It goes on air for about 58 hours a week, of which only about a third is filled with locally produced programs, with a sizeable proportion of them being repeats. The rest of its airtime is filled with imported programs, which are substantially cheaper.

Suria's limited budget and advertising support are perhaps unsurprising given that the entire media industry in Singapore accounted for less than 1% of the value of the Asia-Pacific market, according to a 2007 industry report.[10] Notably, however, a government-led effort has been underway since 2003 to make Singapore a "global media city" by offering a litany of inducements including financial, government, and infrastructural supports. The state plays a proactive role in attracting global media corporations to Singapore, helping to develop and finance local media companies and their productions, and even marketing them overseas. These efforts, however, had not directly benefited Suria as much since Malay-language programs are deemed limited both in terms of commercial support and their appeal beyond the local Malay market. Therefore, Suria and its productions have not been high on the agenda. It is telling that the channel's executives were rarely included in the team to participate in the annual pilgrimage to the international film and television market in Cannes; in which case, they had to entrust their colleagues in another channel to buy programs on their behalf. Suria's minority status in the global and national media marketplace, however, conceals its significance on other registers, particularly the political and cultural.

Border Patrol, or How Suria Came To-Be

Media, although often described as instrumental in creating an imagined community, are also seen as having the potential to undermine the boundaries of nation-states. The latter do not have a monopoly over how its constituents imagine themselves in relationship to the varieties of mediated identities on offer, as local, regional, and global media are, in varying degrees and manner, always implicated in each other. Territorially-defined identities compete with alternative ways of imagining one's identities and modes of belonging. While embracing these challenges, usually within a discourse of globalization that naturalizes them as the inevitable outcomes of techno-logical and economic development, nation-states have also responded by reasserting their boundaries through the development of what Ien Ang described as "ultra-modernist media policies which insists on the equiva-lence of territorial media, culture and nation."[11] These include the erection of market barriers, censorship of foreign media, and the promotion of a national media industry. Arguably, Suria is the outcome of a state's attempt to counter the transnationally porous nature of media and cultural con-sumption and identification.

Before its launch, there were, on average, only about 3 hours a day of Malay-language programming in Singapore, compared with a dedicated 24-hour channel for Chinese-language programming and three English-language channels, one each for entertainment, arts, and news.[12] The disparity was justified on two grounds: demographic proportionality—over three quarters of the population are ethnically Chinese—and the fact that English is the official language. With the introduction of Suria in January 2000, Malay-language programming shot up from 23-hours weekly to 58.

This dramatic increase in Malay-language programming in Singapore may be understood as a reaction to a migration of viewers to television channels from neighboring countries. A spillover of television signals across international borders is not a particularly spectacular occurrence but, in a historical period marked by large-scale political upheavals, civil unrest, and violence in the surrounding region, the loss of a segment of the domestic audience, even if only intermittently, raises concerns of a loss of ideological control. This was the time of the so-called Asian Financial Crisis that began with a destabilization of certain Asian currencies but quickly deteriorated into a crisis of political legitimacy, bringing on dra-matic changes in the region, particularly in Indonesia and Malaysia. Singapore weathered the crisis better than its neighbors, but given its geo-graphical location and deep historical ties with the two countries, it was not spared the ensuing uncertainties and tensions brought home, notably, by media reports from "Western" global media organizations such as CNN, the BBC, and Reuters. Almost daily, satellite pictures of the unrests, often with accompanying commentaries critical of the status quo, were beamed to audiences in Southeast Asia and internationally. Convinced of the influ-ence foreign media seemed to have over the events in the region, the political elite in Singapore reacted by warning of the dangers posed by foreign media to the Singaporean identity and culture.[13]

Furthermore, Singapore's relationships with Malaysia and Indonesia were strained during the crisis. At one point, the Indonesian President derided the island-state as "a red dot" in a sea of green, referring to Singapore's vulnerability as a tiny Chinese-dominated state in the heart of a vast region that some have called the Malay World (*Dunia Melayu*). Indeed, Singapore was once a nodal point in the flux of migrants encouraged by the British colonial powers. With independence, it is caught in an ongoing postcolonial project of imagining itself as a legitimate nation-state in the region.[14] Much of this imagining has been inflected by a historical experience framed in racial terms, which the ruling elite has insisted is an essential and immutable feature of Singapore. Primordialist theories, asserted as facts, have informed the state's approach to governance. Politically, however, this ideological posture makes problematic the position of Malays in Singapore, raising questions about their commitment to the national project vis-à-vis their affective relationships with Malays in the neighboring countries. The ruling elite saw this as potentially problematic. A minister once raised the dilemma of Singapore Malays having to point their guns at fellow Malays from neighboring countries, should Singapore be at war with any of them.

About the same period, an internal survey commissioned at the request of an advisory committee to the Media Development Authority (MDA),[15] ostensibly to find out the viewing patterns of Singapore Malays, highlighted the amount of time they spent watching Malay-language television on a Singapore channel[16] against the time spent on RTM1, Malaysia's exclusively Malay-language channel.[17] About 60% of Singapore Malays spent an equal amount of time watching the two channels. When it came to Malay-language news, 96% of those surveyed reported watching it on the local channel but equally significant was that 71% also watched the news over on RTM1. Finally, the survey also noted the popularity of RTM1's religious program *Forum Perdana Ehwal Islam* (a public forum on a variety of topics led by Islamic teachers) among Singapore Malays. Such overtly religious programming is generally not allowed on Singapore television.

Given the offering of a mere 3 hours daily of Malay-language programming on the Singapore channel, this turn to Malaysian and Indonesian channels, where Malay-language programs are a staple, should hardly be surprising. As noted earlier, the limited allocation of airtime to Malay programming had its logic in the demographic proportion as well as commercial interests. At this juncture, however, there were other considerations. A senior television executive,[18] recounting his meeting with the minister in charge, told me concerns had been raised over "how Singapore Malays

[were] taking in the events and situation as interpreted by the Malaysian and Indonesian media." Read against this geopolitical background, the setting up of Suria as a dedicated Malay-language channel to win back Singapore Malay viewers may be understood as a historically situated attempt to orientate the Malays inwards and thereby reconstitute the national boundaries. The ideological work of forming a "national outlook and identity" in a segment of the population was explicitly expressed at the launch of Suria:

> While reflecting the viewpoints and concerns of the Malay community, the channel will also equip its viewers with the attitudes, values and instincts that make them comfortably vibrant and proud citizens of Singapore . . . The quality of locally produced programs, which reflected the way of life of Singapore, must be maintained and raised. Then, Singaporeans will want to watch them instead of foreign programs.[19]

The launch of Suria was, therefore, premised on encouraging the formation of Malay subjectivities who are culturally befitting of and loyal to the national project. Its claims to *reflecting* "the unique Singapore Malay identity" seems to ignore the mediating role of television in constituting the said identity. Furthermore, if all identities are relational, as we have come to understand it, then the question arises as to what have been excluded in the process as its constitutive outside. What have been represented as foreign to whom and under what circumstances? The state-sponsored form of an ethnicized identity, defined in territorial terms, may serve as a privileged nodal point in the contest for "fixing" the Singapore Malay identity and culture. Given the cultural, linguistic, and historical affinities between the Malays in Singapore and the Malays in the neighboring countries, and even beyond, however, this rendering of the latter as foreign is often at odds with the lived experiences of Suria's producers (and audiences).

Global as Complexity

With very few exceptions, Suria's producers identify themselves as Singaporeans, Malays, and Muslims, while, at the same time, they speak readily about their Javanese, Baweanese, Terengganu, or "half-Chinese" lineages. They are mostly fluent in English, sometimes more than they are in Malay. A fair number of the producers have at least a first degree in media, social sciences, or a related discipline from overseas, most frequently Australia. Perhaps like their imagined audiences, Suria's producers are as likely to be watching the likes of *CSI* and *Flashforward*, Korean soaps, and Hindi movies as well as Singapore-produced Chinese dramas (which airs with English subtitles). With such a complex mix of histories and cultural identifications, Suria's producers are not simply the powerless agents promoting the ideology of an insular Singapore Malayness but neither are they its resistant heroes. Many commentators on media in Singapore point to its political economy and assume that the state-owned media will function unproblematically as an archetypical ideological state apparatus.[20] In this view, Suria's producers will simply do the bidding of the state, devoid of agency. At the level of practice, however, Suria's producers actively participate in articulating and realizing the official discourse, but often in ways inflected through their lived experiences and positionalities. Although they may echo the channel's official lines of reflecting a distinctive Singapore Malay culture and identity in their programming, equally they may also identify strongly with Malays—and Muslims—in the Malay world and even beyond. Production of the channel is, therefore, fraught with contradictions arising from these conflicting and often shifting modes of identification.

When I met Basir Siswo 8 months after he had launched the channel, he related how it was the local talents and artistes, inexperienced as they may be, that captured the attention of the viewers, rather than the established Malaysian stars he had brought in. He said, "They see their friends, relatives, neighbors on TV. They will support them." Hailing this as "something happening in the [Singapore Malay] community," he proudly reminded me that Singapore was once a regional center for Malay film and literary productions. Not content that Suria should remain a channel for the local Malays, he expressed his hope that the channel would eventually go regional and be a channel for other Malay speakers in the region and not just Singapore. A planned project that he often spoke about was a major documentary on "the Malay diaspora," exploring the historical movements and cultural influences of the Malays from China and Taiwan, across Southeast Asia, and all the way to Sri Lanka, South Africa, and even Liverpool in Britain. When he eventually broached the proposal to the MDA, hoping they would help to fund it, they were broadly in agreement— except for one crucial point of difference. The official felt that the documentary should be centered on Singapore Malays and their ventures overseas.[21] The epic documentary was never produced, at least not in the intended form.

The ease with which Basir had been able to shift between different scales of identification was at odds with the neat distinctions between the foreign and the local that underlie the state's investments in Suria. In 2009, writing from the vantage point of a mobile professional who had moved to Al-Jazeera International in Doha, Basir explained that

the pull of language, culture and religion supercede political boundaries and inclinations. While Malay Singaporeans are proud to be
Singaporeans, we also identify closely with the Malay *Nusantara*.[22]
The issue here is whether identification equals to being disloyal to
the country which is what the government fears most.[23]

Another producer I interviewed made a related point: "The Malays are the
fourth largest population in the world! Why do we have to limit ourselves,
and just produce for the Singapore Malay community? Can you imagine
what we can achieve if we can lift this lid off?"[24] In each case, the project of
Suria, imagined by the state as an apparatus for orientating Singapore
Malays inwards, has been reimagined in terms of some broader connections with a world beyond the national boundaries. Informed by a nostalgia
for historical and cultural linkages as well as the desire for pan-Malay audiences, markets, and productions, this has opened up a space for the contestations, unequally matched as they may be, over what constitutes legitimate
cultural expressions and identities.

Global as Empowering

In Suria's corporate literature, its claim of catering to the "unique views,
lifestyle and culture" of Singapore Malays, presumably unique with respect
to those of Malays elsewhere, has been a constant feature in its branding,
the means by which a television channel tries to distinguish itself from
others. What is ostensibly a practice in market differentiation is not just an
attempt to mark the channel in distinctive ways but also acts to interpellate
the audience as particular sorts of subjects. To win back the audience from
the Malaysian channels, Suria describes itself as "hip, modern, and contemporary," hailing its viewers as "modern Malay Singaporeans."[25] Translated
to programming practice, the channel's producers try to privilege productions they regard as lively, up-to-date, and modern. To broaden the minds
of their viewers, Suria regularly schedules imported programs from countries
that they believe their viewers can relate to, while at the same time giving
the channel "an international feel." This was a version of the global popu-
lated by feature films, documentaries, and dramas from selected countries,
notably Japan, Iran, Thailand, the Philippines, and India—countries beyond
"the Malay world." Though the need for translation and dubbing or subtitling made them costlier than programs from the traditional sources of
Malaysia and Indonesia, these programs, as Kharul Rashid, the former head
of acquisition[26] at Suria, put it, offer the viewers a "window on the world that
empowers them, mak[ing] them aware of what is happening in the world.
We don't want them to be left behind." In meetings to discuss acquisitions,

the theme of wanting to expose viewers to "other cultures" and "how others live" is commonly heard. The corollary of this is that a lack of exposure to other worlds is to be backward or unenlightened.[27]

In these ways, the consumption of the global in global media had been imagined as empowering by virtue of the knowledge and acquaintance they offered of some bigger world they represented. This understanding of the global may be usefully contrasted to programs that Suria's producers describe as "*kampung*." In everyday usage, *kampung* is a Malay word for village, but in the production context of Suria, it is a common reason offered for rejecting proposed programs or acquisitions. Its meanings, though typically ill defined and inconsistently applied, are particularly inflected in Singapore where virtually all *kampung* had been demolished in the enthusiastic embrace of urban redevelopment and modernization in the postindependent years. Although the term has been used to conjure the nostalgia of an idyllic, if laid back, community, it has also been used to signify stagnancy or backwardness. One of the more explicit explanations went like this:

> *kampung* means going back to the past, reliving old issues and themes, refusing to be current, not moving forward, afraid to venture into the unknown coz [because] of their comfort zones. They are like people in the village living in their own world. It's a very Malay attitude.[28]

Working against this supposed tendency of the Malays to be insular and bound to the space, time, and ways of the *kampung*, Suria's programming is, at least in part, informed by an imagining of the global as a metaphor of empowerment through the transformation of the Malay mind.

Global through Otherness

As much as the global has been imagined by Suria's producers to be desirable and empowering for its audiences, it has also been experienced as a distant world in which they do not always participate fully. Fuadi's lament at the beginning of the essay tells of the limitations he faced in trying to market Suria's programs overseas, whereas another's disappointment at being left out of the trip to the Cannes Festival underscores those practices of exclusion and inclusion that define the forms and degrees of participation in the global. In the year 2001, however, Suria did send two representatives to Cannes, and Kharul was one of them:

> You never know what you are missing until you are there, and you meet them . . . I ended up with far more screeners [samples of programs] to watch. This genre, that genre, things you never

thought about. I even got to meet some small producers, the niche producers, producing mostly Muslim programs. Never knew there were these kinds of programs . . . Wished we could sell our programs too. Singapore had a booth there, but they were promoting Chinese and Channel NewsAsia a lot. Plus some Central programs.[29] We [Suria] are just not marketable.[30]

In an event like the Cannes Film and Television Festival, the global is produced and experienced but as a hierarchy of differences. Although Kharul spoke excitedly about her experience there, she was also reminded of how small the channel she worked for really was. Limiting as that may be, however, it was not the entire story; for even at its margins, the global may be articulated in surprising ways. Given the miniscule budget, Kharul sussed out some smaller producers to see what "Asian content" they had. By putting together a few productions from different companies, she produced a series on Muslims and Islam in different countries and cultural contexts. What was interesting here was how a bricolage of small productions had been produced as an alternative global—marked by an Islamic theme, a narrative of the interconnectedness of Islamic peoples, places, and cultures. It also opened up a space for circumventing the secular-only programming policy in Singapore.

The state views religion (and race) with ultimate sensitivities. Although Suria's producers are generally sympathetic with the policy, a number of them have also expressed guilt for not using the medium to advance their religious values. In light of this, the series on Muslims and Islam across the world, packaged as a cultural travelogue, was a strategic response to overcome censorship. With religion in the local seen as sensitive ground, the global has been deployed as an avenue to resist the stifling ways of the state—a detour for the expression of a Muslim identity, ostensibly on behalf of the Malay—and Muslim—audience.[31] Here, television representations of Muslims elsewhere are reconstituted locally in ways that claim both differences and similarities with Muslims in Singapore.

Conclusions

Through the above accounts, I have tried to show how the global has been variously articulated in and through the lived experiences and everyday practices of Suria's producers. In each case, the mediation of identities and cultures has served as a rallying point over which the claims to and about the global, as well as the regional, local, and national, are often made. In these senses, although Suria as a television channel lies at the distant margins of what we typically understand by global media, the global remains a relevant frame for analysis. This, I have tried to show, is particularly productive when we think of the global, not as a prediscursive terrain out there, but as an effect of its articulation. What began as a project to produce a distinctive Singapore Malay identity and to "reflect" its "unique" culture—different from other Malays in the region, at home in some bigger world (the global?), but firmly defined within the framework of the nation-state—had also become a site for their contestations.

Competing versions of the global, as produced, imagined, and experienced by the channel's producers, have come to inform the trajectories of Suria. We have seen, for example, how one notion of the global—the interconnectness of peoples, cultures, and histories in the region—has been imagined as a threat to the legitimacy of the nation-state and its claims over the loyalties of its constituents; whereas another version of the global was produced as a desirable counter to the insularity of the *kampung* and a panacea for the supposed closed mindedness of the Malays. It is in the production of such connections and continuities across mediated time and space that the global in global media gets articulated, sometimes as empowering, other times as disempowering.

Equally, however, and this is perhaps ironic, the global may also be constituted through the imagination and experiences of exclusion and the disconnectedness they engender. It is not just in the continuities but also in the discontinuities that the global comes into relief. If this is an uncommon view of the global, it may be because it has come from the vantage point of the margins. For here, where the center or centers sometimes seem so distant, the analyst is forced to consider the possibility of other globals. Suria's productions are not just unprofitable cultural expressions. Like countless others, they are virtually invisible on the register of the global media market. Arguably, this invisibility may be the articulatory effect of the market as a globalizing discourse, which renders particular features of the global thinkable and others unthinkable. However, as the foregoing accounts of the lived experiences and practices of media producers at Suria attest, their struggles over their identities and cultures, and their mediation through media, overlap with their struggles about the kinds and scale of partial connections across time and space to be affirmed, resisted, or transformed.

Endnotes

1. The reference to the "margins" is not to reify its existence as a prediscursive space between the global and its outside. Rather, I use it as an idiom to generate other vantage points from which to consider the global in global media.
2. Arjun Appadurai, "Disjuncture and Difference in the Global Cultural Economy," in *Modernity at Large: Cultural Dimensions of Globalization*, ed. Arjun Appadurai (Minneapolis: University of Minnesota Press, 1996), 33.

3. See, for examples, Joseph Dean Straubhaar, "Beyond Media Imperialism: Asymmetrical Interdependence and Cultural Proximity," *Critical Studies in Mass Communication* 8 (1991): 39–59; John Nyuyet Erni and Chua Siew Keng, *Asian Media Studies: Politics of Subjectivities* (Malden, MA: Blackwell, 2004).

4. Youna Kim, "The Rising East Asian 'Wave': Korean Media Go Global," in *Media on the Move: Global Flow and Contra-flow*, ed. Daya Kishan Thussu (London: Routledge, 2007), 149.

5. Koichi Iwabuchi, "Contra-flows or the Cultural Logic of Uneven Globalization? Japanese Media in the Global Agora," in *Media on the Move: Global Flow and Contra-flow*, ed. Daya Kishan Thussu (London: Routledge, 2007), 73.

6. See, for examples, Jonathan Friedman, "Globalization and the Making of a Global Imaginary," in *Global Encounters: Media and Cultural Transformation*, eds Gitte Stald and Thomas Tufte (Luton, UK: University of Luton Press, 2002), 13–32; Michael Kearney, "The Local and the Global: The Anthropology of Globalization and Transnationalism," *Annual Review of Anthropology* 24 (1995): 547–65; Mike Featherstone, "Genealogies of the Global," *Theory, Culture & Society* 23, no. 2–3 (2006): 387–92.

7. The notion of "scale-making," favored by Khandekar and Otsuki (this volume), makes a similar point about how the global is produced.

8. This understanding of articulation is borrowed from Jennifer Daryl Slack, "The Theory and Method of Articulation in Cultural Studies," in *Stuart Hall: Critical Dialogues in Cultural Studies*, eds David Morley and Kuan-Hsing Chen (London: Routledge, 1996), 115.

9. By "producer," I refer not to a specific occupational category as commonly understood in professional media circles, but rather, to an inclusive term covering a myriad of media professionals engaged with the production, programming, and marketing of media.

10. Datamonitor, *Media in Singapore: Industry Profile* (Sydney: Datamonitor, October 2008), 9.

11. Ien Ang, "Desperately Guarding Borders: Media Globalization, 'Cultural Imperialism', and the Rise of 'Asia'," in *House of Glass: Culture, Modernity and the State in Southeast Asia*, ed. Yao Souchou (Singapore: Institute of Southeast Asia Studies, 2001), 36.

12. By the time of writing, another two television channels were added, bringing the total number of channels in Singapore to seven—all run by the Mediacorp Group, the state-owned monopoly in television broadcasting.

13. Singapore, *Singapore Parliamentary Debates Official Report* 70, no. 6 (March 12, 1999): 682.

14. Lily Zubaidah Rahim, *Singapore in the Malay World: Building and Breaching Regional Bridges* (New York, NY: Routledge, 2009), 15–16.

15. This is the state's agency for regulating and developing media in Singapore.

16. This channel was the predecessor to Suria. Called Prime12, it was a minority interest channel into which Malay-, Tamil-, and foreign-language programs were slotted.

17. RTM1 was of particular interest not just because it was an exclusively Malay-language channel but also because it carried Islamic programs. As it can be received in Singapore, this has the effect of undermining the secular-only broadcasting policy in Singapore.

18. In view of some reservations expressed by the executive, the quote has been edited to conceal the identity.

19. Excerpt of speech by then-Deputy Prime Minister Lee Hsien Loong at the launch of *Suria* as summarized in a news item broadcast on Channel NewsAsia (*Singapore Tonight*, January 30, 2000).

20. See, for examples, David Birch, *Singapore Media: Communication Strategies and Practices* (Cheshire: Longman, 1993); James Gomez, *Self-Censorship: Singapore's Shame* (Singapore: Think Centre, 2000).

21. From fieldnotes (May 17, 2001) by the author at a meeting between Suria and the MDA to discuss new projects and funding.

22. Like *Dunia Melayu*, mentioned earlier, *Nusantara* (Malay Archipelago) is a concept used to mobilize the imagination of the unity of the Malays in the region.

23. Basir Siswo, e-mail correspondence with author, May 11, 2009.

24. Yusoff Ahmad (Chief Executive Officer, Communications 2000), interviewed by author, September 14, 2001.

25. From *Suria*, "About Us," http://www.suria.sg/about_us (accessed November 2008). This site is no longer available.

26. Khairul Rashid, personal communication, May 14, 2009.

27. With its budget shrunk, Suria's vision of offering viewers a window on the world has since been scaled back significantly. To avoid translation and dubbing costs, programs that do not come in Malay or Indonesian languages are now rarely acquired. Ironically, though the channel was set up to win back the Singapore Malay viewers from those two countries, the economics and pragmatics of broadcasting has made the channel partly reliant on them to help fill its schedules and keep the viewers "at home." What began as an attempt to solidify the boundaries of the nation-state has been complicated by time and markets.

28. Basir Siswo, e-mail correspondence with author, May 13, 2009.

29. Like Suria, Central (arts and children channel), Channel NewsAsia (news, current affairs, and documentaries channel), and the Chinese-language channels are part of the Mediacorp Group.

30. Khairul Rashid, personal communication, May 14, 2009.

31. The reader may notice a slippage here between Malays and Muslims. In fact, Malays in Singapore are often referred to, in official discourse, as "Malay-Muslims," on the grounds that 99.7% of Malays are at least nominally Muslims. There are obvious problems with this, not least of all because these classifications were generated for the purposes of state administration, including the applicability of *Syariah* (Islamic) laws and obligations.

CHAPTER 9

Remediation and Scaling

The Making of "Global" Identities

AALOK KHANDEKAR AND GRANT JUN OTSUKI*

Chapter Description

This chapter analyzes the processes through which coherent claims about global identities are articulated. It argues that invocations of scale, such as the global, are contingent: they become meaningful in specific historical and cultural contexts. Two sets of media productions—"Global Indian" branding commercials and representations of "Hapa" identities centered in North America—constitute the empirical basis of the analysis. The chapter proposes that the construction of global identities is gainfully interrogated through the notions of *scale-making processes*[1] and *remediation*[2]: understanding media representations of global identities as remediated, scale-making processes disrupt straightforward conceptions of media and draw attention to the ways in which they are embedded in specific historical and cultural contexts. The chapter brings together theories of remediation and scale-making processes to highlight the ways in which particular

*Parts of this chapter were presented at the May 2009 joint annual meetings of the American Ethnological Society and the Canadian Anthropology Society. We thank Kim Fortun, Nancy Campbell, Nicole Cook, Maral Erol, Brandon Costelloe-Kuehn, Shiho Satsuka, and Joshua Barker for their comments on drafts of this essay. We also thank Atsushi Akera and the other participants of the INES-affiliated Regional Workshop on Engineering Identities for useful discussions of the arguments made in this chapter. Finally, we also thank Rohit Chopra and Radhika Gajjala, the editors of this volume, for their generous support.

imaginations of scale and media forms are choreographed into coherent articulations. In doing so, it also offers a methodological contribution toward analyzing claims to the "global."

* * *

The cover image of the August 1999 issue of the *National Geographic* magazine features two women—one older and clad in a South Indian sari; the other younger, wearing a tight, shiny black dress unzipped halfway down to her abdomen.[3] They are seated on a marble-topped bench—outdoors, but nowhere in particular. The younger woman, perhaps the daughter, is resting her right arm on the mother's shoulder. The mother is glancing sideways at the daughter, fondly, and perhaps with a hint of nostalgia. The younger woman is staring straight at the viewer, confident, and daring to be challenged. The clothing, jewelry, and accessories that these women wear hint at their affluence. Her clothing and jewelry help to identify the older woman as an Indian; the younger woman is made conspicuous by the absence of such ethnic markers. The image, contained within the familiar yellow borders shared by every issue of the *National Geographic* magazine, is captioned "Global Culture."

One interpretation of this image suggests that the "global" here is the movement, in time and in space, from the "traditional" to the "modern": the older woman displays specific ethnic markers, whereas the younger one does not. The movement is from *some*where to *no*where, or perhaps *every*where. The contrast in age between the two subjects—the maternal glance of the older to the younger woman, who does not return the glance but directs her eyes toward the reader—marks a linear, outward progression. The passage of time is accompanied by a movement away from the maternal figure, from a culture that is not global. The *National Geographic* masthead sits in the top half of the cover but is relegated to the background, creating a sense of transparency that is crucial for imagining an immediate connection between the viewer and the women in the image. The image caption "Global Culture," placed in the foreground over the subjects' feet, mediates between its subjects and viewers.

What makes this an image of global culture? Is it the play of contrasts, between the traditional and the modern, and the local and the worldly? Is it the provocative gaze of the young woman, captured in a photograph? Or is it the neat, commodified, reproducible, mass-mailed container of the magazine? In this chapter, we view these questions as inseparable. We are interested in understanding how such imaginings of the global are produced through interlocking processes of mediation and scale making. Our overarching argument is that the global is far from universal. Claims to the global are contingent: they emerge from and are articulated alongside particular imaginings of other scales. Paying attention to the ways in which the global is constituted helps to uncover these specificities and draws attention to its omissions.

To make our argument, we use examples from two sets of imaginings of global identities. The first set derives from television commercials aired in India, which stake a claim to a "Global Indian" way of being. The other set concentrates on representations of "Hapa"[4] identities in North America.

For the analysis, we draw on two distinct concepts: *remediation* and *scale-making processes*. Remediation has been used in media studies to understand the ways in which digital media represent developments of older media even as they create new forms of mediation. We draw upon the idea of scale-making processes to see how scales such as the global, the national, the regional, and the local are mutually intertwined and acquire meaning in relationship to each other. We make two related arguments: (i) the global assumes meaning only alongside other spatial imaginaries, and (ii) the global assumes meaning and significance through the interplay of various media forms. We use these cases to show how attention to remediation creates possibilities for critical reflection on claims to the global by highlighting the synergies that link these examples to culturally and historically specific modes of representation and broader projects of scale making.

Scales, Remediation, and the Global

Anna Tsing defines scale as "the spatial dimensionality necessary for a particular kind of view, whether up close or from a distance, microscopic or planetary."[5] Scales are frames through which cultural practices become intelligible. These frames are not neutral: scales mediate and impart meanings to cultural projects. They are neither static nor universal: they are tied to particular historical moments. According to Tsing, scale-making projects become powerful by enrolling other scale-making projects—globalisms and localisms can reinforce each other, as they become intertwined in the process of producing a particular representation of the world. Successful scale-making projects naturalize their products and create the appearance of universality and transparency in what Tsing playfully calls APHIDS—Articulations among Partially Hegemonic Imagined Different Scales.[6] Tsing argues that, when APHIDS are successfully produced, their constructedness is hidden and they become self-evident and transparent. Scales articulate and mediate claims that attempt to produce privileged views on the real by drawing together diverse sets of culturally available resources.

Remediation refers to the "representation of one medium in another."[7] The content of any medium is always another medium (the written word is the content of print, and print is the content of the telegraph), that is, *every medium is always already remediated.* Remediation, according to Bolter and Grusin, is defined by the interplay between the logics of *immediacy* and *hypermediacy.* Immediacy refers to an attempted erasure of the medium while producing representations, that is, the desire to provide unmediated access to that which is being represented. The immersive nature of virtual reality, for example, demands that the technology of mediation disappear. In contrast, by hypermediacy, they refer to the multiplication of media forms. A web page, for example, may simultaneously contain text, pictures, and video. Rather than an attempted effacement, it is the sense of fullness and presence that such environments create, which provides the viewer with a perspective on reality.

As such, immediacy and hypermediacy are in tension with each other and mutually constitutive. Hypermediated productions strive to create a sense of reality by drawing in other forms of media. Immediacy is threatened by this appropriation and juxtaposition with other media. In other words, media productions that emphasize hypermediacy cite, deconstruct, and critique those that attempt to produce immediacy, and vice versa. Remediation makes it possible to read certain differences between media representations not just as contingent and local stylistic choices but also as negotiations within cultural spaces where only some paths are available. Analyzing media representations through the lens of remediation allows us to map these spaces.

Remediation disrupts straightforward conceptions of "media" by seeing each media form as a *cultural* production.[8] By recognizing remediation and scale making as cultural processes at work in media representations of the global, we show how such representations produce, on one hand, a seemingly self-evident and transparent view of the global and, on the other hand, the possibility of deconstructing these representations. We analyze two sets of examples, one focusing on the production of transparency and the other on its deconstruction. A primary contribution of this chapter, then, is to examine the production of scales, by drawing on theories of remediation. A second contribution is methodological: we provide a way of unpacking the processes through which coherent articulations of scale are made possible.

Global Indians: In the Immediate Presence of the Global

In this section, we highlight the ways in which different scales articulate and reinforce each other to produce the global through the interplay of various media. We use examples of advertisements aired by two Indian corporations that seek to make Indianness a defining feature of their brand identity. Both ads follow a similar narrative trope—they highlight their

Indian roots while also foregrounding their desire for global expansion. The first ad is a branding commercial for Videocon,[9] a leading Indian manufacturer of consumer electronic goods, and the second is for an Indian conglomerate, the Aditya Birla Group (henceforth ABG),[10] which operates in a highly diverse range of industries. Though very different in size and scope, both these companies make the idea of "taking India to the world," while firmly holding on to their Indianness, a central part of their brand identity. The question generated by these advertisements is, how can India be taken to the world without being taken by the world? The question suggests a tension between individual/national uniqueness and a collective global homogeneity and the basis for reconciling them. By comparing these two ads through the lenses of scale and remediation, we can discern the cultural work expended to seamlessly present the interface of different nations as one that also serves to link transnational corporate identities to Indian national selfhood.

Consider the ad for brand Videocon. To articulate the Global Indian, the ad uses three different kinds of media—video, audio, and text. Individually, each of these media is deployed in very different ways to construct the global and the Indian, and it is their interplay that creates the desired effect of a transcendental Indianness. The video depicts a series of stereotypical images of very diverse people across space and time, from a Mongol tribesman to a businesswoman on Wall Street, and from Bushmen in the sub-Saharan African desert to Inuit in the ice-covered Arctic region—who are all chanting the Gayatri Mantra, an important chant in Hinduism. Also present continuously in the backdrop is a world map that very literally indexes the global, suggestive of the Indian company's counter/neocolonial aspirations.[11] Overall, the series of images in the video creates a sense of heterogeneity and an all-encompassing globalism.

The audio, which consists of various people chanting the Gayatri Mantra, creates a first layer of uniformity. The chant is repeated twice over the course of the video (about 50 seconds long)—during the first cycle, different people chanting the Gayatri Mantra are introduced successively, and each of their voices is layered onto the ones preceding them to form a uniform chorus. Other than the sounds of subdued bells, there is little background music. The overall effect of the rhythm and the tone of chanting is not unlike that of priestly chanting during Hindu rituals. The sound of a flute precedes the second cycle of the chant. In contrast to the first cycle, the second cycle is marked by the presence of prominent drumbeats in the background. The voices continue in chorus, until the very end when a female operatic soprano departs from the chorus, with the effect of highlighting the uniformity of the chant even further. The drum and the soprano together create a sense of fusion, of a blending of different cultures.

The text overlaid on these images creates yet another level of uniformity. A semitransparent Sanskrit text depicting the Gayatri Mantra appears throughout this video. The Devnagari script indexes the distinctly Indian roots of Videocon. The translucence of the text further creates an effect of an undergirding Indian core of a world otherwise in flux. The penultimate shot of the video reads: "Taking India to its rightful place in the world." The text appears against the background of the world map mentioned earlier—in white Roman characters, but stylistically presented with a hint of the Devnagari script, enhancing the sense of cultural fusion. Against the video and audio that precede it, the text suggests that being its spiritual basis is India's "rightful" place in the world. The ultimate shot reads "Videocon: New Improved Life" in bold, metallic silver letters, suggesting that Videocon is the means through which this rightful place will be attained.

As a hypermediated representation, the Videocon ad represents global Indianness as something that works at a level other than visual human difference. Aural uniformity and transcendence through text are the primary means through which India becomes global and vice versa. By juxtaposing individuals representing different cultural stereotypes with uniformities performed in text, sound, and maps, Videocon becomes the means through which the rest of the world becomes Indian, overcoming superficial physical and cultural difference by colonizing and structuring thought and utterance. Videocon takes India to the world by making the world Indian.

Like the Videocon commercial, the brand advertisement for ABG also foregrounds its Indian identity while emphasizing its global outreach. As in the previous example, the ABG advertisement depends on a specific choreography of aural, visual, and textual media to construct both the global and the national (Indian) scales. This commercial, aired in 2006, was part of an advertising campaign begun in 2005 that sought to project the 125-year-old company, with its more recent international presence, as "India's first multinational company."[12] The ad exemplifies the globalism that it seeks to depict: an executive describes the production of the ad film thus, "In the end it was a team of 500 highly charged creative technicians who worked across 3 continents for 8 months, to give shape to this epic commercial."[13]

The ad film depicts protagonists whose representations highlight their diverse roots. Using computer-generated graphics (CG), the protagonists in the commercial are shown harnessing the elements of nature—wind, water, fire, and earth—to bestow them with mystical and superhuman powers. The text passing over this movie reads, "Over 70,000 people . . . Across 9 countries . . . 20 nationalities . . . 4 continents . . . 1 Team." The final text crawl, simultaneously narrated in an assertive male voice, reads, "Aditya Birla Group: Bringing India to the world." "Vande Mataram"—a

Sanskrit mantra which translates as "[I] worship the Mother[land]"—forms the background chant for this video.

The ad suggests that its protagonists are deploying mystical powers toward global expansion. "Bringing India" to the world consists in showing globalism as the complementarity between naturalized and essentialized ethnic cultures, symbolized by its Oriental protagonists. This along with the use of CG to heighten and emphasize the human/nature interface as magical and superhuman can be read as an attempt to show that globalism not only includes all nations but also exceeds them and that technological supplementation (CG/magic supplementing film) is also what makes the human or natural into the superhuman or supernatural. The background chant suggests that a strong patriotic sense of duty, rather than the desire for corporate expansion, drives the company's quest for global outreach.

In both these examples, the global is constructed through the interplay of visual, aural, and textual media. In the Videocon commercial, the global is created through a series of images of spatially and temporally dispersed people. In the commercial for the ABG, it is created through the use of a CG-generated movie and a text that explicitly foregrounds its global reach. In both cases, the global is constructed in relation to multiple localities, some concrete, and others abstract. In both examples, India is created primarily through the use of audio and the narrator's synthesis at the very end. In the branding of Videocon, India is presented as that which unites, which provides coherence to otherwise unrelated peoples and places. In the branding of ABG, global expansion is presented as an act of obeisance to the motherland. Furthermore, through its use of computer-generated effects, the ABG advertisement emphasizes the seamless transition between the everyday worlds of industrialization and global expansion and the supernatural realm in which national difference becomes essential, elemental, and empowering. In its attempt to produce a sense of immediacy, national differences are naturalized into complementary elements, which point to a larger global order. India becomes one among many who constitute the globe, and ABG takes on a life independent of the Indian nation as one manifestation of a globalist cosmology. Compared with Videocon's nationalism, the ABG is supernational.

The synergies between different scale-making processes that Tsing suggests in her use of APHIDS are apparent here. Particular ideas of the globe and the nation converge in both these ads to articulate a consumer-nationalism. The global here is articulated on a consumerist register; Indianness, on the other hand, is enacted on a cultural-nationalist register. By attending to the cultural work of remediation, we see that Indian consumer-nationalism is not all of a kind but defines a space in which different ways of placing India in the world can be articulated. The hypermediated consumer-nationalism exemplified by the Videocon advertisement places India as a hypernationalizing, colonizing entity that operates by drawing the rest of the world into India's cultural sphere of influence. By contrast, ABG occupies the consumer end of the space, emphasizing a shared global order that ABG itself embodies and to which India, imagined as one among many, is subordinated.

Hapa Cosmopolitanism, Remediated Globalisms, and Nationalisms

Although the last section focused on how different scales articulate to produce a sense of the global, this section will look at how various media forms are drawn together to produce the global. This section offers readings of Jeff Chiba Stearns' short animated film *What Are You Anyways?*[14] and Kip Fulbeck's photobook *Part Asian, 100% Hapa*[15] to show how different media are brought into mutual articulation to produce a Hapa identity. In Stearns' film, different media are used to situate the individual Hapa in relationship to hegemonic ethnoracial categories and various scales. In Fulbeck's book, hypermediated parodies of bureaucratic manifestations of identification construct a formal unity that produces a view on the authentic but multiple Hapa subject.

Jeff Chiba Stearns' film *What Are You Anyways?* is situated in this space of cultural production. *What Are You Anyways?* is an animated narrative of the filmmaker's struggles with ethnicity growing up in Canada. It is presented as a journey of self-discovery through which Stearns comes to recognize a Hapa subjectivity, outside race and racelessness, which promises a coherent individualism versus the partial Japanese/Caucasian subjectivity he occupies at the beginning of his story. We focus on two visual features in the film. First, the film exploits a characteristic of hand-drawn animation known as "line boil" that we interpret as a remediation of the still image into the motion picture that embodies the artist's agency and his immediate presence to the subject and viewer. Second, the film invokes images of the Earth as a visual metaphor for Stearns' rejection of one kind of globalism and its replacement with a different one that affords him a space to exercise his individual agency.

The film begins with Stearns as a child in the small community of Kelowna in the interior of British Columbia. Not initially seeing himself as an ethnic other, his classmates' jibes impose Japanese ethnicity on him, which creates the narrative tension that structures the rest of the story. The story follows Stearns into adulthood in Vancouver, where he comes to understand himself as Hapa and not "half-Japanese" through a series of encounters that culminate in a romantic relationship with a Hapa named Jenni. At the beginning of the story, Stearns' character goes through experiences that spark uncertainty regarding his own identity that lead him to reject his half-*Japanese*ness. At its conclusion, Stearns resolves this uncertainty by following Jenni's lead and asserting his *Hapa*ness. Stearns narrates, "No longer would I have to tell people I was a half-breed."

Visually, the film is rendered in a rough, hand-drawn style that evokes cartoonish sketches done in pencil on a paper. The lines of the animated characters quiver through the use of line boil, an artifact of hand-drawn animation in which variations between frames make lines appear to wobble. Line boil is used here as a device for evoking a sense of the rough, in progress, and the personal. The film attempts to draw the viewer into imagining the work's producer as the single author with pencil in hand.

The story told by these moving sketches contains a commentary on the tension between global cosmopolitanism and localism. Images of the globe appear at key points to illustrate the remaking of Stearns' identity that takes place against an unstable set of spatialities that need to be rethought and reconstituted to arrive at a sense of self. The first moments of the film show a spinning Earth set against a field of stars. The picture fades just as Japan passes the middle of the frame and disappears over the horizon. The world continues to turn, eventually centering on North America. As Stearns' narrative begins, a series of satellite photo-style images bring us closer to Kelowna. The sound of a camera shutter accompanies each step toward the ground. National, provincial, and state borders become visible in succession as we zoom in on southern British Columbia, until eventually we are shown the location of Stearns' hometown, on a map where political borders, major cities, and topographical features such as the Rocky Mountains provide visual signposts. In images that string together planetary, international, and regional perspectives on the Earth, we are given an initial glimpse into spaces of belonging that are imagined as a nested hierarchy of globe, nation, province, and city. Within this hierarchy, the nation is privileged as a determinant of identity. The first borders we see appearing on the globe highlight national divisions. Later on, we see an early stage of Stearns' search for identity—in which he recognizes his ability to "pass" for a variety of ethnicities in a scene midway through the film, which equates ethnic and national identities. Stearns narrates "I can be Filipino when I visit the Philippines, or Brazilian when I travel to Brazil . . ." accompanied by images of his character in settings and attire stereotypically associated with those places.

This equation is soon disrupted. At the climax of the film, Stearns introduces his high-school nickname, "Super Nip," and the globe is shattered. Super Nip is Stearns' alter ego in the film, an anime-inspired superhero that embodies his frustrations and feelings of alienation. With cape waving in the wind and eyes peering out from beneath the shadow cast by his conical hat, Super Nip stands across from three "redneck" adversaries wearing work boots and lumberjack shirts. During the battle, the rednecks mock Super Nip with ethnic stereotypes, taunting him with fake karate moves and offering to pose for his tourist pictures. Super Nip, speaking in Japanese with a deep, menacing tone, flies into the sky to prepare his counterattack, momentarily leaving the Earth behind. Against a backdrop of stars and with a distant globe below, we see Super Nip let loose a terrifying scream that is muffled by the vacuum of space before he propels himself back toward the ground with superhuman speed. The impact shatters the landscape, sweeping his adversaries away. The scene closes with the victorious Super Nip laughing, levitating among fragments of the ground on which he and his enemies had been standing.

The final appearance of the image of the globe occurs at the very end of the film, when we once again see it whole and spinning. There are no discernible national borders now, and Stearns' voiceover tells us that he had come to appreciate "just how lucky [he was] to be a Hapa living in Canada." As North America spins out of view, Stearns' parting message appears: "Hapa'ly Ever After."

Taken together, these representations of the globe narrate how Stearns comes to see himself as the bearer of a global, postnational subjectivity that cites nation, race, and ethnicity but is not defined by them. Prior to the imagined destruction of the globe, Stearns is constrained by nations, but afterward, the globe remade becomes the scale on which Stearns' individuality can be truly expressed. It diverges from conventional cosmopolitanisms, because Stearns' Hapa subjectivity is not positioned to mediate between the East and West. However, it is still imagined as cosmopolitan through its desire to allow the individual to transcend parochial categories and carve out a space for self-definition. At the film's conclusion, Stearns is not half-Japanese-Canadian or Hapa-Canadian, but a Hapa living in Canada.

In contrast to Stearns' work, which focuses on the perspective of the individual Hapa artist, Kip Fulbeck's book *Part Asian, 100% Hapa* presents 116 Hapa subjects, each allocated two pages in a volume of alternating pages of sketches and texts done by hand and spartan color photographs. Fulbeck's book is driven by the same question as Stearns' film: "*What are you?*"[16] It not only shares a pencil-on-paper immediacy but also draws heavily on forms of identification closely associated with the nation-state. The American national imaginary is brought into an articulation of a Hapa global that exceeds it. Although Stearns traces the life of an individual over time, Fulbeck considers a cross section of people in a hypermediated rendering of Hapa diversity and unity, which carefully places them in relationship to several frameworks of identification. Considered together, Fulbeck and Stearns' works highlight how Hapa identity emerges as both subjective lived experience and collective identification, each of which cannot be encompassed by the other. Responding directly to a *Time* magazine framing of Eurasians as the "poster children of globalization for the 21st century,"[17] Fulbeck writes, "That's a lot of expectation placed upon a group that's been ignored for centuries. And now it's our time because we're in vogue? The way I look at it, it's always been our time."[18] For Fulbeck, Hapas have always been global and closest to the most authentic way of being human. This book can, therefore, be interpreted as both the emergence and the recovery of an identity; made present and visible by combining still photography, sketches, and texts and playing off of the individual, national, ethnoracial, and global. Fulbeck's book aligns several strategies for producing immediacy into a hypermediated rendering of Hapa identity that produces a view on the real subject by stressing diversity, unboundedness, and uncategorizability.

Fulbeck presents his book as giving voice to a silent but significant group within American society that has been without a voice because it does not easily fit within ethnic categories. For Fulbeck, this is a symptom of American "laziness," the desire for straight fits into simple categories. For example, the U.S. census, he writes, has only recently let him answer the question on ethnicity "accurately" when multiple answers became acceptable.[19] Each set of two pages in Fulbeck's book begins with a typeset string of ethnic categories, printed in small lower-case text for each subject. "chinese, english, scottish, german" follows "filipina, japanese, german" follows "chinese (toisan), jewish (russian, polish)." Fulbeck explains in his introduction that this is a response to the "ethnic guessing game" that Hapas are often forced to participate in by curious others, but in this case, the game is appropriated as an expression of the value of diversity and the lived experience of mixedness. "In this scenario, it gets used with assertion, with claim. 'Name that Asian' becomes *our* game."[20] The astounding variety of categories listed exceeds the list of races in U.S. censuses. Along with racial and ethnic categories appear "wasp," "shanghainese," "cherokee," and "palauan" all rendered in the same typeface and occupying similar positions on each page. They cite a range of scales through and against which the other elements of the person's record take on meaning.

On opposing pages are color photographs that show each subject from the shoulders up without any visible clothing, jewelry, or makeup. The 116 subjects include men and women, from infants to the elderly. Fulbeck explicitly seeks to evoke familiar forms of photo identification, such as the driver's license or passport. But, over pages and pages of similarly framed photographs depicting people stripped of similarities and differences performed through dress or makeup, Fulbeck presents the participants' bodies as a collective embodiment of irreducible diversity. In contrast to the ethnoracial categories listed beside them, the photographs assert difference and sameness that cannot be rendered precisely in text. They stand as an incitement to think through and against textual labels.

In the white space below the list of ethnicities, participants offer drawings, prose, and poetry that range from messy scribbles to dense blocks of text. Some offer lists of their most cherished roles in life or other things they take pride in, whereas others refer to more immediate, banal life occurrences. One explains, "This morning I thought I was going to the movies. Then my mom made me come here."[21] Where in another kind of identification practice we may find names, dates of birth, hair and eye color, and height and weight, in this book the space beside a photograph is filled by a reproduction of that person's own sense of what constitutes their identifying traits, expressed through short statements ("Queer Eurasian"),[22] longer responses ("What are you? Hard to say, except maybe self-contained, leftist and humorous . . . and increasingly impatient with the nonsense of others? . . . Is Hapa enough for you?"),[23] or drawings (one submitted by a young boy shows himself and four members of his family).[24] Here, as in Stearns' film, we are invited to imagine the subject of the photograph putting pencil directly to paper. The words and pictures appear to us as faithful reproductions that leave intact the person's handwriting, the words crossed out or squeezed in, the grammatical misses and the spelling mistakes, which authorize the sense that we are seeing the unedited work of the person depicted. Working around the mechanical uniformity of the industrially printed book, the pages recall the moment of their production and locate the ability to define an identity with their creators.

Through the orchestration of these three modes of representation—ethnic categories, identifying photographs, and writings and sketches done by hand—the book creates a hypermediated perspective on Hapa identity. The use of photographs and ethnic and national categories seeks to critique and appropriate institutionalized forms of identification associated with the nation-state, whereas the white space embodies a freedom in which identities can be presented. It is also the form in which these media are presented—the book—that allows an additional dimension of diversity to be enacted. Hapa identity is recognizable not through any straightforward shared characteristics or traits but is represented in the book as a collective artistic performance. The juxtaposition of more than a hundred similar records establishes a new ground on which to represent diversity.

Stearns and Fulbeck are both driven by the same question—"what are you?" Both answer "Hapa," but reading their works as remediated, scale-making projects shows that the referent Hapa remains unstable. Fulbeck, in particular, draws attention to the diversity of people for whom Hapa has deep personal meaning. But it is not unstructured. Imaginings of the nation, the globe, and the individual permeate both accounts, and these circumscribe the kinds of selves and worlds that can be represented. If Hapa cosmopolitanism and a view of the global had been seen as straddling the gap between tradition and modernity, the exotic and the familiar, and the East and the West, then the works of these two artists reject these binaries, one by focusing on the individual's negotiation through a racialized landscape and the other by emphasizing a collective performance of diversity. Together they show how the constraints and play inherent to representations of racialized subjectivities structure a space in which new imaginings of the global can take shape.

Conclusion

In this chapter, we have offered interpretations of two sets of representations of the global—the Global Indian and Hapa—figuring identities as remediated, scale-making projects. In our account, representations of various scales such as the global, the national, and the individual are wrought from the choreography of media forms, which are brought into alignment along with a "real" identity. In the examples from India, globalisms are produced through remediations that make an Orientalist traditional cultural form of "India" into its necessary counterpart for a consumerist globalization. In the North American Hapa examples, national imaginaries that evoke the state or discrete national cultures are brought into hypermediated representations that awaken and subvert hegemonic ethnoracial categories.

In many ways, this chapter embodies the very globalism that it engages. From inception to conclusion, the chapter took shape on two different continents and three different countries. The chapter itself is also an instance of remediation. Descriptions of books, pictures, and videos comprise its empirical base. The visual is remediated and rendered meaningful in textual form. Hypermediation defines both the chapter and its constitutive examples. The "excess and fullness" of its constitutive examples is deliberately subverted to imagine a different kind of hypermediated space—one in which contingencies within hegemonic constructs are highlighted. Remediation is repurposed toward a critical awareness of scale, rather than its disavowal. It is precisely in cultivating a critical awareness of scale that, we believe, lies the promise of analyzing scale making through the lenses of remediation.

Endnotes

1. Anna Lowenhaupt Tsing, *Friction: An Ethnography of Global Connection* (Princeton, NJ: Princeton University Press, 2005).
2. Jay David Bolter and Richard Grusin, *Remediation: Understanding New Media* (Cambridge, MA: MIT Press, 1999).
3. *National Geographic* 196, no. 2 (August 1999): cover.

4. According to Pukui and Elbert (1986, 58), "Hapa" refers to fragments, parts, and mixed blood. Mary Kawena Pukui and Samuel H. Elbert, *Hawaiian Dictionary: Hawaiian-English, English-Hawaiian*, rev. and enlarged ed. (University of Hawaii Press, 1986). In North America, the word has been appropriated to refer to individuals of mixed Asian and European background. Hapa is often taken to be synonymous with terms such as Eurasian, which have been used to address mixed Asian and Caucasian heritage exclusively.

5. Tsing, *Friction*, 58.

6. Ibid., 76.

7. Bolter and Grusin, *Remediation*, 45.

8. Teri Silvio, "Remediation and Local Globalizations: How Taiwan's 'Digital Video Knights-Errant Puppetry' Writes the History of the New Media in Chinese," *Cultural Anthropology* 22, no. 2 (2007): 285–313; Karen Strassler, "The Face of Money: Currency, Crisis, and Remediation in Post-Suharto Indonesia," *Cultural Anthropology* 24, no. 1 (2009): 68–103.

9. Videocon, "Gayatri Mantra," http://www.youtube.com/watch?v=-iuEOUhdxqs (accessed January 14, 2011).

10. Aditya Birla Commercial, "Taking India to the World," 2006, http://www.vgc.in/film2006/home.html (accessed March 27, 2009).

11. The image can be read as the remediation of a certain genre of map. Anderson (2006) has argued that colonial maps, conceived of as projections of the real world on to paper, played an important role in the formation of the nation as an "imagined community." The nation becomes a privileged determinant of identity, and the constant world map in the backdrop is suggestive of novel configurations (i.e., "globalization") in which identities exceed the frame of the nation-state. *Imagined Communities: Reflections on the Origin and Spread of Nationalism*, rev. ed. (New York, NY: Verso, 2006).

12. Atul Hegde, "The Making of an Epic," 2006, http://www.vgc.in/film2006/home.html (accessed March 1, 2009).

13. Hegde, "The Making of an Epic."

14. Jeff Chiba Stearns, *What Are You Anyways?* (Meditating Bunny Studio, 2005).

15. Kip Fulbeck, *Part Asian, 100% Hapa* (San Francisco, CA: Chronicle Books, 2006). Hereafter cited as *PA*.

16. *PA*, 11.

17. In 2001, the Asian edition of *Time* published an article subtitled with what has become one of the most often invoked statements about Hapas: "Why Eurasians' multicultural heritage has made them the poster children of globalization." Hannah Beech, "Eurasian Invasion," *Time Magazine*, April 4, 2001.

18. *PA*, 17.

19. Ibid., 14.

20. Ibid., 16.

21. Ibid., 116.

22. Ibid., 182.

23. Ibid., 216.

24. Ibid., 58.

CHAPTER 10

A New Hollywood Genre
The Global–Local Film

NOLWENN MINGANT

Chapter Description

Globalization has led to the growing economic importance of the foreign market for Hollywood. Hollywood majors have had to increasingly pay attention to a foreign audience that is extremely heterogeneous in taste and character. This chapter examines the cultural consequences of globalization on the Hollywood majors and on the Hollywood big-budget film. This chapter focuses on the "global–local film," which combines traditional Hollywood elements such as stars, action-adventure, and special effects (which it terms the strategy of the spectacular) and foreign elements such as foreign themes, locations, actors, and directors (which it terms the strategy of the familiar). The result is a more complex, stratified, and highly polysemic Hollywood film that combines American and foreign elements aimed at the global audience, is open to diverse interpretations, and is particularly well adapted to the diversification of distribution channels.

* * *

In the past two decades, the Hollywood majors have been deeply influenced by the process of globalization. Structural and operational transformations have been the most visible signs of this influence, such as conglomeration or an increase in overseas location shootings. Authors such as Toby Miller and Janet Wasko have recently looked at these phenomena from a political angle, notably evaluating the impact of Hollywood's globalization on the rest of the world.[1] Determining the cultural impact of globalization, however, is a tricky exercise. Two main approaches can be identified in discussions about the cultural impact of globalization. On the one hand, one can consider that Hollywood movies have an influence on world culture. Theories of cultural imperialism, and of Americanization under the pressure of American media, have been presented with clarity by John Tomlinson in *Cultural Imperialism: A Critical Introduction*.[2] Since the 1980s, this perspective has been supplemented by a range of engagements with the idea of globalization, of the creation of a global culture, under the influence of marketing and management sectors.[3]

One can also reverse the question and wonder what impact globalization has on Hollywood. Here, researchers tend to underline the impoverished content of films. Mattelart explains how, under the aegis of global culture, cultural industries are looking for "cultural universals" that could appeal to the widest audience possible.[4] As early as 1987, Charles-Albert Michalet predicted that Hollywood would turn into a "world cinema," which would erase any Anglo-Saxon specificities to get wider appeal.[5] Recently, Jonathan Rosenbaum concluded that Hollywood films were not American anymore.[6] This chapter focuses on how globalization is influencing Hollywood movies, but its arguments will counter some of the perspectives in the literature described earlier. Although Michalet, Rosenbaum, and other researchers analyze the evolution of the Hollywood film in terms of their impoverishment, I will argue here that globalization leads to an enriching of the content of these films. Although some researchers have felt that national specificities were disappearing, I aim to show that globalization actually leads to a resurgence of local characteristics in the world of culture in general and in Hollywood in particular. Indeed, by the late 2000s, the inner paradoxes of globalization had become visible, and thus, a reinterpretation of the evolution of Hollywood films seems necessary.

The 1990s seemed to promise the advent of a global market characterized by a homogenized culture. The Hollywood majors welcomed globalization notably for two reasons. First, more countries were opening up to a model of the free-market economy and Western products (South Korea in 1988, Eastern Europe after 1989, and Vietnam in 1994). Since the mid-1990s, theatrical revenues from abroad have become more important than revenues from the domestic market. In 2007, 66% of worldwide theatrical revenues came from the foreign market.[7] Second, the creation of a global culture would be favorable for export by allowing the creation of films based on a common cultural ground. A likely assumption among scholars and critics was that this global culture would be based on American culture, spread around the world by CNN and MTV.

However, in the very midst of globalization, researchers started to notice the forceful resurgence of local characteristics. For Benjamin Barber, the world faced two possible futures—McWorld, a homogeneous world market, and Jihad, a retribalization of humanity.[8] Globalization also turned out to be accompanied by a countermovement of relocalization. Mel Van Elteren identified oppositions present within the process of globalization—universalization versus particularization, homogenization versus differentiation, and integration versus fragmentation.[9] For the Hollywood majors, the realization that globalization did not hold all its promises took place in the late 1990s. Although more markets did open up to Hollywood films, they had to face growing competition from local media industries. Confronted with the vitality of local cultures and particularities, the majors realized that profitable global practices such as worldwide day-and-date release had to be balanced by more local strategies such as adapted marketing campaigns or dubbed versions in local languages. The very diverse censorship systems in the world were cases in point of the persistence of strong cultural differences. Europe, for example, is very strict regarding violence in films, whereas the Asian countries are more watchful of obscenity.

By the early 2000s, it became obvious that globalization thus led to specific paradoxes for the Hollywood majors. Although globalization involved increasing markets and profits, it also meant that the Hollywood majors had to deal with more and more culturally disparate audiences. The heterogeneity of the world has thus shattered Hollywood's dream of homogenization. The area of production is especially impacted by the paradoxes of globalization. Although the worldwide audience has become vitally important to the majors, they can no longer rely on their traditionally U.S.-oriented films. In the past 10 years, production practices have thus been evolving. An analysis of the decision-making process of the committees choosing which films are to be financed showed that they have increasingly focused on foreign preferences before taking any decision.[10]

To identify the influence of the economically important—but heterogeneous—global audiences on contemporary Hollywood films, this chapter takes an empirical approach. To understand the decision-making process of the majors and their criteria, a list of films was studied based not on box office results, as is usually the case, but on budget. For the purpose of this study, any film whose budget was 30% more than the average industry budget was considered a "big-budget" production. A list of more than a hundred films was thus compiled, from *Eraser* in 1996 to *Catwoman* in 2004. For each film, a complete information sheet was then created including elements such as the nationality of the director, actors, characters, and financing, the story location, the source material, and the languages spoken. The database thus created was subjected to statistical analysis that identified the evolution of the presence of American and foreign elements in the film. A selection of films was also subjected to content analysis (Hollywood style, ideological subtext). On the basis of this research, I argue that a new type of film has become predominant in Hollywood—the global–local film.[11]

The Global–Local Film

As the importance of the global market pushes the Hollywood majors[12] to take foreign preferences into account, they have had to adapt their production strategy, first by retaining the qualities that make Hollywood films popular around the world and second by including elements that would please specific segments of international audiences.

Global Films

Hollywood films are internationally associated with high-quality production values. The presence of stars, well-crafted screenwriting, and the use of state-of-the-art special effects, all of which are made possible by large budgets, are some reasons for the popularity of the Hollywood films around the world.[13] A first response to the importance of the international market is thus to emphasize this aspect, to play on what marketers call the "made in effect."[14] Two elements are particularly important—the stars and the spectacular quality.

The choice of the main actors is based on the idea of bankability that refers to the commercial value of a star depending on his or her ability to draw audiences. To ascertain the world bankability of a star, the majors rely both on internal market research and on information given by the press. In the late 1990s, the trade magazine *Variety* featured a regular column called "Star Translation" that evaluated the popularity of an actor, based on the performance of his or her films in the United States, Great Britain, and Germany. In 1998, *Variety* identified the most popular American actors worldwide—Tom Cruise, Mel Gibson, Harrison Ford, Tom Hanks, and Julia Roberts.[15] The majors also favor actors who are very popular in the foreign market even if they are less popular in the domestic market. Sylvester Stallone, Arnold Schwarzenegger, Kurt Russell, Bruce Willis, and Sharon Stone have all benefited from foreign fame and have been, for this reason, regularly hired by the majors. For example, a major will tend to hire Brad Pitt for an internationally oriented big-budget film, rather than Denzel Washington, although the former is less popular in the U.S. market.

The second basic element, which is linked with the idea of high production value, is the spectacular quality of traditional Hollywood films. When one observes films in which world bankable stars appear, one notices the predominance of action-adventure films—*Mission Impossible* (Tom Cruise), *Air Force One* (Harrison Ford), *Armageddon* (Bruce Willis), and *National Treasure* (Nicolas Cage). Star presence and the action genre are mutually reinforcing elements of production value. The popularity of action-adventure films in the international market enables the stars to ask for larger salaries. With respect to production, the presence of a bankable star will be an asset for a producer who wants to obtain a larger budget for his or her film. Action-adventure films, including epics such as *Gladiator* (2000) or *Kingdom of Heaven* (2004), are the tent poles on which the majors' distribution slates lean. As Joseph D. Phillips[16] noted, the "American film industry's search for formula with international appeal has led to an increasing reliance on standardized 'spectaculars.'" The emphasis put on special effects is also an important part of this search for spectacle.[17] Pleasing global audiences implies, for the majors, an emphasis on the traditional Hollywood quality of their films. I call this the *strategy of the spectacular*. This spectacular quality is universally accepted and appreciated for two reasons: first, as it aims at the spectators' emotions and not their brains, it is more readily accepted by culturally diverse audiences; second, for decades, audiences have been educated to expect this from Hollywood films. A way to reach global audiences is thus to provide them with what Hollywood does best—spectacular, star-driven, special-effects-laden big-budget films.

Local Films

As the majors must now take into account the cultural diversity of their international audience, they increasingly resort to a localization strategy. The foreign spectators must feel that they are taken into account in the production process, that is, films are specifically made for them. To achieve this, the majors tend to include more foreign elements in their films. Such non-American and non-Hollywood ingredients are visible in three different areas—the story, the cast, and the director. Stories can be inspired by foreign elements in two ways. The "*Indiana Jones* formula" depicts an American protagonist going through a number of adventures around the world. Films such as *Mission: Impossible* (1996), *Congo* (1995), or *Ocean's Twelve* (2004) fall into this category. The "*Braveheart* formula" depicts a non-American hero and his trajectory completely unrelated to American concerns or history, such as the history of a Scottish rebel in Mel Gibson's 1995 film. *Seven Years in Tibet* (1997), *Man with the Iron Mask* (1998), and *King Arthur* (2004) fall into this second category.

A film can also acquire a foreign touch through its casting decisions, such as the French Sophie Marceau in *The World Is Not Enough*, the British

Clive Owen in *King Arthur*, or Hong Kong's Jackie Chan in *Rush Hour*. Finally, directors can also introduce a foreign vision to Hollywood films. French director Jean-Pierre Jeunet rejuvenated the *Alien* series in 1997. In the same way, Warner Bros. turned to Mexican director Alfonson Cuarón for the third film in the *Harry Potter* series. The growing inclusion of such foreign elements in the Hollywood film is a localizing strategy that I call the *strategy of the familiar*. Indeed, making these foreign elements highly visible is an attempt at creating bonds with the audience. It is a way for the spectators to recognize themselves in the film and thus to endorse it. For example, the scenes that take place in a French railway network [Train à Grande Vitesse (TGV), Thalys] in *Mission: Impossible* and *Ocean's Twelve* have a special resonance with French spectators. In the same way, foreign spectators from specific countries can be targeted by the presence of certain actors. The presence of Michelle Yeoh in *Tomorrow Never Dies* (1996) or Chow Yun-Fat in *Pirates of the Caribbean: At World's End* (2007) is a clear step toward Asian audiences. Because the audiences know the personae of the actors and have seen them in films of their country, they tend to identify with them more easily.

The identification factor also works with directors. French film magazine *Positif* recognizes Jeunet's typical style in *Alien: Resurrection*,[18] and *Cahiers du cinéma* spots "signature effects" in John Woo's *Broken Arrow*.[19] This strategy of the familiar translates into economic results. Michelle Yeoh's presence in *Tomorrow Never Dies* is credited with having increased the film's gross by US$ 20 million. Taking a localized approach to filmmaking and targeting specific national groups in production choices is thus a viable and profitable answer to the expansion of the majors' foreign market.

A New Trend

International stars have been present in Hollywood films long before the 1980s and the rapid development of a globalized world. Many artists settled in Hollywood, either fleeing their countries because of historical circumstances, such as wars or dictatorships, or because they were invited by the majors. Hiring foreign artists has also always been part of a constant quest by the majors for differentiating themselves from competitors. Hollywood experienced two important foreign waves—in the 1930s and 1960s. In the 1930s, European immigrants fleeing Nazi Germany and a beleaguered Europe deeply influenced Hollywood filmmaking.[20] This artistic transfer might be understood in terms of the dynamics of exile. In the 1960s, American audiences, and especially youth influenced by the development of a strong counterculture, were quite interested in the rest of the world. European films, notably the French New Wave, were appreciated in the

United States. This context of internationalism led to the presence of European stars in Hollywood films (such as Claudia Cardinale in *The Professionals*, 1966, or Anouk Aimée in *Model Shop*, 1969), as well as European films (such as Truffaut's *L'Enfant sauvage*, 1970) being financed by Hollywood.[21]

The 1990s and 2000s context is, however, very different. Foreign films are hardly popular in the American market. As a consequence, the majors' interest in foreign films and artists derives only from the foreign market's growing importance in terms of revenues. The American audience is slowly losing its importance as foreign audiences take center stage. A second difference is that, in the 1960s, Europe was the center of interest. In the late twentieth century, Hollywood turned not only to Europe but also to Asia and Latin America for plot ideas and talent. Finally, the most important difference is that taking the foreign market into consideration has now become systematic practice, as shown by the presence of foreign marketer teams in the green-light committees. No big-budget film can be produced nowadays without the question of its foreign potential being debated. The upstaging of the domestic audience by the foreign audience and the geographically wide sphere of influence and the systematization of pre-existing but more marginal practices are the new elements governing Hollywood's relationship with the foreign market. At the dawn of the twenty-first century, one cannot talk about a wave of foreign influence as the foreign market and its spectators have become a constitutive part of the Hollywood film industry. Inspired by older practices and systematized under the strong influence of the foreign market, the global–local film is thus more than a passing fad. It is a new way to conceive film production. As they head in this new direction, Hollywood films tend to become increasingly polymorphous and polysemic.

Polymorphy and Polysemy

Hollywood films cannot be described as univocal any more. They are made of multiple elements, can take different shapes on different distribution platforms, and can be interpreted in various ways. The global–local film is thus a mixed product. First, it combines Hollywood and non-Hollywood elements. The *Pirates of the Caribbean* series (2003, 2006, and 2007) is a good representative of this trend. It has Hollywood elements—large production value, established Hollywood star (Johnny Depp), action, state-of-the-art special effects. It also includes many foreign elements—the setting (the Caribbean, Singapore), the context (the British presence), the main couple (the British Keira Knightley and Orlando Bloom). But such mixing and combining is not limited to pirate escapades any more. Even American-oriented films now include foreign elements—British Alfred Molina is Dr. Octopus in *Spider-Man 2*, whereas Australian Eric Bana impersonates an American superhero in Ang Lee's *Hulk*. Such Hollywood films are global as the Hollywood elements, especially the constant emphasis on the spectacular, are recognized worldwide. Such films are also *local* as some elements are familiar and appealing to specific segments of the foreign audiences.

The global strategy of the spectacular and the local strategy of the familiar do not conflict but, on the contrary, complement each other. Hollywood's internationally oriented big-budget films are currently defined by what we can call a *mariage des contraires* (marriage of opposites). Hollywood movies can both transport you to exotic sceneries and feature places you know, both sweep you off your feet with breath-taking special effects and make you identify with actors from your own country. Instead of playing these opposite elements against one another, the global–local films play on all of them at the same time. Complementary, not oppositional, is the important word.

Although the importance paid to stars, actions, and special effects has its critics who denounce the extreme simplification in Hollywood production, the process of *mariage des contraires*, born of the necessity to appeal to world audiences, actually shows a trend toward complexification. Diverse elements now compose the Hollywood film. Not only are there several juxtaposed layers but also the same element can be interpreted differently according to the context in which the film is received. Although the different layers of a same film are directed at different types of audiences, the very same element can be understood differently. The mix of Hollywood and foreign elements inevitably leads such films to play simultaneously on the familiar and the exotic. This is also a way for these internationally oriented films to keep appealing to American audiences. The elements inserted to attract a certain portion of the foreign market appear as pure exoticism for the domestic audiences. Americans who have traveled around Europe will also appreciate *Mission: Impossible*'s scenes taking place in the TGV but for a different reason. What was familiar to the French audiences is exotic and linked to holidays for American audiences. Pixar's *Ratatouille*, which was clearly created with the foreign audiences in mind, deliberately plays on these two levels. A French person might laugh at the clichés but would also enjoy recognizing their capital city and depiction of their national culinary culture. A Parisian may even recognize the morbid window of the shop Destruction des animaux nuisibles, 8 rue des Halles, which exhibits dead rats caught in traps. For a non-French viewer, the film is filled with exotic images—1950s Paris, DS cars, sunny Provence, and bérets. In general, the presence of foreign actors, such as Vincent Cassel in *Ocean's Twelve*, also participates in this familiar/exotic dimension. The accumulation of layers and multiple-meaning elements is then a characteristic of the complexification at work in the production process of Hollywood big-budget films now. As a consequence, the global–local films are highly polysemic.

Because of this high degree of polysemy, global–local films are also polymorphous. The same film can take different shapes according to the context of distribution and reception. Marketing teams are particularly instrumental in this routine reshaping of the Hollywood film. They can choose which elements they are going to highlight from among the different layers of the film. Again, although this practice is not new, it is deployed to a very high degree with the global–local film. As foreign marketers are present in the green-light committee, they participate in the development of the product that they will later advertise. A global–local film can, therefore, be considered a marketer's dream, full of potential hooks. Marketers can choose to emphasize the spectacular facet of the film, thus following a uniform global campaign generally provided by the American marketing team. But they very often take advantages of the possibility of highlighting local elements in some markets. The films' local facets are very much in keeping with a traditional marketing emphasis on proximity. Global–local films are thus frequently repositioned for certain markets. French actress Sophie Marceau was featured more prominently on the *World Is Not Enough* posters in France. Warner Bros. held *Batman & Robin*'s European premiere in Schwarzenegger's native Austrian town. When it comes to distribution practices, the films are also highly mutable. To sell *Pearl Harbor* (2001) in Japan, Touchstone not only had some dialogues modified but also had the film recut, adding a scene. Through such practice, the film is modified not only in its appearance but also in its substance.

Although the global–local film trend clearly derives from a growing concern for foreign audiences, it is also part of a more general evolution toward mutability. Robert Allen describes "the new logics of Hollywood film-making and marketing produced by the confluence of technological, demographic and social change."[22] Films are not so much produced for theaters as for a large number of different distribution channels and formats, from video to merchandising. The evolution of a film's life in turn influences its content—"The rise of the post-Hollywood cinema . . . also manifests itself in a number of narrative and representational strategies within films themselves. Ambivalence and indeterminacy are the distinguing formal qualities of text that are subject to protean refashioning as commodities."[23] Ambivalence and indeterminacy are indeed among the characteristics of the polymorphous and polysemic global–local film.

The Cultural Content Issue

Although more and more non-American elements are included in current Hollywood big-budget films, long-standing stereotypical depictions of foreigners seem to die hard. In terms of plot and setting, foreign countries are still very much linked with adventure and exoticism, not only in *Ocean's Twelve*'s postcard-like Europe but also in *Saving Private Ryan*'s Normandy. As for foreign characters, they still tend to epitomize the figure of the Other. When represented in a positive light, the Other can be the attractive Kate Beckinsale in *Pearl Harbor* or the amusing Gérard Depardieu in *102 Dalmatians* (2001). But foreign actors are very often cast in negative roles. Women are *femmes fatales*, such as the treacherous and deadly Emmanuelle Béart in *Mission: Impossible*. Men are terrorists (Gary Oldman in *Air Force One*), drug dealers (Jordi Mollà in *Bad Boys II*), or demented scientists (Kenneth Branagh in *Wild Wild West*). Foreign actors are often chosen to impersonate characters who are barely human—ghosts (*The Haunted Mansion*), mutants (*X-Men*), androids (*Artificial Intelligence: AI*), or cannibals (*Hannibal*).

Recent evolutions can, however, be noted. First, positive roles are increasingly given to foreign characters. Such films tend to show the evolution of a partnership between American and non-American characters. Significantly, this phenomenon can be noted in very different genres. Jackie Chan teamed up with Chris Tucker in the comic *Rush Hour* series (1998, 2001, and 2007). In the adventure drama *The Last Samurai* (2003), Tom Cruise is encountering a new culture through his conversations with Ken Watanabe. In post-9/11 thriller *The Kingdom*, an American FBI agent (Jamie Foxx) collaborates on equal terms with a Saudi Arabian officer (Ashraf Barhom). A notable evolution is that the nationality of the character increasingly corresponds to the nationality of the actor. For example, although in *Robin Hood: Prince of Thieves* (1991), most of the actors were American, the majority of *King Arthur*'s (2004) cast was British. In parallel to this more authentic and sympathetic representation of foreign characters, one notices the presence of American villains. Kevin Bacon is a demented sadist in *Hollow Man*. Sharon Stone is a greedy and inhuman character in *Catwoman*. These two evolutions can be interpreted as attempts to please the foreign audiences. Representing foreign characters in a less stereotypical way ensures a better reception abroad, whereas turning American characters into villains plays on a certain anti-American feeling pervasive around the world. Besides, this evolution also reflects the difficult choice of finding a Hollywood villain in today's geopolitical context. After the fall of the Berlin Wall, Hollywood lost its Communist villain. After 9/11, Hollywood could not use Arab villains without many precautions. In a way, American villains are a safer choice for Hollywood.

These films' global facet does not only correspond to the Hollywood spectacular tradition but also to the American cultural component that continues to be relevant. This American component remains fundamental for two reasons. First, the domestic market still represents almost half of revenues.[24] Besides, most of the Hollywood personnel are American and tend to think first in terms of the American audience. The non-American local elements thus cannot totally upstage the American elements. Second, foreign viewers are also partly attracted to Hollywood film precisely because they represent the American dream. This American cultural substratum is thus what constitutes exoticism for the foreign audiences.

Indeed, foundational American values still form the ideological substratum of the global–local film. These values, identified by Anne-Marie Bidaud in her seminal *Hollywood et le rêve américain*, are, for example, a strong belief in the American democratic system, especially through the star-spangled banner and the figure of the president, a condemnation of any revolutionary idea, and a defense of individualism, through the figures of the common man and the self-made man.[25] Let us consider *Enemy at the Gates* directed by the Frenchman Jean-Jacques Annaud for Paramount in 2001. An American actor Ed Harris and British actors Jude Law, Joseph Fiennes, and Rachel Weisz embody German and Russian characters in this big-budget reenactment of the battle of Stalingrad. Although there is no actor/character nationality concordance, one notices that congenial characters are played by British actors, whereas the villain is played by an American actor. Although the film is heavily tilted toward foreign elements, an American ideological substratum is still obvious. Vassili Zaitsev (Jude Law) is represented as the "common man," the ordinary man whose hunting skills, taught by his father, are put in service of his country. This sincere patriotism is opposed to the character played by Joseph Fiennes. Although Commisar Danilov is also a patriot, he is above all presented as a manipulative intellectual. This classical negative representation of intellectuals is reinforced by the young girl falling in love with Zaitsev. The scene in which Danilov dies is extremely significant. Not only does he recognize his uselessness as an intellectual but his last tirade also puts into question the Soviet Revolution as a whole.

> We tried too hard to create a society that was equal, where there would be nothing to envy your neighbor. But there is always something to envy . . . In this world, even the Soviet one, there will always be rich and poor,

says the unhappy lover. This echoes the classical fashion in which any revolutionary idea is brought into disrepute, a trend identified in earlier films by Anne-Marie Bidaud.[26] The film also classically ends with the image of the reunited lovers, an image of love as the "final reward," which is also one element of the American dream.

Many other global–local films can still be read in terms of common American values: the tramp can be interpreted as a common man character in *The Day After Tomorrow*; Dracula's plot in *Van Helsing* can be seen as a revolutionary movement and is clearly discredited; *Minority Report* describes the fight of an individual against a system gone wild; in *The Last Samurai*, the hero never accepts fate as inevitable.

In cultural terms, Hollywood big-budget films thus privilege their global facet, perpetuating the tradition of an American ideological substratum, which can be an asset both in the domestic and the foreign market. The local facet, that is, the representation of the foreign elements, however, leaves much to be desired. Indeed, many stereotypes are still conveyed. This can be deeply problematic because too much stereotyping can derail the familiar effect expected. Clichés in *Ratatouille* or *National Treasure: Book of Secrets* can indeed unnerve the French viewer and lead to bad word of mouth instead of identification. In this sense, the trend toward actor/character nationality concordance is fundamental as it reinforces the identification factor.

Conclusion

The growing importance of the foreign market in a globalized world has led the Hollywood majors to change their production strategy. Taking the foreign market into account, they have initiated a new trend. Their internationally oriented big-budget films can be called "global–local" in that they are made of several layers—a Hollywood layer (stars, action, and special effects) for the worldwide audience and a foreign layer (story, actors, and directors) for specific foreign markets. The possibility to emphasize some layers over others, whether in the marketing campaign or in the reception process, has made such films highly polymorphous and polysemic. The global–local film's polysemy is to be understood not only in formal terms but also in cultural terms. Although the Hollywood-foreign elements seem quite balanced formally, there is still a strong imbalance in cultural content. The fundamental American ideological substratum is still very much present, and the evolution toward a more authentic use of the foreign elements is very slow. Although only a dozen films can be truly called global–local (*Mission: Impossible, Gladiator, Rush Hour, Pirates of the Caribbean, Troy, The Last Samurai, Van Helsing, Ocean's Twelve, King Arthur*, . . .), the global–local trend does infuse the Hollywood production as a whole, with foreign elements also being included in U.S.-oriented films. This trend is more than a passing fancy. Several elements show that it has become ingrained in the Hollywood system itself. No production decision can be taken without considering at one point the foreign potential and one can surmise that the influence of the foreign marketers in green-light committees will continue to grow alongside the foreign market revenues. The systematization is also visible in the fact that the global–local trend pervades all types of filmmaking: internationally and U.S.-oriented films, as well as films from many different genres. The global–local film, through its system of Hollywood/America/foreign layers, seems to be the best cultural strategy to maintain the position of Hollywood films in the world. What we are witnessing today is, however, only the early days of this global–local trend. Because of the very complexity of its layered structure, and because of the cultural finesse needed, achieving a convincing global–local film is still very difficult. Some films, such as *Ocean's Twelve*, still largely rely on exoticism. Some, like *King Arthur*, tend to get lost in the attempt. But other films, such as *The Last Samurai* or *Enemy at the Gates*, seem reasonably successful attempts and possible models for the future.

Endnotes

1. Toby Miller et al., *Global Hollywood* (London: British Film Institute, 2001); Toby Miller, Nitin Govil, and John McMurria, *Global Hollywood 2* (London: British Film Institute, 2005); Janet Wasko, *Hollywood in the Information Age* (Austin: University of Texas Press, 1995); Janet Wasko, *How Hollywood Works* (London: Sage, 2005).
2. John Tomlinson, *Cultural Imperialism: A Critical Introduction* (Baltimore, MD: The Johns Hopkins University Press, 1991).
3. Armand Mattelart, "La nouvelle idéologie globalitaire," in *La mondialisation au-delà des mythes*, ed. Serge Cordellier (Paris: La Découverte/Poche, 2000), 86.
4. Ibid.
5. Charles-Albert Michalet, *Le Drôle de drame du cinéma mondial* (Paris: La Découverte/Centre fédéral FEN, 1987), 93–4.
6. Jonathan Rosenbaum, *Movie War: How Hollywood and the Media Conspire to Limit What Films We Can See* (Chicago, IL: A Capella Press, 2000), 133.
7. MPAA, *Theatrical Market Statistics*, 2009.
8. Benjamin Barber, "Jihad vs McWorld," *The Atlantic Monthly*, March 1992.
9. Mel Van Elteren, "Conceptualizing the Impact of US Popular Culture Globally," *Journal of Popular Culture* 30 (1996): 56.
10. This analysis of the decision-making process was based on varied clues, as industry leaders tend to be quite secretive about it. I gathered allusions in studies on Hollywood written in the past 40 years, clues from the trade papers, as well as statistical evidence uncovered by my analysis of a list of films produced by the majors. A detailed account can be found in Nolwenn Mingant, *Hollywood à la conquête du monde* (Paris: CNRS Editions, 2010), 205–10.
11. A similar database was created for big-budget films produced from 1966 to 2004, which enabled comparative analysis. The complete list is available in my PhD dissertation; see Nolwenn Mingant, "Les Stratégies d'exportation du cinéma hollywoodien (1966–2004)" (PhD diss., Université Paris X-Nanterre, Paris, 2008), 529–33.

12. The Big Six are now News Corporation (20th Century-Fox), Sony (Columbia, MGM, UA), Time Warner, Viacom (Paramount), Disney, and General Electric (Universal).

13. See, for example, Philippe Meers' research project on young film audiences in Belgium. Philippe Meers, "'It's the Language of Film!': Young Film Audiences on Hollywood and Europe," in *Hollywood Abroad: Audiences and Cultural Exchanges*, ed. Melvyn Stokes and Richard Maltby (London: British Film Institute, 2004), 158–75.

14. Charles Croué, *Marketing international: Un consommateur local dans un monde global*, 5th ed. (Bruxelles: De Boeck, Perspectives Marketing, 2006), 62.

15. "Fewer Stars Lay Claim to Fame," *Variety*, February 13, 1998.

16. Joseph D. Phillips, "Film Conglomerate Blockbusters: International Appeal and Product Homogenization," in *The American Film Industry*, ed. Gorham Kindem (Carbondale: Southern Illinois University Press, 1982), 325–35.

17. Michael Allen, "From *Bwana Devil* to *Batman Forever*: Technology in Contemporary Hollywood Cinema," in *Contemporary Hollywood Cinema*, ed. Steve Neale and Murray Smith (London: Routledge, 1998), 109–29.

18. "Alien, la Résurrection," *Positif*, December 1997, 442.

19. "Broken Arrow," *Cahiers du cinéma*, March 1996, 500.

20. Jean-Loup Bourget, *Hollywood: Un rêve européen* (Paris: Armand Colin Cinéma, 2006).

21. Thomas Guback, *The International Film Industry: Western Europe and America since 1945* (Bloomington: Indiana University Press, 1969), 165; Michael Allen, *Contemporary US Cinema* (New York, NY: Longman/Pearson Education, 2003), 67–8.

22. Robert Allen, "Home Alone Together: Hollywood and the 'Family Film,'" in *Identifying Hollywood's Audiences: Cultural Identity and the Films*, ed. Melvyn Stokes and Richard Maltby (London: British Film Institute, 1999), 109–34.

23. Ibid., 125.

24. MPAA, *Theatrical Market Statistics*, 2009.

25. Anne-Marie Bidaud, *Hollywood et le rêve américain: Cinéma et idéologie* (Paris: Masson, 1994), 119–60.

26. Anne-Marie Bidaud, *Hollywood et le rêve américain: Cinéma et idéologie* (Paris: Masson, 1994).

CHAPTER 11

The Discursive Disjunctions of Globalizing Media

Scalar Claims and Tensions at the French–German and European Television Channel ARTE

DAMIEN STANKIEWICZ

Chapter Description

This chapter interrogates the meaning of "global media" through an examination of the programming and production practices at the television channel *Association Rélative aux Télévisions Européennes* (Association Relative to European Televisions; ARTE). ARTE, which calls itself "the European culture channel," understands itself to promulgate French–German, European, and global perspectives. The chapter examines how ARTE staff deploy ideas about the channel's "transnational" structure and mission and how ARTE programming circulates among audiences. ARTE programmers tend to understand Europeanness in terms of European high "Culture"—roughly correlating to the fine arts—even as they understand the channel's mission as more broadly "cultural" in the word's anthropological and sociological sense. High Culture and culture are, therefore, mutually defined, and are often superimposed, as ARTE programmers and staff produce "European" television. The chapter considers the implications of this culture/Culture conflation for the circulations of the channel's programming beyond Europe—to Eastern Europe and the Caucuses, the Middle East, and parts of Africa. The chapter concludes by arguing that media scholars must pay close attention to the claims of international, transnational, and "global" media, which perhaps increasingly claim that they produce extralocal perspectives, knowledge, and narratives that escape local and national cultural perspectives, politics, and ontologies.

* * *

The Terms of Global Media

Though for some time now scholars of media have acknowledged that their analytical gaze must shift toward the ways in which images and sounds circulate through increasingly transnational and global circuits, there have been relatively few attempts to describe, in concrete terms, what such "global media" look like from producers' perspectives: we lack the ethnographic data and detail that might describe how these nascent media function on the ground as producers, programmers, and others construct and interpret what Brian Larkin has felicitously phrased "the imagined realities of other cultures."[1] Scholars have a sense that traditional media continue to delocalize and denationalize, albeit in partial, scalar, and multivalent ways,[2] and they have begun to map out the circuits that international and global media industries have burrowed, rhizome-like, around and through local and national borders.[3] However, global media remains more an analytical premise than a located set of social practices rooted in the technological infrastructures[4] and institutional logics[5] of particular forms of media.

Part of the difficulty of assembling what anthropologists Faye Ginsburg, Lila Abu-Lughod, and Brian Larkin articulate as "a media theory that is genuinely transnational," so that we might, as they put it, "remap the presence and circulation of specific media forms,"[6] may be the very terms of analysis in which scholars of "global" media tend to traffic. Indeed, although Ginsburg, Abu-Lughod, and Larkin write of "transnational" media, Jean Chalaby writes of "trans-border" television,[7] and these are more or less synonymous with what Michael G. Elasmar refers to as "international television":[8] global, "globalizing," trans-border, transnational, "international," and a sprinkling of other modifiers interchangeably find themselves before "media" as if these all approximate the same kind and range of phenomena, collapsing the distinct scalings and scopes of what are discrete media circuits and circulations. Some of this imprecision may stem from the wider scholarship on transnationalism and globalization, which has not always defined its terms clearly;[9] but with media, in particular, which especially lend themselves to the facile assumption that image and sound—and their concomitant messagings—simply flow above and through borders and boundaries, a more careful and systematic definition and application of terms may be in order. One might better characterize the BBC, CNN, and, to a lesser extent, Al Jazeera, for example, as primarily *inter*national ("among, amid"[10]) rather than *trans*national ("across, through, beyond"[11]) channels because none of these media organizations are joint or shared projects between two or more nations, but in certain meaningful ways must be understood as projections and extensions of primarily national headquarters, funding structures, and production ideologies of the United Kingdom,[12] the United States,[13] and Qatar,[14] respectively.

In this chapter, I am mindful of such distinctions not to perform a glib semantic revisioning but because my fieldwork research at one such globalizing media organization—a television channel that is understood by its administration and many of its staff to be, indeed, the first truly *trans*national television station in the world—has led me to understand that media producers themselves are keenly aware of, and draw upon, these scalar labelings and categories, in their production activities. Producers and programmers who perceive their role as constructing a broadcast or website for an *international* audience, rather than a *national* one, or a *global* viewership rather than a *regional* one, employ these conceptions of place, function, and scope-of-audience in making sense of their daily work in a world of increasingly stratified and competing media. If staff at a once primarily national channel such as the BBC begin to imagine the channel, and their work there, as now international, or global (which do not, I would argue, amount to exactly the same sort of claim), it seems clear that we should understand the BBC not somehow as wholly, *ipso facto*, to be included in this latter, "later" category, but rather to regard the national and international—or national and global—as held *in tension*. In this way, the global might be scrutinized as a socially located and discursively produced set of aspirations—what Anna Tsing has termed a "global *project*"[15]—rather than as a foregone, globalized conclusion, thereby allowing for richly productive queries about modalities, strategies, and the inevitable partialities and hybridities of globalizing processes.

In this chapter, I illustrate some of the possibilities for this kind of analysis through discussion of the French–German and European television channel "ARTE," where I completed 15 months of fieldwork, at both its Strasbourg headquarters and national offices, between the summer of 2006 and early 2009.[16] I refrain from pronouncing on whether the French–German and European television channel ARTE is "binational," "cross-border," transnational, global, or something else, to emphasize, instead, the complex interplay of these categories, as these geographies are imagined and put into practice by ARTE producers and programmers. With this kind of analysis, we might begin to map the disjunctures between *discourse about* media circulations—how an organization conceptualizes its place and role in a global media landscape—and the circuits through which its media actually circulate, thereby revealing what are often deeply held ideologies about audience, ethnicity, and the meaning of culture. We must more fully account for cultural producers' understandings and conceptions of what transnational and global media are, whom they are for, and what they are meant to do.

The Case of ARTE

Almost 20 years after beaming its first broadcasts from its headquarters on the French–German border, in Strasbourg, not far from the European Parliament building, the television channel ARTE remains an anomaly in the landscape of media. It is among very few media initiatives to split funding 50/50 between two nations, France and Germany, not only to divvy up production responsibilities but also to negotiate differences between French and German production practices (e.g., how news stories should be constructed), language use among a mostly bilingual staff, corporate bureaucratic practices (such as accounting formats), right down to the food served in its cafeteria (today *Weisswurst*, tomorrow *saucisse merguez*).

ARTE's production activities, mostly funded by French and German governments, and split between France and Germany in an exquisitely complex delegation of budgets and responsibilities, are too complex to fully outline here. In brief, the channel's Strasbourg headquarters has the responsibility of evaluating programming proposals that arrive from the channel's national offices in France and Germany, which work with Strasbourg in coordinating and monitoring production. Some of ARTE's programming is coproduced with its eight European partners (RTBF in Belgium, TVP in Poland, ORF in Austria, SRG SSR in Switzerland, YLE in Finland, ERT in Greece, the United Kingdom's BBC, and SVT in Sweden), and certain productions may find further financial support through European film funds such as the Council of Europe's *Eurimages* program. ARTE's programming is broadcast, at roughly the same time,[17] in both French and German; in France, German programs are subtitled or dubbed, and vice versa. Elsewhere in Europe, ARTE programming is dubbed or subtitled in postproduction by the receiving channel.

ARTE was partly the outgrowth of a French project initiated by Prime Minister Laurent Fabius in 1985 called "LA SEPT," which was more or less a pool of production funds, which was meant to encourage the production of high-quality film and documentary to supplement the more mainstream programming of the major French networks. François Mitterand's socialist government introduced LA SEPT, which refers to cinema (in France, cinema is *la septième art*, the "seventh art"), partly as a means of balancing the ongoing privatization (and *de facto* Americanization) of French media markets.[18] The idea for a French–German cultural television channel was first envisioned, however, by a German working group (composed of three regional Minister-Presidents), which brought the idea for a cultural television channel, initially French–German but eventually to expand to become a more broadly European channel, to the French government in early 1988. In November of that year, French and German governments announced that the project was under consideration, and in France, it was soon understood that LA SEPT might already provide the basic structures, on the French side of things, to accommodate this new European channel. It was the joint support of François Mitterand and Helmut Kohl which perhaps most guaranteed a still inchoate and visionary project the visibility and political legitimacy it required to move beyond ideas on paper. Indeed, the French and German leaders' friendship has become something of an origin myth in the halls of ARTE, where I was told by one administrator that the channel would "never have seen the light of day were it not for these two men." On October 2, 1990, the evening of German reunification, the French government, and the 11 regional governments of Germany, signed the international treaty that established the foundations of ARTE.

The channel's inception was both a potent symbol of the French–German reconciliation and a benchmark of the ongoing shared leadership of France–Germany as the *de facto* "motor of Europe," the driving force behind what was at that time a fast-integrating continent.[19] ARTE's charter mandates its task, in part, as the production of television programming aiming to encourage the "understanding and coming together [*rapprochement*] of peoples in Europe."[20] Its first President, Jérôme Clément, wrote in a 1992 *Le Monde* editorial, "ARTE is a European project . . . What could be more important for Europe, now under construction, than to forge in common a memory, an imaginary, a common view of the world that surrounds us?" He continued:

> To change mentalities, frame of mind, and to create the conditions of a veritable united Europe, it isn't enough to have a money, an army corps, and legal directives, though they may be well made. What's necessary is a common imagination. To think Europe together. So that the Germans, French, Italians, Spanish and all the others, even the English, learn to look at the world and to think the world together . . .[21]

It should be clear from this brief history that the delineation of ARTE as national, transnational, international, or global would be ill advised; it is instead in identifying the overlappings, contradictions, and ambiguities, between and among these labelings, that leads us to raise questions about the possible implications, unintended or otherwise, of this "European project" (Figure 11.1).

Figure 11.1 An ARTE Flyer Handed Out at ARTE-Hosted Events; It Translates as "ARTE, Europe Every Day," or "Everyday Europe"

French, German, French–German, (Western) European?

"*ARTE, c'est la naissance de l'Europe*" ("ARTE is the birth of Europe"), one longtime programmer at the channel's headquarters in Strasbourg told me, with conviction, when I asked her whether Europe actually meant anything to its staff. Opinion among ARTE staff was quite divided, however, when I would query if ARTE were more properly to be understood as *European* or as *French–German*. "I think that we are first a French and German channel, and second, a European channel," one administrator told me. "We are always *both*." However, ARTE's status as French–German (the channel is primarily funded by French and German national television taxes) and European (as stipulated in the channel's founding charter) constitutes an ambiguity, tension, and sometime contradiction for ARTE staff, informing how they negotiate nearly all aspects of their daily work.

One of ARTE's recent major programming initiatives provides an initial example of these tensions. *The Great Playwrights* (*Les Grands Dramaturges/ Die großen Dramatiker*; 2008) was launched with a survey (in French,

German, and English) on the channel's website asking viewers from across Europe to vote, from a list of 50 preselected nominees, for those that they believed were Europe's greatest authors of theatre. ARTE then produced and broadcast 30 min segments about each of the top 10 dramaturges and asked viewers to tune in for a live "voting countdown" special that culminated the series, during which one of these 10 playwrights would be crowned king (there happened to be no women in the final 10) of European theatre.

Some of the most interesting moments of the live broadcast finale came when the program hosts periodically checked the voting results, which expanded on-screen into colorful bar graphs. Although the program was, in some ways, trans-European—it included in its top 10 not just Molière and Schiller but also Sophocles, Chekhov, and Beckett—in its final minutes, votes for Molière and Schiller suddenly spiked and came close to surpassing those for Shakespeare, who had been firmly in the lead (Figure 11.2).

The burst of competition between French and German viewers—egged on by the French and German presenters ("Let's go, French people! Are we going to let the Germans outdo us?")—was an unanticipated reminder that

Figure 11.2 *ARTE* Magazine's Advertisement for the Finale of the "Great Playwrights" Series
Source: Reproduced with permission of ZDF, Stefan Schmitt.

the audience of this trans-European competition of playwrights was not quite trans-European but mostly just French–German.

French and German programmers had disagreed about the program from its inception: These "ranking shows" were "too German," one audience studies staff commented during a programming meeting. Were not they the domain of the private, lower-brow RTL channel in Germany, full of game and ranking shows, and so "not for the high-quality brand that ARTE represents"? German staff advocating the project bristled at this, pointing to the program's very "cultural" content, and to ARTE's deflated audience numbers, which suggested that drawing on the populism of mainstream German channels might help to bolster the channel's viewership, at least in Germany. In the end, it did not: All 11 parts of the series went mostly unnoticed by audiences, and several ARTE programmers I spoke with considered the series a failure.

In ARTE's studios and studio boardrooms, in awkward or acrimonious moments like these, still regnant (national) historical and geographical limitations of a channel that understands itself to be transnational, and European, resurface and are laid bare. ARTE has only one other national partner—ARTE Belgique (in French-speaking Belgium), having unsuccessfully attempted several years ago to sustain a long-term programming relationship with Spain's public TVE channel. Although ARTE has negotiated several coproduction and programming exchange agreements with public channels across Europe, only one such agreement has been established with a non-Western European nation—Poland's TVP.

What does ARTE's claim to be the first "European" cultural television channel mean, then? To emphasize the "Europeanness" of *The Great Playwrights* series, ARTE added the subtitle: "Europe's heritage" (*Patrimoine européen/Europas Erbe*); after the finale, some publicity materials proclaimed that *"l'Europe a voté!/Europa hat gewählt!"* [Europe has voted!]. One could argue, however, that French and German, or French–German, sensibilities and ideologies are in this case merely relabeled, and rescaled, as European. Who is included in and precluded from what are, to some degree, still-French, still-German, and still-Western European constructions of a wider and demographically dynamic continent? Are Schiller and Beckett as appreciated as part of some "European heritage" in Finland or Romania as they are in France and Germany? If across much of ARTE's publicity materials one reads "ARTE: The European culture channel" (*Der europäische Kulturkanal; La chaîne culturelle européenne*), a central question we must ask not only of ARTE but also of all media, and especially those that claim extranational, even global, relevancies, purviews, and audiences, is about whether and how this supposedly "broadened" perspective is warranted or achieved. In this case, what kind of "European culture" does ARTE claim to represent, and to bring to its audiences? Is ARTE the European *culture channel* or the *European culture* channel? Indeed what sense of "culture" is being promulgated here and to what end?

"Culture" and "culture" at ARTE

When ARTE claims to be "the European culture channel," one might presume that the channel means *Culture* with a capital "C," in what we may not challenge as a conventional sense of the term roughly encompassing the "fine arts." Indeed, much of ARTE's programming tends exactly toward this definition, with a schedule full of classic film, documentary, series about painting, architecture, theatre, opera, and classical music. When culture is capitalized, there is little definitional problem for ARTE production staff, be they French, German, or Spanish, who understand what is meant by Culture this way, as it has long been enframed and patronized by the State at national theatres, museums, and public parks.[22] However, just 2 years ago, controversy erupted at ARTE when ARTE's administration decided to eliminate a weekly night of programming called the "culture theme night" (Figure 11.3).

Figure 11.3 From the Cover of One of ARTE's Promotional Glossy Brochures; It Reads, in German, "The European Culture [/Cultural] Channel"

"It never worked," one programmer told me, "because we were always debating what subjects were 'cultural' subjects." She recalled that there was a particularly heated discussion about whether homeopathic medicine was appropriate for the "'culture' theme night." Previously programmed topics ranged from social issues to those related to the arts to pop culture. The ambiguity of culture as a category of programming eventually brought about the "culture theme night's" cancellation, but this only amidst uproar and near-revolt on the part of the THEMA programming department, a social drama that makes clear the high stakes of the meaning of culture at ARTE.

The problem is that the definition of culture at ARTE rests uneasily between one that mostly has to do with the arts, and one which is more all-encompassing, closer perhaps to Edward Tylor's classic anthropological premise that culture is the "complex whole which includes knowledge, belief, art, morals, law," and so on, of a people.[23] Indeed, ARTE ultimately benefits from the ambiguity of what a European culture channel means: its producers and administrators, when challenged about the meaning, or responsibility, of representing European identity or belonging for millions of viewers, can fall back on the more limited meaning of a "Culture channel" by capitalizing the C in culture. As one programmer explained to me, "We don't think about things in terms of what 'Europe' means or doesn't mean. That's not our job." Their job, instead, as it was often described to me, is to produce "quality programming," understood as more or less synonymous with "cultural programming," which might help audiences to appreciate and understand opera, cuisine, philosophy, or architecture. They are not, say the programmers, constructing ideas about Europeanness, or European identity, but rather, much more simply, producing "quality" programming that is generalist in nature, if mostly Western European in scope.

However, the channel leans on its European moniker in substantial ways. For one, because the channel's structure and bureaucracy is trans- or supranational, it benefits from a special financial designation (*"groupement européen"*) that absolves it from certain national taxes. Furthermore, when national media politics heat up and budget cuts hang in the air, as was the case in France in the summer and fall of 2008, ARTE is quick to underline the European in European culture channel, to argue, as it did successfully in 2008, that national policy changes in the financing of national public channels did not, could not, apply.

Furthermore, European Culture—glossed as "the arts"—often provides a means, explicit or metaphorical, of addressing transnational European politics and social issues in the channel's programs. One of the clearest examples of this is ARTE's programming about food and cuisine. On

ARTE's long-running *Cuisine des Terroirs*, or *Zu Tisch* in German, viewers travel to various European regions to watch how Bavarian desserts, Hungarian goulash, or Spanish tapas are made, often in rural villages. But at some point during these 30 min magazine programs, the camera leaves the kitchen and moves around the village, introducing us to ordinary villagers (and Europeans), who help us to understand rural depopulation, the double-edged sword of tourism, and about how problems with the fishing industry are affecting the local economy. I asked a programmer in the *Documentary* magazines programming department if there was not a strategy on the part of the department to use these seemingly ordinary topics to introduce viewers to more complex trans-European social issues. She smiled. "Of course we always try to bring viewers new experiences, new knowledge," she told me. In ARTE's programming strategies, we often find a sort of Trojan horse. During a series about island paradises, we learn about renewable energy; during a documentary about Moorish Spain, we learn that this part of Europe flourished because of its trans-European cosmopolitanism; a biography of Picasso focuses on his European identity. In programming like this, then, Culture subtly meets up with, and discreetly overlays, culture in its broader anthropological sense of belongingness and, in a Geertzian sense, of shared webs of meaning.[24]

ARTE's equivocal deployment of culture, sometimes implying "high culture," at other times referencing what are assumed to be popular and everyday ways of life, seems problematic when we consider that, not only are the channel's staff and audience mostly French–German, but so too, in the main, are its ideas about geopolitics, its experience of history, its ideas about race and ethnicity, and so on: there are, in short, no doubt deep discursive consequences for rendering European *Culture* interchangeable with European *culture*. When one considers, furthermore, the demographic dynamism of Europe—that, for example, the number of Western Europeans over the age of 60 years will almost double by mid-century[25] and that this aging labor force will likely be substantially replaced with migrant and immigrant labor[26]—one can appreciate the extent to which Cultural representations of Europeanness are quickly growing outmoded and inadequate, if they have not already been.[27]

Producing the "Universal"

Cultural producers rarely have a singular or narrow sense of their audience,[28] and most journalists, production staff, and programmers at globalizing media organizations are likely to define the scope of their work through multiple registers, which are often held in tension.[29] Producers at ARTE most often contend with distinctions between the channel's national funding and transnational-regional mandate, but many producers I spoke with either complemented this tension, or elided it, with another: that between ARTE as a transnational channel and a global channel. ARTE producers often spoke to me about ARTE's programming as "overcoming borders" in not just a European but global sense. If ARTE could find common ground between French and German sensibilities and audiences, the logic was, it is because many of the stories it tells in documentaries or fiction films are universal. For example, "There are good stories—universal stories—that will work as well in France as in Lebanon or Africa," one audience studies official told me.

Indeed, ARTE's programming travels down paths of circulation and distribution that extend well beyond Europe. ARTE is available via satellite in much of the Middle East, and since 2002, ARTE is available via Multichannel Multipoint Distribution Service (MMDS) or satellite across a large part of sub-Saharan and Central Africa; about 80,000 African households have already subscribed to ARTE.[30] One audience study poll found that ARTE is a familiar television channel to more than 30% of Israelis and 50% of Moroccans, and that in Tunisia ARTE is watched more frequently (more than 36% of those polled watch it more than once weekly) than BBC World.[31]

Crucially, however, it is not through this sense of geographical reception that ARTE producers tend to imagine the globalness of the channel but rather through an assumed aesthetic and narrative translatability of its programming. One programmer in the documentaries department at ARTE told me that his formula for successful cross-border programming is "love, life, sex, and death." This formula derives from something like common human experience, he explained. Everyone knows these things, regardless of his or her cultural disposition. "It's the emotional quality of the stories," as he put it—the ways in which humans everywhere can affectively engage with the experience of finally recovering from a life-threatening illness or the physical exhilaration of an early sexual encounter—which might qualify these films as "transcultural cinema," in David MacDougall's theorization of the term.[32]

However, the stakes of this "aesthetic universalism" are high. ARTE has very little sense of, or concern for, the ways in which its documentaries about World War II or Jean Renoir might be read and understood beyond Europe. If in some skeletal sense aspects of its narratives might be transparently universal, they may be substantially less so when they dwell in the cultural and political particularities of European metropoles, which feature prominently in its programming. Lila Abu-Lughod has noted, for example, that rural Upper Egyptians often see in "educational" programs broadcast to them from well-meaning producers in Cairo not transparency or connectedness, but rather the stark contrasts between urban modernity and the realities of their daily lives. For these rural poor, certain television programs only confirm the obliviousness of elites to the ways in which they have been marginalized, reproducing these hierarchies through the sense of distance imparted by an imperfect picture on a small screen.[33]

Localizing the Production of Global Media

ARTE claims to be the world's first European cultural television channel, but its staff and administration remain largely French–German; its conceptions of Europe are mostly Western European, yet are exported to Northern, Eastern, and Central Europe; meanwhile, many of its programmers believe that certain narratives or histories are universal, transcending such cultural geographies and ontologies.

It is not my purpose to excoriate ARTE; indeed, I might easily have written about some of ARTE staff's efforts to grasp the channel's responsibilities toward its growing and extra-European audiences. But ARTE, exactly because its newfangled mandate is caught awkwardly between the national, regional, and the global, must be held up to scrutiny because it illuminates, through its many hybridities and contradictions, the contemporary predicament of globalizing (but not fully globalized) media: while these media are called, and call themselves, "regional," transnational, or global, such labelings and discourse elide the ideological webbings that still hang together the national and global or transnational and international. These tensions form the cracks and gaps between ARTE's transnational purview and its regional and global claims—and between the global-cosmopolitan BBC and CNN of today and their preglobal chic, more self-avowedly *national* predecessors of not-so-long-ago.

Crucial to understanding transnational and globalizing media is the ongoing work of mapping how the producers and staff at these located media understand, and discursively produce, their scope and role in what are ever more complex, and diversifying, media marketplaces. One means of approaching this complexity, I hope to have shown, is by paying close attention to the scalar projects of these media, especially when they claim to simply "bring us" the Middle East, Europe, or the world. ARTE's glossy statement that it is "*L'Europe au quotidien*" (everyday Europe), the BBC's assertion that through it you "Connect to the world," and Al Jazeera's ad that reads "Every angle, every side" must be understood as claims to represent cultural worlds without any particular cultural perspective of their own. Part of the task of an anthropology of media is to resituate these claims in social sites of production and to follow the hermeneutic paths that these media travel: What and whose sensibilities, politics, and ideologies are folded into production practices? Who and where are audiences real rather than imagined? In what more specific ways do producers who select programming, or news stories, understand the global and global audiences?

There are no doubt quite complex, theoretically fraught intersectionings of cultural producers' discourses about what they are doing, and scholars' own sense of what global or transnational media might actually be. However, whether we speak of ARTE as an international channel, a regional project, a transnational organization, or as part of the global media, the exercise of trying to set down what these categories may or may not include, and where globalizing media such as ARTE may fit into such a taxonomy, is less crucial than understanding the ways in which producers and media outlets themselves draw on these categories as they go about constructing global media—not out of thin air or airwaves but through the immediate, and ultimately finite, ideological, moral, and political tools at their disposal (Figures 11.4 and 11.5).

Figure 11.4 Al Jazeera Online Banner Advertisement

Figure 11.5 BBC World Street-Level Poster Advertisement
Source: Photo by Damien Stankiewicz.

Endnotes

1. Brian Larkin, *Signal and Noise: Media, Infrastructure, and Urban Culture in Nigeria* (Durham, NC: Duke University Press, 2008), 16.

2. Arjun Appadurai, "Disjuncture and Difference in the Global Cultural Economy," in *Modernity at Large: Cultural Dimensions of Globalization* (Minneapolis: University of Minnesota Press, 1996); Faye D. Ginsburg, Lila Abu-Lughod, and Brian Larkin, *Media Worlds: Anthropology on New Terrain* (Berkeley: University of California Press, 2002), 14–17; Lisa Parks and Shanti Kumar, *Planet TV: A Global Television Reader* (New York: New York University Press, 2003); William Mazzarella, "Culture, Globalization, Mediation," *Annual Review of Anthropology* 33 (2004): 345–67.

3. Jinquan Li, *Chinese Media, Global Contexts* (New York, NY: Routledge, 2003); William Mazzarella, "'Very Bombay': Contending with the Global in an Indian Advertising Agency," *Cultural Anthropology* 18, no. 1 (2005): 33–71; Mayfair Mei-hui Yang, "Mass Media and Transnational Subjectivity in Shanghai: Notes on (Re)Cosmopolitanism in a Chinese Metropolis," in *Media Worlds*; Jean K. Chalaby, *Transnational Television in Europe: Reconfiguring Global Communications Networks* (New York, NY: I. B. Tauris, 2009).

4. Brian Larkin, *Signal and Noise*.

5. Georgina Born, *Uncertain Vision: Birt, Dyke and the Reinvention of the BBC* (London: Secker & Warburg, 2004).

6. Faye D. Ginsburg, Lila Abu-Lughod, and Brian Larkin, eds, *Media Worlds: Anthropology on New Terrain* (Berkeley: University of California Press, 2002), 14.

7. More recently, Chalaby has written, too, of "transnational television" but continues to refer to these media interchangeably as "trans-border"; see Chalaby, *Transnational Television*.

8. Michael G. Elasmar, *The Impact of International Television: A Paradigm Shift* (Mahwah, NJ: L. Erlbaum Associates, 2003).

9. See Michael Kearney, "The Local and the Global: The Anthropology of Globalization and Transnationalism," *Annual Review of Anthropology* 24 (1995): 548; Anna Tsing, "The Global Situation," *Cultural Anthropology* 15, no. 3 (2000): 327–60.

10. Etymologies from the *Oxford English Dictionary* (3rd ed.).

11. Ibid.

12. Born, *Uncertain Vision*; Glen Creeber, "'Hideously White': British Television, Glocalization, and National Identity," *Television and New Media* 5 (2004): 27–39.

13. Edward S. Herman and Robert Waterman McChesney, *The Global Media: The New Missionaries of Corporate Capitalism* (Washington, DC: Cassell, 1997).

14. Olivier Da Lage, "The Politics of Al Jazeera or the Diplomacy of Doha," in *The Al Jazeera Phenomenon*, ed. Mohamed Zayani (Boulder, CO: Paradigm Publishers, 2005); Sam Cherribi, "From Baghdad to Paris: Al-Jazeera and the Veil," *Harvard International Journal of Press and Politics* 11 (2006): 121–38.

15. Tsing, "The Global Situation," 328, 347; also see Anna Tsing, *Friction: An Ethnography of Global Connection* (Princeton, NJ: Princeton University Press, 2005).

16. This research was generously funded by the Social Science Research Council, the National Science Foundation, and the Wenner Gren Foundation for Anthropological Research.

17. Until very recently, all of ARTE's programming was simultaneously broadcast to French and German households. In 2008, ARTE introduced a slight lag between French and German programming (*"décalages,"* in French) to accommodate French viewers' slightly later prime-time viewing habits.

18. Serge Regourd, *L'Exception Culturelle* (Paris: Presses Universitaires de France, 2002), 11–45.

19. Laurent Bouvet, *France-Allemagne: Le bond en avant* (Paris: O. Jacob, 1998); Colette Mazzucelli, *France and Germany at Maastricht: Politics and Negotiations to Create the European Union* (New York, NY: Garland, 1997).

20. Founding treaty/charter of ARTE [*Traité fondateur d'ARTE*], http://www.arte.tv/static/c5/pdf/traite_inter-etatique.pdf (accessed October 28, 2008).

21. Jérôme Clément, "ARTE, enfin l'Europe!" *Le Monde* (September 26, 1992).

22. Marc Fumaroli, *L'Etat Culturel: Une religion moderne* (Paris: Fallois, 1991); David Lloyd and Paul Thomas, *Culture and the State* (New York, NY: Routledge, 1998).

23. Edward Tylor, *Primitive Culture* (New York, NY: G. P. Putnam's Sons, 1920 [1871]). In both French and German, "culture" can refer to each or both of these in a way that is somewhat less fluid at least in American English.

24. Clifford Geertz, *The Interpretation of Cultures: Selected Essays* (New York, NY: Basic Books, 1973).

25. Wolfgang Lutz, Brian C. O'Neill, and Sergei Scherbov, "Europe's Population at a Turning Point," *Science* 299, no. 5615 (2003): 1991–2.

26. Anthony M. Messina, *West European Immigration and Immigrant Policy in the New Century* (Westport, CT: Praeger, 2002), 49.

27. Nina Glick-Schiller, "Racialized Nations, Evangelizing Christianity, Police States, and Imperial Power: Missing in Action in Bunzl's New Europe," *American Ethnologist* 32, no. 4 (2005): 526–32; Ruth Mandel, "A Marshall Plan of the Mind: The Political Economy of a Kazakh Soap Opera," in *Media Worlds*; Paul A. Silverstein, "Immigrant Racialization and the New Savage Slot: Race, Migration, and Immigration in the New Europe," *Annual Review of Anthropology* 34 (2005): 363–84.

28. Maureen Mahon, "The Visible Evidence of Cultural Producers," *Annual Review of Anthropology* 29 (2000): 472–4.

29. John Caldwell, *Production Culture: Industrial Reflexivity and Critical Practice in Film and Television* (Durham, NC: Duke University Press, 2008).

30. ARTE-commissioned Oxford Research International study, 2008.

31. Ibid.

32. David MacDougall, *Transcultural Cinema* (Princeton, NJ: Princeton University Press, 1998).

33. Abu-Lughod, *Dramas of Nationhood: The Politics of Television in Egypt* (Chicago: University of Chicago Press, 2005), 57–79; Richard R. Wilk, "Television, Time, and the National Imaginary in Belize," in Faye D. Ginsburg, Lila Abu-Lughod, and Brian Larkin, eds, *Media Worlds: Anthropology on New Terrain* (Berkeley: University of California Press, 2002), 171–86. Richard R. Wilk makes a different, but not altogether opposed, argument in his discussion of the shift of Belizean notions of time after real-time satellite television became widespread in that country: "Instead of seeing themselves as backward or stuck in the past, Belizeans have come to understand their difference from the metropole in cultural and political terms" (172). He concludes, "The beam from satellites provides a new image of the foreign 'other' that furthers an emerging consensus about the content and identity of Belizean culture" (184).

PART III

Digital Mediations in the Global Era

CHAPTER **12**

Toward a Global Digital History

PAUL LONGLEY ARTHUR

Chapter Description

Digital history spans disciplines and can take many forms. Computer technology started to revolutionize the study of history more than three decades ago, and yet genres and formats for recording and presenting history using digital media are not well established and we are only now starting to see large-scale benefits. New modes of publication, new methods for doing research, and new channels of communication are making historical research richer, more relevant, and globally accessible. Many applications of computer-based research and publication are natural extensions of the established techniques for researching and writing history. Others are consciously experimental. This chapter discusses the latest advances in the digital history field and explores how new media technologies are reconfiguring the study of the past.

* * *

Technological innovation in the early twenty-first century is transforming the study of the past. At no time arguably since the invention of the printing press has history been so popular, so richly documented, so accessible, and reached and influenced so many people as it now does. Global interconnections enabled by the digital media environment are a central factor in these transformations. They have opened the way for new approaches to record and communicate the complexity of the past. The explosion of interest in history has not only been generated by research organizations and collecting institutions. In fact, history departments have generally been slow to embrace the possibilities that new media innovation offers. Rather, the surge of interest has come from the public. People everywhere are studying the past with a new degree of sophistication, partly because they have access to a vast and ever-increasing store of online information that was previously unavailable. In turn, people are using digital tools and online services to tell their own stories and track their own histories. This is creating new sorts of primary documents that will form the records for future historians.

This everyday history making is often aligned with the larger *democratic* turn in historical studies. Perhaps this democratic turn is just another "turn"—following closely on the *spatial* turn, the *linguistic* turn, and the *cultural* turn—but it is arguably much more powerful because it has drawn so many more people to the study of the past.[1] When Edward Ayers referred to democratization more than a decade ago in his important essay "The Pasts and Futures of Digital History" (1999), he was arguing for greater public access to digitized primary sources.[2] Ayers' vision is coming to fruition on an immense scale. The future is full of the promise of even greater access and public benefit from the availability of digitized primary material. Digital media and associated global communication channels are enmeshed with this democratization of history in further, equally important, ways. They have made it possible for "ordinary" people to create their own historical archives by recording their stories in affordable formats that can be readily exchanged and stored.[3]

In 1996 Gertrude Himmelfarb made a negative assessment of the Internet and of postmodernism, implicating both in a leveling of authority when she writes,

> Like postmodernism . . . the Internet does not distinguish between the true and the false, the important and the trivial, the enduring and the ephemeral . . . Every source appearing on the screen has the same weight and credibility as every other; no authority is "privileged" over any other.[4]

Some historians have been especially skeptical of the challenge to expert authority facilitated by the Internet and by postmodernism. William Thomas sums up this pattern of response, explaining that these "historians have viewed computing technology variously as the handmaiden of postmodernism, as a witless accomplice in the collapse of narrative, and as the silent killer of history's obligation to truth and objectivity."[5] Many would counter that readers or users have now developed new media literacies that allow for effective discrimination between information sources online. Indeed, there are many "signposts." For example, most major cultural institutions now have a presence online, and this lends a traditional status and credibility to the information they present. The national biographical dictionary projects in the United Kingdom, the United States, and Australia, for example, have relatively recently launched full online versions, and in fact, in some cases, the definitive (continually updated) version is only available online.[6] Nevertheless, it is also true that competition between specialist and nonspecialist voices (and the difficulty of telling the two apart) is having repercussions for historians, biographers, librarians, archivists, museum curators, and collectors. Currents of user-generated content increasingly flow alongside the work of academic and professional specialists. In this context, the resurgence of interest in history worldwide is demonstrating that specialist historical scholarship is required more than ever before—to secure pathways through the multiplying data and to provide reliable alternatives to nonspecialist interpretations. Projects such as the "September 11 Digital Archive" and the "Hurricane Digital Memory Bank" of the Center for History and New Media at George Mason University are models for collaborative history writing that bring together specialist and nonspecialist input, showing the possibilities as well as the dangers of an often fraught alliance.[7]

The World Wide Web is a growing global network of interconnected nodes for people anywhere to instantly communicate and share information. The community-forming role of the Internet is one of its most important functions, and it has dramatically changed the nature of societal interactions. A complex collective record of the immediate past is being produced constantly via myriad electronic channels. This facilitates intercultural dialogue, but it tends to highlight differences as much as it does similarities in perspective and experience, across places and cultures, in different languages, and between young and old. Furthermore, the immediacy of the global response to scandal or crisis, via Facebook, Twitter, and YouTube (and any number of other online services), shows how partial and political any interpretation of events always and inevitably is. Citizen journalism is thriving in this environment. "World history" is a small but growing field within historical studies that seeks to understand events in terms of global patterns and contexts.[8] It is unlikely that we will ever be able to speak of a truly "global" history that could accommodate the endless competing perspectives that make up the collective knowledge of the past. Nevertheless, people's diverse experiences, and our recording of them as history, now have global, instant reach.

The advantages of embracing digital media for history center on: greater access to information (for specialists and nonspecialists alike), the potential for more sophisticated analysis of information, and newly flexible structures to present the plurality of voices and historical experiences. Furthermore, investment in cyberinfrastructure will ultimately enable new modes of publication, new methods for doing research, and new channels of communication to make historical research richer, more relevant, and more widely accessible. This chapter explores a range of issues related to the evolution of "digital history," including definition of the term, scope of the field, the character of "hypermedia textuality," and the influence of media change on the study of history over the course of the twentieth century.

Defining Digital History

With its dependence on diverse kinds of information and evidence, the study of history is perfectly positioned to be a major beneficiary of advances in the digital media environment. That is because history's own progression over two centuries from authoritarian to democratic approaches, from a focus on "big" history (Carlyle's "The history of the world is but the biography of great men"[9]) to multiple and partial histories, and from trusted high authority to participant and processor, has attuned history to the fragmentary and deterritorialized global world of digital media. However, as an emerging field and set of practices, the scope of digital history is difficult to pin down.

Many applications of computer-based research and publication are natural extensions of the established techniques for researching and writing history. Others are consciously experimental. One of the barriers to any straightforward definition of digital history is that the activities that constitute the field are spread across disciplines. The embrace of interdisciplinary approaches means that many aspects of the past are now studied as much in English and cultural studies departments, library and information studies departments, even media and communication departments, as they are in history departments. In universities, this has highlighted the value of history as a lens through which to understand social behavior and change and has extended its reach. The digital media environment has played its part in helping to facilitate this interdisciplinarity. Researchers once working in relative isolation in very different fields now draw upon a common set of digital tools and services and similar modes of producing and communicating their work. For better or worse, new technology and interfaces have created an environment where researchers arguably even use similar methodologies and procedures because the technology itself encourages this. Software, whether designed for a general or a specialized market, routinely includes templates that ensure people will work in similar ways. The digital environment has become a common denominator.

It is difficult to draw a line around the range of work that constitutes the digital history field, not only because it spans disciplines but also because new opportunities continue to open up. It is worthwhile reflecting on how much digital research culture has evolved even since Dan Cohen and Roy Rosenzweig's book *Digital History: A Guide to Gathering, Preserving, and Presenting the Past on the Web* (2005).[10] In this seminal book—which helped to draw attention to the field of digital history as a distinct area of study within the digital humanities and remains the only substantial practical guide devoted to designing digital history resources—the authors list seven qualities of digital media and networks that point to new directions that historical research can take in the digital environment: *capacity, accessibility, flexibility, diversity, manipulability, interactivity,* and *hypertextuality* (or *nonlinearity*). They also refer to five dangers or hazards: *quality, durability, readability, passivity,* and *inaccessibility*. Although these possibilities and challenges remain open, the book was published just after the beginnings of Web 2.0-style services around 2004 and so does not take into account the major transformations of recent years. *Digital History* met a need, in its time, for an introductory book with an applied focus. As a reflection of how quickly the setting had already changed by 2005, the authors note in their introduction that they could not have imagined writing such a book 10 years earlier.[11]

There is no agreed definition of digital history. Vernon Burton describes digital history as "the process by which historians are able to use computers to do history in ways impossible without the computer."[12] Expanding on this, I would suggest that digital history can refer to all aspects of the study and appreciation of history, heritage, and material culture that involve digital media in their presentation, storage, and access. It can also refer to a stand-alone text, in the sense of "a digital history of" a particular topic. In the latter context, it does not refer to a genre but rather to the digital means of delivery itself. Digital history can be found in physical settings, including in museums or galleries as interactive displays. Digital history can also be stored and delivered on CD or DVD. Most commonly, however, it is presented and accessed online, in the form of databases of historical information and digitized material that often involve some kind of digital curation to lead users through paths of information. The latest working definition on Wikipedia links digital history to the movement in the 1960s and 1970s in social science history, when, for the first time, there was widespread use of mathematical modeling in historical studies. The extracts below from Wikipedia, introducing, defining, and setting out the scope of digital history, underline its global reach and indicate diverse uses of digital media:

Digital history is the use of digital media and tools for historical practice, presentation, analysis, and research. It is a branch of the Digital Humanities and an outgrowth of Quantitative history, Cliometrics, and History and Computing. Some of the previous work in digital history includes digital archives, CD-ROMs, online presentations, interactive maps, time-lines, audio files, and virtual worlds. More recent digital history projects focus on creativity, collaboration, and technical innovation, all of which are aspects of Web 2.0. Future work in digital history will likely include projects such as text mining . . . Digital history is a rapidly changing field. New methods and formats are currently being developed. This means that "digital history" is a difficult term to define. However, it is possible to identify general characteristics. Digital history represents a democratization of history in that anyone with access to the internet can have their voice heard, including marginalized groups which were often excluded in the "grand narratives" of nation and empire. In contrast to earlier media formats, digital history texts tend to be non-linear and interactive, encouraging user participation and engagement . . . Digital history is studied from various disciplinary perspectives and in relation to a range of interrelated themes and activities. The field includes discussion of: archives, libraries, and encyclopedias; museums and virtual exhibits; digital identity and biography; digital games and virtual worlds; online communities and social networks; Web 2.0; and e-research and cyber-infrastructure.[13]

It is clear that the category of digital history is in an uneasy position—related to the digital humanities in its techniques and motivations but grounded fundamentally in an interest in the past and the complexity of its textual representation across time and across media.

Unlike area studies, or the study of periods or movements or particular people, digital history has more to do with the *processes* of recording and presenting history in the digital media environment than with a traditional historical domain of study. It is certainly linked with media history and the history of technology, and it is also increasingly linked with the study of digital culture and community—which is a vast, related area. One of the most common mistakes is to think of digital history simply as a tool for interactive learning—which is, in fact, a dominant view. A related view is that digital history is the domain of librarians and archivists who have responsibility for digital capture, preservation, and organization of historical resources. This view is that information managers look after the information and historians *use* it. For the full potential of digital history to be realized in creative new interpretative formats as well as for informational purposes, this model needs to change, and for that to happen, historians must be more engaged with the production of digital resources.

Because there is not yet a set of established genres and formats for digital history, there are great opportunities—the chance to reconfigure publishing formats, for example, not necessarily with the aim of superseding the printed book, but with the goal of making best use of the inherent characteristics of digital media, to better capture the plurality and complexity of the past. In turn, new ways to measure or evaluate scholarly value and standards would need to be devised.[14] The challenge in any digital history project is to transform the presentation of history in the digital media environment and to make best use of that environment's inherent capacity for hyperlinking—but to do so in a way that preserves, respects, and builds on the very basic principles that are the foundation of evidence-based historical studies.

Media Change and Hypermedia Textuality

On one level, it is reasonable to think that academic history should be at arm's length from technological transformations. By its very nature, the discipline of history has tended to stand back from technological change, as an observer, not engaging with passing experiments but rather seeking to create reliable, trustworthy, and enduring historical records for the future. But history has grown beyond its originally clear intentions and neat disciplinary boundaries. It is caught up, as much as any discipline, in the new interdisciplinary drive of humanities and social science research today. When historians choose to adopt today's very latest media formats (at this relatively early stage in their development) historical scholarship is taken out of its comfort zone and brought face to face with the very processes of change it seeks to document. This means that, for all the apparent possibilities, there are many challenges.

More than 20 years on from the beginnings of the publicly available World Wide Web, digital history today faces many of the same issues as do other areas of the digital humanities more broadly. Although history, literature, philosophy, anthropology, and art, along with many other disciplines of the humanities and social sciences, have been moving increasingly online into a networked environment, the research community has not yet discovered, developed, or at least has not agreed on common formats that information and interpretation should take. It could even be argued that the digital history field has not moved far beyond the innovation represented by the very earliest projects such as the University of Virginia's awarded "Valley of the Shadow: Two Communities in the American Civil War" and the American Social History Project's "Who Built America?"

(both released in 1993, available on CD-ROM, and later migrated to the web).[15] This may be because the digital environment does not lend itself as well as do earlier media formats to *narrative* interpretation, on which historians have relied; it is better suited to interactive, nonlinear, and ultimately non-narrative textual forms.[16] The most sophisticated experiments investigating the possibilities and constraints of digital narrative forms are certainly taking place outside history departments, in initiatives such as the long-term database narrative program of the Labyrinth Project of the Annenberg Center for Communication, University of Southern California.[17] The lack of established formats, the endless array of different standards and the problems of obsolescence of software and hardware, and flow-on problems of preservation and access mean that, despite the seeming abundance of information now in the hands of anyone with access to the Internet, actually there is a great risk that many of today's works of digital scholarship will not survive into the future—the phenomenon often referred to as the "digital dark ages." However, experience shows that historians have in the course of time made very good use of new media once they have matured.[18] We can assume that, in the future, it will be as commonplace for history to be presented in the digital media environment as through established written or visual documentary forms. The stage we are at is one of great experimentation—a stage that arguably has been seen early in the life of all forms of new media, in their time.

The digital media environment is only the latest of many different "technologies of representation" including print, photography, and the moving images of film. Each has its own set of possibilities and constraints for presentation, storage, and access, unique qualities that relate in fundamental ways to the underlying technology. In the case of the printing press, for example, this underlying technology includes the machinery itself; there have been limitations or possibilities, in different eras, of printing only onto certain sizes of paper or material. In the case of the computer, the underlying technology is the digital machine language of bits and bytes; this is related to limitations or possibilities associated with processing power and the characteristics of magnetic or other kinds of storage, as well as the native "hypermedia" format for hyperlinking of information. Ultimately, genres develop that make best use of new media formats but always in view of what has come before. The history of centuries of media format changes can offer clues to help to understand these processes.

As new technologies of representation have emerged, they have not generally superseded or eclipsed previous forms. For example, although many predicted the "death of the book" when electronic publishing became widespread, the book form has remained remarkably resilient even in the face of apparent threats from digital devices such as Amazon's Kindle and competing e-book readers. This shows how multiple technologies of representation can thrive side by side. It may also be a sign that applications of digital media have not yet matured to a point where these can seriously challenge the primacy of print. Likewise, photography did not lose its popularity when the moving images of film emerged as a technology of representation (intriguingly, in 1915 D. W. Griffith predicted that children soon would be "taught practically everything by moving pictures" and "never be obliged to read history again"[19]). There have been in-between phases too, such as the transition from silent film to sound film. With the development of film, the still images of photography could be animated, to tell history as a visual and aural kind of simulation—something that both confused and expanded notions of history telling by offering the possibility of vivid, lifelike reenactment. Documentary film has evolved, through its many subgenres developed over time, to something that has its own long heritage. Technologies of representation, then, do not start and finish in eras. They exist as continuities, building on what has come before and evolving alongside the new forms.

In view of these historical patterns of media change, it is important to consider what the enabling and constraining factors are that underlie the digital environment, and how this may impact on the presentation of history. The digital media environment builds on previous technologies of communication in a unique way by acting as a mechanism for their assemblage via a digital interface. That combinatory impulse (of multimedia) in turn has its own long genealogy in disparate prior formats. Norman Klein traces this impulse back to 1671 with the earliest known attempts to create immersive environments using optics and mirrors, and even further to prototypes in Florence and Rome around 1510.[20] The concept of networking also has its own long history through different forms of social organization and connectivity.[21] Although there is no scope for in-depth exploration here, the history of changing terminology is directly relevant to the discussion of digital history. Some terms have recently come and gone out of favor and they cast a particular light on the changing nature of the digital media environment. These terms include "multimedia" (literally bringing together the earlier media in combination), "interactive multimedia" (self-consciously emphasizing the arguably often over-hyped potential of interactive modes of engagement), and "network media" (a more recently adopted term that foregrounds the interconnected communication networks that are providing the infrastructure—both physical and intellectual—for today's research and knowledge generation). Digital modes of presenting information are full of the traces of older genres (with remnants of their traditions of production and reception) but mask the original distinctions between them. Parallels can be drawn between this convergent aesthetic and that of the nineteenth century with its spectacular display of knowledge in the age of the great exhibitions and encyclopedias of culture, language, and knowledge. The Internet itself can be thought of as a vast cabinet of curiosities. Barbrook and Cameron's vision in "The Californian Ideology" (1995) was that convergence would create something which, as they put it, "is more than the sum of its parts."[22] Indeed, online resources such as encyclopedias, atlases, and exhibitions now bring together all kinds of documents, information, and reflections in super-archives that open many pathways to information as well as featuring advanced search facilities.[23]

What sets this hypermedia textuality apart from the earlier forms it brings together in combination in the digital environment is a reliance on the database. One of the main mechanisms for digital convergence,[24] databases underlie all manner of digital history projects, from simple informational websites, online community history forums, multimedia documentaries, and interactive narrative CD and DVD projects, through to large-scale repositories of digitized primary sources at major research organizations and collecting institutions. The database in its very basic form is open-ended, unlike a book. In the shift toward a database-driven textuality, there is a new emphasis being placed on the collection, collation, and positioning of information rather than information itself being solely the substance on which interpretation rests and relies. This positioning is illustrated most clearly in GIS (geographic information system)-based projects, where interactive, dynamic maps provide a structured interface to and framework for information. The "Texas Slavery Project"[25] of the University of Virginia and the "Gallipoli: The First Day"[26] project of the Australian Broadcasting Corporation utilize maps and timelines in very different but equally impressive ways. Many projects position information on the world map by employing freely available and customizable Google Maps or Google Earth services, and these have become user-friendly default interfaces for presenting all manner of location-specific information to global audiences.[27]

Most crucially for historical information, information in a database can be corrected—new editions no longer need to be published. Databases are endlessly open to revision and renewal, and as micro adjustments are made within the system, databases tend to keep on growing—especially if they store a record of adjustments and improvements rather than only preserving the latest version. The database has had a profound effect on how information is presented and collected, even for the old media in their digitized forms. The magic of database forms is precisely that they offer a way of making links and relationships between disparate pieces of information, creating new kinds of order within a system at the request of a user. They provide a remarkable vehicle for history to capture some of the fragmentariness and multiplicity of the world in which we live without seeking to fit all the pieces of the jigsaw together. Digital history is arguably more about creating pathways through information and interpretation than about achieving a whole picture or a final product.

Conclusion

There is no doubt that global communication networks are changing the character of society in fundamental ways. People meet online, political campaigns are conducted online, lives are recorded in all their detail online through shared correspondence, photographs, and videos—and there are many other examples. These social transformations are well documented and have been studied within interdisciplinary fields such as cultural, media, and communication studies, as well as literary and film studies. Historians are increasingly using and creating digital resources and are also starting to seriously document the massive production of historical records that goes on daily on the World Wide Web. However, history as a discipline continues to be one of the least engaged with discussions of online transformations that are having a global impact—literally "changing the course of history."

There are many factors that impact on the study of the past in today's global networked media environment, and the evolving digital history field takes so many forms as to defy easy definition. Perhaps the most important factor continues to be the basic capacity to communicate instantly with a global audience. This potentially allows researchers to collaborate without any of the traditional barriers to working remotely—although opportunities for collaborative e-research are in their infancy in the arts and humanities in general. More visible are the online communities that form organically on a day-to-day basis, producing new kinds of historical records in the process. There is no time to wait (or need to wait) for the guiding hand of official commentators or media outlets—let alone learned historians or cultural critics. The Internet is awash with competing accounts and perspectives that construct, analyze, communicate, and preserve the memory of major social events as well as everyday ephemera. The ability to comment immediately to a potential global audience of millions of people has helped to underline and facilitate a movement toward the democratization of knowledge. This movement is not only spurred by the technical capacity for instant communication but also grounded in philosophical insights that have emerged from postmodernism and related movements that have questioned the basis of western knowledge systems.

There is no doubt that future digital history texts will not be stand-alone products; they are likely to use the hypermedia textuality to recombine information available through any number of online services to create new forms and new portals to information. In doing so, they will increasingly mirror the patterns of global communication that make up today's communities. The recombination of information across online services will help to frame history in new ways. It may no longer be possible to simply call these texts: they will be composite and shifting information resources that are defined by their very distributed nature rather than by their location within a particular institution, discipline, or domain. As we move from the Web 2.0 to Web 3.0 semantic web environment, historians, for the most part, lag behind in their understanding of the impact and possibilities of digital media technologies. A cultural shift is taking place but only slowly. There are important issues to face and questions that need to be asked. One thing is certain: it is necessary for historians to be involved in setting the direction that digital history is to take at this critical turning point in its own development.

Endnotes

1. This democratization began long ago with the idea that history should be available to anyone—that it should not only be the domain of specialists. Collecting institutions increasingly opened their holdings to the public rather than only to scholars. In the last century, there was a widening of the topics of history that corresponded with developing poststructuralist and postmodernist approaches, resulting in general agreement that all subjects are worthy of study and all kinds of lives and experiences should be recorded as accurately as possible, even (or especially) if this highlights conflicting perspectives.
2. Edward L. Ayers, "The Pasts and Futures of Digital History," 1999, http://www.vcdh.virginia.edu/PastsFutures.html (accessed April 17, 2010).
3. This personal exchange and storage is being actively encouraged by major national collecting institutions. For example, the National Archives of Australia project "Remembering Our Anzacs" allows users to create and share "scrapbooks" of digital material of interest. See http://mappingouranzacs.naa.gov.au/login.aspx (accessed May 15, 2010).
4. Gertrude Himmelfarb, "A Neo-Luddite Reflects on the Internet," *Chronicle of Higher Education*, November 1, 1996, A56. Quoted in Dan Cohen and Roy Rosenzweig, *Digital History: A Guide to Gathering, Preserving, and Presenting the Past on the Web*, 2005, http://chnm.gmu.edu/digitalhistory/introduction/#_ednref3 (accessed December 20, 2009).
5. William Thomas, "Computing and the Historical Imagination," in *A Companion to Digital Humanities*, ed. Susan Schreibman, Ray Siemens, and John Unsworth (Oxford: Blackwell, 2004), 61.
6. See, for example, the *American National Biography*, http://www.anb.org (accessed December 1, 2009), the *Oxford Dictionary of National Biography*, http://www.oxforddnb.com (accessed December 1, 2009), and the *Australian Dictionary of Biography*, http://www.adb.online.anu.edu.au (accessed December 1, 2009).
7. See http://911digitalarchive.org (accessed December 18, 2009) and http://www.hurricanearchive.org (accessed December 18, 2009).
8. See Patrick Manning, "Navigating World History: A Synopsis," http://www.historycooperative.org/journals/whc/1.1/manning.html (accessed December 28, 2009).
9. Edward H. Carr, *What is History?* (London: Penguin, 1961), 49.
10. http://chnm.gmu.edu/digitalhistory (accessed December 12, 2009).

11. http://chnm.gum.edu/digitalhistory/introduction/#_edn3 (accessed December 20, 2009).

12. Orville Vernon Burton, "American Digital History," *Social Science Computer Review* 23, no. 2 (2005): 206–20.

13. See http://en.wikipedia.org/wiki/Digital_history (accessed December 19, 2009).

14. For a related discussion, see Michael Coventry, "Moving beyond 'the Essay': Evaluating Historical Analysis and Argument in Multimedia Presentations," *Journal of American History* (March 2006), textbooks and teaching section, http://www.journalofamerican history.org/textbooks/2006/coventry.html (accessed May 15, 2010).

15. See "The Valley of the Shadow," http://valley.vcdh.virginia.edu (accessed December 12, 2009) and "Who Built America?" http://ashp.cuny.edu/who-america (accessed December 12, 2009).

16. Teachers may lament the loss of what are referred to as basic reading skills, and yet today's students have arguably developed a new kind of literacy that is difficult to assess but includes the ability to take in "chunks" of information without the preset order that narrative structures typically provide. Perhaps better thought of as "digital dexterity," this skill set includes the ability to interact with software, often in a very tactile manner.

17. See the project website http://www.college.usc.edu/labyrinth (accessed December 15, 2009). Well-known projects include *The Dawn at My Back: Memoir of a Black Texas Upbringing. An Interactive Cultural History* (2003) [DVD-ROM] (Blue) and *Mysteries and Desire: Searching the Worlds of John Rechy* (2000) [CD-ROM] (Kinder).

18. The recording of oral history using tape recorders of various kinds is one of the very obvious examples of historians embracing new media formats. Photography, of course, also revolutionized recording and communication of events.

19. Rosenzweig, "So, What's Next for Clio?: CD-ROM and Historians," *Journal of American History* 81 (1995): 1621.

20. Norman Klein, *The Vatican to Vegas: A History of Special Effects* (New York, NY: The New Press, 2004), 21, 96, 304.

21. For a wide-ranging overview, see Armand Mattelart, *Networking the World, 1794–2000* (Minneapolis: University of Minnesota Press, 2000).

22. Richard Barbrook and Andy Cameron, "The Californian Ideology," *Alamut*, 1995, http://www.alamut.com/subj/ideologies/pessimism/califIdeo_I.html (accessed September 13, 2009).

23. Recent examples of this increasingly popular, emerging genre include the *Encyclopedia of Melbourne*, http://www.emelbourne.net.au/home.html (accessed November 1, 2009), the *Dictionary of Sydney*, http://www.dictionaryofsydney.org (accessed November 1, 2009), and *Te Ara Encyclopedia of New Zealand*, http://www.teara.govt.nz (accessed November 1, 2009).

24. Lev Manovich and Andreas Kratky, *Soft Cinema: Navigating the Database* [pamphlet with accompanying DVD-ROM] (Cambridge, MA: MIT Press, 2005), 1.

25. See http://www.texasslaveryproject.org/maps/hb (accessed September 10, 2009).

26. See http://www.abc.net.au/innovation/gallipoli (accessed November 12, 2009).

27. For example, "America's Highway: Oral Histories of Route 66" links oral histories and photographs with a Google Map interface, http://sites.google.com/site/route66map (accessed August 28, 2009). The "Gallipoli: The First Day" project (see endnote 26) is also available in a "light" Google Earth version, http://www.abc.net.au/innovation/gallipoli/google_earth.htm (accessed December 20, 2009).

CHAPTER **13**

Subtitling Jia Zhangke's Films

Intermediality, Digital Technology, and the
Varieties of Foreignness in Global Cinema

HUDSON MOURA

Chapter Description

Globalization, subtitles, and new technical filming devices bring new possibilities to contemporary Chinese cinema. This potentiality is revealed in the work of Jia Zhangke, through intermediality, which examines the imposition of technology and industrialization on contemporary Chinese society, two phenomena that cause the alienation and estrangement of Chinese people. This paradoxical result, expressed through Jia's characters, is central to his films, such as *The World*, *Still Life*, *Dong*, *Useless*, and *24 City*, that focus on the isolation of transplanted individuals in urban settings and the breakdown of community. In his films, Jia subverts the government's attempts at globalization without media democracy—in other words, without citizens' ability to question the consequences of such transformation. This phenomenon is creating a huge "gap" between the government's projected ideal society and the experience of Chinese people themselves. Jia's films give a different approach to Chinese society's perception of their place in the world, their identity, and their "real" isolation from global society.

* * *

Introduction: Global Virtual Village—Migration and Identity

In the past few decades, cinemas from all over the world have experienced increasing popularization, film production has internationalized, and filmmakers have begun to develop screenplays on an international basis. New technical strategies have been developed to respond to international grants and global audiences, especially those from the international film festivals. Filmmakers have been shaping a global grammar of cinematic storytelling and producing films with a combination of national and international funds, as well as cultures. Filmmakers have been adopting transcultural perspectives and working in transnational productions to criticize and to respond to a lack of production in some countries. For those reasons, terms such as *world, transnational,* and *national cinema,* in their historical and cultural contexts, as well as *globalization in cinema,* signal important issues that must be reconsidered, rethought, with a contemporary perspective.

In *The World* (2004), Chinese filmmaker Jia Zhangke creates a new approach to subjectivity in global cinema through intermediality. Subtitles and digital media are part of this intermediality to transpose to the screen the film's characters' "understanding of modern life." Jia's China reflects global conditions and trends that affect us all, both Chinese and foreign audiences. This approach is essential in creating new narratives that correspond with the experiences of new generations that are living through and connecting via media.

The comprehension of world cinema audiences can be undermined by subtitling that avoids complex issues or local ("foreign") subjects that would be difficult for a foreign audience to understand. How can we be sure about our understanding of some films' sequences? Audiences must rely on the intermediation of the written text to understand the dialogues and even the images. Sometimes this is not revealed by the translated subtitles of the dialogues. How do filmmakers manage these possible losses in translation? In addressing the topic of subtitles, I want to stress the idea of the experience of foreignness in film and question how we can say that we understood a film through the mediation or intermediation of subtitles.

Subtitles are a cross-cultural intermediation that enables Jia Zhangke to show his films widely, while avoiding the Chinese government's censorship. Subtitles also allow him to participate in screenings overseas without official approval and, in some cases, despite official protests and bans. Audiences around the world have been discovering the new face of China, at the same time as becoming familiar with Jia's unique film style. He has been acclaimed internationally in many important film festivals such as those of

Cannes, Venice, and Berlin. His films have also been shown in many retrospectives around the world, and this is before they have been widely shown within China due to censorship issues. What happens in China is just a reflection of what happens around the world: migration, interculturality, and displacement. Chinese filmmaker Jia Zhangke understands cinema as a medium that can communicate worldwide without frontiers.

To avoid any kind of government censorship, Jia relies on the devices of digital video (DV) to widely circulate his films. The new "cheap and accessible" technologies permit a great number of filmmakers to develop their projects and to institute a national or independent cinematography. Filmmakers' independence from their official funding sources and from commercial markets has been crucial to new Chinese cinema in establishing an important role in contemporary cinema.

Jia's generation of filmmakers has been developing a new form of cinematographic style revealing daily life and having ideological implications that have subsequently influenced their own approach to make fictional feature films. Documentary and documentary style in fiction films allow them to question and make statements as a self-liberation and a self-reflection process.

The "revolution of digital video," as Jia calls it, allows him to film quickly, using non-actors in public spaces, thus enabling him to avoid questionable situations where he could be threatened by authorities or subject to government surveillance. Video was long considered a suitable medium for documentary but not for fiction. Although film connotes an ideal or fictional world, video has a connotation of reality. Thus, when filmmakers use the inexpensive medium of DV, they import those documentary connotations into the fiction world.

With this approach, everything seems to be improvised, and this unpretentiousness allows a precise encounter between fiction and documentary and the exploration of intermediality between cinema, video, animation, and computer screens. How does this approach shape a particular Chinese style in global cinema? How does this global production process impact local media, art, and culture? Should we conceive of cultural globalization as a cross-cultural translation that promotes the comprehension of a work or access to this work? Is cultural globalization a creation or a transformation of the senses? This chapter will discuss and attempt to answer these and related questions.

Subtitling Global Cinema: Interculturality and Displacement

The interrelation of image and text, the movement from one to another, creates a terrain of culture negotiation in foreign films, especially in a transnational context. Subtitles engage us in a double exercise of reading the text and seeing the image. Today, subtitles are more easily integrated in a film; often there are multiple versions of languages on a screen. In Asian countries, it is very natural to have different subtitles at the same time on the screen.

Subtitles draw attention to the limits of translation, as well as to the text's intermediation on the screen. As Lo Kwai-Cheung says, "Subtitles tell us about the dialectical interactions of words and images taking place in the transborder film viewing process under the heightened speed of globalization."[1] According to Lo, "As a specific form of making sense of things in cross-cultural and cross-linguistic encounters, subtitling reveals realities of cultural domination and subordination and serves as a site of ideological dissemination and its subversion."[2] In contrast, Hamid Naficy states that *multilinguality*, an extensive titling on screen, has become a part of intercultural films. According to him, "There is no single or original source language for many accented films, which are made in the interstices and astride several cultures and languages. Subtitling is thus integral to both the making and the viewing of these films."[3] Certainly, the globalization creates a great advance in the use of subtitles; however, it does so through a process of impeding foreignness and heterogeneity between cultures and languages. The main purpose, in this matter, is to achieve a perfect symmetry between discourses—texts, voices, and images—to facilitate and eliminate any disturbance to the film's consumerism.

Subtitles mean different things to different people in a global context. "Every film is a foreign film" to someone, somewhere. How do we translate a work of art or media—when behind that art/media there is an entire culture with its own particular values?

Subtitles enable audiences to have access to foreign films. Globalization expands the subtitling industry as new demands in interlingual practices are created. For example, one single DVD can provide subtitling in several languages. Because of new methods of distribution, images are more and more readily crossing barriers of language and making inroads into markets that are mostly dominated by commercial and standard narrative films.

Jia Zhangke's film *The World* (Shi jie, 2004) is punctuated with references to subtitles, questioning their real necessity in a film to provide access to "meaning" in a globalized and media-saturated society. Can contemporary images be understood beyond the subtitles? In a dialogue between the dancers Tao (a Chinese) and Anna (a Russian), each speaks their mother tongue. However, internationally distributed, their speech is subtitled uniformly into one language. The lack of comprehension between these two characters is diminished as a result of this subtitling. This particularity of the film completely bypasses the viewer for whom the entire dialogue is clearly subtitled. Also, at times, incomprehensible words in the dialogue of a film are only partially heard by the original public. However, the technique of leaving some words unheard, or not understandable, is not possible with subtitles that make everything "audible." Subtitlers may, therefore, consciously or unconsciously "recontextualize" some of the resulting ambiguities when writing the subtitles, introducing nuances that otherwise would exist in the scene only in an unexpressed form. Subtitling has become one of the creative ingredients of the filmmaking process. Different meanings of subtitled lines can be more understandable through prior scenes that contextualize the subsequent situations. With Jia's dialogue between the Russian and the Chinese characters, the director seems to emphasize the need for subtitles to enable people to understand each other's situation or subjectivity.

However, these qualities are diminished in translation. Also, it is doubtful that the foreign audience is experiencing the original audience's understanding. Although subtitles in a film can maintain the original language and sound of the film, in some countries subtitling is just not "allowed." Their films and TV shows are dubbed. Thus, subtitles offer viewers a way of thinking beyond borders and viewing different worlds, enabling them to experience foreign cultures.

Jia's film is divided by intertitles, as book chapters, that introduce the audience to the subject of each part of the film: Paris in Beijing Suburb, Ulan Bator Night, Tokyo Story, and Ever Changing World. Subtitles allow the characters to achieve immediacy, individuality, and complexity and also a "right" to be heard by a non-Mandarin-speaking audience. Subtitling provides the audience with a new pathway to the characters' thoughts and feelings.

The relationships among the workers who also live in a theme park, on the outskirts of Beijing, are artificial and ambiguous. The characters are difficult for viewers to empathize with and there is no plot line in the film, just some random events. Most of Jia's films show a gap between national expectations of modern China and the expectations of Chinese people who are migrating from the countryside to the city and suffering from displacement. At the same time, these people are searching for meaning in their lives in their "reconstructed" urban world.

The enigmatic ending of *The World* maintains some complex issues while denying some possible interpretations and different translations. Because the screen has faded to black, the audience hears only the voices and has to rely on the subtitles to understand the last scene. Even the famous film critic Jonathan Rosenbaum[4] admitted to not understanding the last sequence of the film. Viewers may ask themselves: "Did something get lost in translation?" Does this lack of understanding result from not knowing Chinese culture or is this subjectivity of nonunderstanding inherent in the film itself? Critical and debated sequences, such as the last scene of *The World*, are complicated by the need to trust the translated dialogue, when there are many possible translations.

Taisheng says:
<Wo men shi bu shi si le?>
"We are / aren't dead?"
(Are we dead yet?)
Tao says:
<mei you>
"not have"
(we haven't)
<Wo men chai gong gong kai chi>
"We just now (this instant) start"
(We're now just starting / We've just started / We've just begun)

When Taisheng asks Tao "Are we dead?" she replies, "No." Tao concludes, "It's just the beginning."

In summary, what she says has the connotation of "we're not yet dead, this is just the beginning." These last crucial words could mean the characters are heading for death but have not yet arrived; in Chinese culture, this suggests the idea of the afterlife that has no ending.[5] But the subtitles simply say, "This is just the beginning."

According to MacDougall "no forms of speech are culturally neutral."[6] I agree: translations do not take place between words, rather they occur between cultures and, through subtitles, between media or "meaning or sign systems." Subtitles provide cross-cultural understandings that traverse the barriers and frontiers of language and nation-states and transform language into a cultural commodity that allows foreign audiences to consume foreignness.

Chinese "Transforming" Reality: Censorship, Documentary, and Digital Cinema

Emergent cinemas from small or poor nations have great difficulty in gaining access to international markets due to lack of money and, in many cases, lack of government support. New technologies permit a great number of filmmakers to develop their projects and to institute, in some cases, a national or independent cinematography. This independence from official funding sources and from commercial markets has been crucial to Chinese filmmaker Jia Zhangke in establishing one of the most respected careers in contemporary cinema.

Jia Zhangke became the most prominent of the sixth-generation film-makers from Mainland China. The so-called urban generation, independent or underground cinema, includes filmmakers such as Wang Xiaoshuai, Zhang Yuan, and Li Yang. These filmmakers were born during the Cultural Revolution, between the 1960s and 1970s. They are known for filming the contradictions of urban life in China. These filmmakers have constituted the almost nonexistent production of independent films in China, opting for private and international funding, instead of the official system. Their independence from official funding has meant lack of money, low-budget films, small crews, and screenplays that they avoided being scrutinized and censored by the government film system. The DV revolution, which began in 1998,[7] was a prerequisite for emerging independent filmmakers.[8]

However, Yingjin Zhang remarks that if we understand the term *independent* as

> works produced independently of direct state funding and administrative control, we come to realize that Chinese independent productions had actually begun with documentaries in the late 1980s [*Bumming in Beijing: The Last Dreamers* (1988–1990) directed by Wu Wenguang and the series *Tiananmen* (1991) directed by Shi Jian] when China was undergoing an unprecedented intellectual transformation.[9]

For Jia's generation, the incident at Tiananmen Square has changed their ideological approach, and it was also fundamental to build their social collectiveness and interaction among Chinese independent filmmakers.

Those sixth-generation filmmakers have adopted an interest in new, experimental cinematographic forms, and they are also very critical toward the modern China. Filmmaking for them is a kind of self-expression. Their concern is with the individual, the local, and the current reality, which is different from those of fifth-generation filmmakers, such as Zhang Yimou and Chen Kaige, who aimed to revise Chinese history and tradition. Contemporary Chinese cinema has replaced emperors and concubines with marginalized and excluded people, losers, and victims of modernization and globalization. These characters have become the central driving interest since the late 1990s. Documentaries, and documentary style in fiction films, allow for a questioning and statement of self-liberation and self-reflection. According to Yingjin "we should not indiscriminately accept Chinese independents' typical claims to *truth*, *reality* and *objectivity* but, instead, must investigate their preferred means of achieving their perceptions of truth and reality."[10] This style has subsequently influenced their own approach to make fiction feature films.

Jia Zhangke's first feature film was *Pickpocket* (Xiao Wu), shot in 16 mm, in 1997, just after his graduation from the Beijing Film Academy. Influenced by French filmmaker Robert Bresson, this film is about a pickpocket in Jia's home city of Fenyang. Jia's technique employs different approaches in camerawork, mise-en-scène, and narrative style from scene to scene, adopting or "stealing" different cinematic approaches from other directors such as Jean-Luc Godard and Vittorio De Sica. Jia's second film, *Platform* (2000), shot in 35 mm, was an autobiographical epic of the young post-Cultural Revolution generation. Tremendous socioeconomic changes occurred during the 1980s. The film "stage," the country's postsocialist system, reveals the replacement of Maoist culture by westernized popular culture in everyday life. *Platform* is also much more personal; Jia considers it a statement in response to his father's incomprehension of him and to generational incommunicability. *The World*, produced in 2004, was Jia Zhangke's first film that was cofinanced by the government. His three prior films were prohibited from being shown in China.

Screenplays can be censored whether or not the films were government funded. There are three steps in the Chinese censorship process, explains Jia Zhangke (2002): "First, you have to hand over your script. Then they go through your rushes, during the shooting. The last step is to watch your final product." According to the Chinese censors, there are some areas that nobody can film: prostitution, drugs, and homosexuality. Chinese characters are not even allowed to swear or reveal weakness or bad conduct. Characters are obligated to show optimism toward their own lives and to closely watch the behavior of others.

In 2004, new censorship policies were announced. Instead of needing to present a whole screenplay, it is now only necessary to get approval of a character/plot summary before starting to shoot the film. Furthermore, although it was previously the responsibility of the national Ministry of Radio, Film, and Television, now six different regional offices have the authority to approve films. Jia said,

> Originally, all of us so-called independent directors, or underground directors, were that way because the censorship apparatus was to a large degree restricting our freedom of choice. But now it looks like we'll have the chance to express ourselves freely.[11]

The struggle between freedom and censorship has defined Jia's unique film aesthetic: shooting cheap and fast in real locations, using China as the main character, and working with nonprofessional actors.

In 2001, Jia shot a digital documentary, *In Public*, and since then he has become an ardent advocate of DV. His 2002 feature film, *Unknown Pleasures*, is also a DV (later transferred to 35 mm); it originally started as a documentary project about industrial architecture. But gradually the idea to insert characters in these settings became essential for Jia. He has pursued this technique of filming fiction as documentary in his subsequent features.

According to Jia, the freedom that DV provides has enabled him to choose a space in which to wander freely and to capture the most *theatrical moments*. His exploration of cinematic style with DV images is what is most remarkable in his filmmaking production. Jia is concerned about documenting this crucial moment in Chinese history, at the same time expressing his own point of view instead of creating a reality portrait. Furthermore, rather than concentrating the whole plot on one couple's "particular" situation, the story is shown by different characters' perspectives. Jia says,

> Everybody is experiencing a process of growing up, during which [their] capacity of realizing and thinking gradually grows as well. This is what I called [the] "gap" in our life. For me it's interesting to live in such a gap [between rustic origin and urban existence].[12]

This gap is expressed in his long and slow shots of people wandering about and contemplating emptiness in front of urban scenes in the process of transformation, such as a construction site, the deserted roads that surround the park, or the empty settings such as the Arc du Triomphe in Paris, the pyramids of Egypt, or St. Mark's Square in Venice, Italy. Some critics compare these shots with that of Italian filmmaker Michelangelo Antonioni. Certainly, Jia's films are far more realistic,[13] but his fiction films can render reality more real than any apparent "optimism" that Chinese official rhetoric insists on "displaying" in contemporary China.

If fiction films are products of filmmakers' imagination and are "impressions of life," then documentaries require an open attitude to "understand life." Amazingly, this is exactly what critics and scholars perceive as central to Jia's fiction films. He is able to *incorporate* in personal and ordinary stories a *strangeness* and an understanding of Chinese people's lives that goes beyond our average perception. This *transforming world* seen by one's perspective is fully explored in Jia's most acclaimed film, *Still Life* (2006). The film tells stories of two people looking for missing partners in a town about to disappear as a result of the Three Gorges Dam flooding. Both have good and bad experiences and try to find some kind of peace. A contemporary world that concurrently brings technology and alienation is one of Jia's most cherished subjects.

One often finds in his films many references to international filmmakers such as Robert Bresson, Jean-Luc Godard, Yasujiro Ozu, Michelangelo

Antonioni, Roberto Rossellini, and others. As well, cinema is a result of an international copartnership with foreign producers, in his case especially Japanese such as Takeshi Kitano. Independent filmmakers, trapped between the limitations of the official film system and the desire for self-expression, have been searching for alternative forms of funding. His recent films were created with foreign financial support and also with the cooperation of foreign technicians, producers, and filmmakers. According to Kevin Lee, Jia's films about Chinese society are as important to Chinese culture as to cinema itself: "Jia's importance on the global cinematic stage is inextricably tied to his depiction of contemporary China, if only because Jia's China reflects global conditions and trends that affect us all."[14]

We may relate the contemporary international cinema to Gilles Deleuze's argument about the historical emergence of modern cinema. After World War II, the map of the globe was almost completely changed and many cultures were displaced from a region, culture, or nation to another. For Deleuze, Italian Neorealism (1944–1952) was the beginning of cinematographic modernity. He refers to the new image that the Italians created in the postwar era as an image that could not be understood, because the war was not logically comprehensible or intelligible. Therefore, they created something very close to their reality with nonprofessional actors and real décor but with disconnected actions, to show how illogical our lives and miseries could be.

The crisis of representation creates in cinema history the separation between the modern and the classical (narrative) of cinema in the post-World War II era. "The first things to be compromised everywhere are the linkages of situation-action, action-reaction, excitation-response . . ."[15] Classical cinema is characterized by the linkage (action) between images for the purposes of the continuity and meaning of the narrative and of representation of time. "A new kind of image is born that one can attempt to identify in the post-war American cinema, outside Hollywood."[16] Furthermore, modern cinema, which presents time directly and breaks with the contract of linkage between images, incorporates essential discontinuities and ambiguities of the real.

Intermedial Global Community

Jia Zhangke's documentary films, such as *Dong* (2006) and *Useless* (2007), create a dialogue with filmmakers' fiction films, such as *The World* (2004) and *Still Life* (2006), even making critics consider these last ones as documentary films as well. However, different factors are brought to this analysis such as the use of the DV, non-actors, real sets, and especially the contemporaneity of China's social and economic life depicted by Jia's films. In *24 City*, the filmmaker implements a more aggressive way of depicting contemporary China and its recent history. In a series of interviews, he tries to know and understand what happened to the workers in China's military industries. Among the interviewees, Jia places actors to interpret some of the testimonies. One cannot in fact distinguish between real people and the actors, except in the case of famous actresses Joan Chen and Zhao Tao. It seems that boundaries between fiction and documentary are neither that important nor matter from a filmmaker's perspective when he crosses the line between real and fictional characters and stories. In fact, the actors are depicting real stories in real locations.

With this approach to historical fact, everything seems to be improvised, and this unpretentiousness allows a precise encounter between fiction and documentary and the exploration of a distinction between present "becoming" and history. As Gilles Deleuze states, it is not an opposition between the eternal and history, but the event in its becoming escapes the history. The fact of the moment of the interview is what matters as much as a true story has been told in a real setting. Jia emphasizes and creates a possibility of making the people inhabit the screen as much as possessing their history. What history captures of the event is its execution in the state of affairs. In the same way, what the film documents is the encounter between the filmmaker and his interviewees. In that moment, they can create something historical while inventing a people that would otherwise be missing in the official history. Jia's films are questioning the historical Chinese archives as much as people's participation and place in the creation of the modern China.

"The most 'healthy' illusions fall,"[17] Deleuze says. He refers to the new image that modern cinema creates to jeopardize the classical narrative that offers us the idea of the whole. "If the people are missing, if there is no longer consciousness, evolution or revolution, it is the scheme of reversal which itself becomes impossible."[18] The characters in Jia's films try to create a place despite this gap between people's expectations and the increasing modernization of Chinese society.

The documentary approach to fiction gives Jia great liberty in his work. His films do not force one aesthetic onto another, but in a way, he is able to manage the genres to achieve a more "realistic" tone by fully exploring the characters and settings. The characters "seem unable to communicate with people in immediate physical proximity to them in any meaningful way."[19] As Jia states, they do not really understand what the modern world is like; however, they are completely integrated with "modern" habits like any other contemporary society, such as the use of cell phones, the Internet, and text messages. These media create communities with "no sense of place."[20]

They are not yet thinking like modern people. That's the main idea behind *The World* . . . You can walk from the Eiffel Tower to the Pyramids with ease. You can visit different countries without a passport or a visa. It gives the impression that the whole world has become a global village.[21]

What do we understand in Jia's ideas regarding the conceptions of globalization and the world?

For Jia, the term world[22] does not mean much; it is more a convention, especially for people who cannot rely any more on their own environment, and globalization is only a "small village." These notions are apparent in Jia's films, and maybe because of that he incorporates in *The World* a foreign character, the Russian girl who was not able to speak Chinese. In her conversations with Tao, the Chinese dancer, they do not speak a word of one another's language, though they share thoughts and gestures of mutual recognition and comprehension. Jia maintains that even when we do not come from the same city or culture or speak the same language, we share basic human feelings of longing, sadness, and hope. These are all feelings that we mutually understand.

Everything in *The World* seems to be improvised, enabling Jia to explore freely the intermediality between cinema and video discourses. The intermediality results from the encounter of media or meaning or sign systems within a single medium. The objective of intermediality is to question existing media forms by the encounter of various media (radio, TV, film, and also theatre, literature, painting, music, etc.) within a single media, creating a third discourse. In this way, intermediality shows a media crisis that one single medium is no longer able to express. Intermediality evokes tensional differences between media (a medium is always in relationship to another medium), modes (text, image, and sound), and frames (interactions of different screens).

Jia states,

> We're living in a globalized age, in a world saturated by mass media, in an international city, as it were. But despite all that, the problems we're facing are our own problems. So these landscapes are intimately related to what's going on in the film.[23]

The idea of globalization seems to approach a translation task asking: should we translate a work literally or completely? It means that what defines global culture products is their foreignness (distance) or seamlessness (proximity).

For Arjun Appadurai, societies are living a new form of shared experience through imagination:

> The image (mechanically produced), the imagined (community in Anderson's sense), and the imaginary (constructed landscape of collective aspirations)—these are all terms which direct us to something critical and new in global cultural processes: *the imagination as a social practice.*[24]

Appadurai sees the globe as crosscut by fluxes that he calls "scapes," that shape the constantly changing worlds of the new global landscape. How should this landscape be conceived in cinema? How can we understand intercultural cinema in the age of globalization? What exactly is a global community—is the distance so close that people become indifferent to it?

Films are showing, through this evolution of the world, that the complexity of the subject requires a complexity of cinematic forms and narratives: video and cinema, and also through flash animation, a virtual version of the globe. This virtuality is reinforced by intermediality in the film, with its convergence of DV, cinema, and animation of the main characters revealing their inner world or yet their electronic "avatar" personas: those that can control and fully exist in a small-scale dimension of the globe, completely alienated from the rest of the world. In this sense, Jia agrees with Appadurai that we share and live in another social practice, that of the imagination.

Conclusion: Globalization versus Mondialisation

Decentralization in China and globalization of film production and film audiences have challenged Chinese filmmakers to deal with these new problems while permitting them to explore their own subjectivity. Jia relies on the devices of DV, cinema aesthetic, and subtitles to produce his films. These also enable him to globally circulate his films while avoiding any kind of censorship.

The film *The World* manages to recreate the *perfection* of the cinema analogy by the imperfect *numerical-pixel* images of the video. Jia also accomplishes this on another level by exploring even more the imaginative, virtual wandering and, by animation, the dematerialization of the characters and of the globe giving them a new dimensional degree.

Jean-Luc Nancy, in his book *The Creation of the World or Globalization,*[25] distinguished the English term *globalization* from the French one *mondialisation*. Although *mondialisation* preserves something untranslatable, *globalization* has already translated everything in a global idiom. In both ideas, those differ in many aspects. It is in those differences that a definition for the word "world" comes out. Nancy argues that "a world is a totality of meaning," which applies to the word globalization that "has already translated everything in a global idiom," whereas *mondialisation* (world-forming) does not have such a set-in-stone meaning but leaves a "space of possible meaning."[26] The problem with a word such as globalization is that it encompasses so much and has already given a set of definitions for what it does entail, whereas *mondialisation* "would rather evoke an expanding process throughout the expanse of the world of human beings, cultures, and nations."[27] Despite the untranslatability of these terms, the question remains the same: *Can what is called "globalization" give rise to a world, or its contrary?* This question raises a series of possibilities of thinking of Jia's film in the way the filmmaker represents his idea of globalization and how his films have circulated globally in a dynamic way, allowing audiences all over the world to celebrate his aesthetics and his subjects' approaches, more freely than within Chinese territory. In *The World*, Jia is concerned not just with representing the globalization (world circulation) of his work but also with a consciousness—the awareness and knowledge—of globalization itself.

Endnotes

1. Lo Kwai-Cheung, *Chinese Face/Off: Transnational Popular Culture of Hong Kong* (Urbana: University of Illinois Press, 2005), 46.
2. Ibid.
3. Hamid Naficy, "Epistolarity and Textuality in Accented Films," in *Subtitles on the Foreignness of Film*, ed. Atom Egoyan and Ian Balfour (Cambridge/London: MIT Press, 2004), 29.
4. The critic Roger Ebert makes an observation in his film review of *The World* regarding the last sequence:

   > After the screening, I rode down on the elevator with the great film critic Jonathan Rosenbaum. 'I've seen it five times,' he said. 'It's one of my favorite films. I still don't understand the ending.' I was not only afraid to ask him what he didn't understand about the ending, I was afraid to ask him what he thought the ending was. In a sense, *The World* is about a story that never really begins.
   >
   > (*Chicago Sun-Times*, July 29, 2005)

5. In the last scene of the film, Taisheng and Tao are next to each other as in a cocoon (wrapped in blankets), an image that approaches the Chinese legend of Lian Shango and Zhu Yingtai, the *Butterfly Lovers*, set in ancient China in the Eastern Jin Dynasty (265–420). Despite the lovers not being able to live together, they are reborn as butterflies for eternity.
6. David MacDougall, *Transcultural Cinema* (Princeton, NJ: Princeton University Press, 1998), 171.
7. Yiman Wang, "The Amateur's Lightning Rod: DV Documentary in Postsocialist China," *Film Quarterly* 58, no. 4 (2005): 16–26.
8. This had to do with the fact [that] young filmmakers eventually obtained their access to filmmaking as medium of art. Filmmaking formerly was an officially monopolized art . . . Thanks to DV, normal people obtained their access to filmmaking and a new generation of filmmakers came into being.

   Jia Zhangke in Yi Sicheng, "A Window to Our Times: China's Independent Film since the Late 1990's" (PhD diss., Kiel University, 2006), 79.

9. Yingjin Zhang, "Styles, Subjects and Special Points of View: A Study of Contemporary Chinese Independent Documentary," *New Cinemas: Journal of Contemporary Film* 2, no. 2 (2004): 2.

10. Ibid., 3.

11.   I think the biggest change has been that the pressure is greatly reduced . . . Most of my earlier films were shot within two to three weeks, 21 days or so. But this time [*The World*, 2004] I was shooting for eight weeks and so had a lot of time to think things over. My last film [*Unknown Pleasures*, 2002] was shot in only 19 days, because at that time finances were very tight.

Jia Zhangke in Valerie Jaffee, "An Interview with Jia Zhangke," in *Senses of Cinema* (June 2004), http://www.sensesofcinema.com/2004/feature-articles/jia_zhangke (accessed January 14, 2011).

12. Yi Sicheng, "A Window to Our Times: China's Independent Film since the Late 1990's" (PhD diss., Kiel University, 2006), 79.

13.   China looks like a modern country, but if you look underneath the surface, it isn't . . . I take everything very slowly so that I can make sense of things. The real China is a mess, and it takes a measured approach to make it understandable. On the poster for *The World* in China, it says, We have become too fast. We have lost the art of being slow.

Jia Zhangke in Richard James Havis, "Illusory Worlds: An Interview with Jia Zhangke," *Cineaste* Fall (2005): 59.

14. Kevin Lee, "Jia Zhang-Ke," *Senses of Cinema*, http://www.sensesofcinema.com/2003/great-directors/jia/ (accessed January 14, 2011).

15. Gilles Deleuze, *Cinema 1: The Movement Image* (Minneapolis: University of Minnesota Press, 1986), 206.

16. Ibid., 207.

17. Ibid.

18. Ibid., 208.

19. Jonathan Rosenbaum, "Workers' Playtime," *Sight & Sound*, 16, no. 9 (2005): 92.

20. Arjun Appadurai, "Disjuncture and Difference in the Global Cultural Economy," in *Media and Cultural Studies: Keyworks*, ed. Meenakshi Gigi Durham and Douglas Kellner (Malden, MA: Blackwell Publishers, 2006), 586.

21. Jia Zhangke in Havis, "Illusory Worlds," 59.

22. "My opinion is that there's no such thing as the so-called "world." People can only see their own lives . . . , and our impressions of the world are just our impressions of the environment we live in." Jia Zhangke in Jaffee, "An Interview with Jia Zhangke."

23. Ibid.

24. Appadurai, "Disjuncture and Difference," 587.

25. Jean-Luc Nancy, *The Creation of the World or Globalization* (Albany: State University of New York Press, 2007).

26. Ibid., 28.

27. Ibid.

CHAPTER 14

Women Seeking Women

*Identity Constructions in German and
Taiwanese Online Personal Ads*

MATTHEW HEINZ AND HSIN-I CHENG

Chapter Description

With public access to the Internet, there came, in nations that had the
needed technological resources and a widely literate population, online
matchmaking. Online matchmaking has created, quite rapidly, an intrigu-
ing new way of somewhat safely meeting other people for the purposes of
correspondence, friendship, travel companionship, casual sex, or lifelong
committed relationships. For lesbian, gay, bisexual, transgender, and
queer (LGBTQ) people, the World Wide Web (where accessible) has dras-
tically changed communication and identity-related practices and perceptions; seeking for partners online is no exception. Personal ads can be
perceived as a discourse that encourages idiosyncratic linguistic expressions and representations, which are simultaneously molded by salient
social and cultural values. This chapter offers insights about the locality
and universality of global LGBTQ discourse as manifested in personal
ads of women seeking women posted on Web sites originating in
Germany and Taiwan.

* * *

Introduction

Millions of people visit matchmaking sites,[1] and the trend shows no signs of slowing down today. Both free usage and paid subscriptions of dating sites increased through 2009; in the United States, an estimated 20 million of 100 million single people visited online dating sites.[2] Online matchmaking has emerged as a significant Internet-based business activity;[3] the reliance on online personal ads and Internet dating may increase, rather than decrease or stay constant, with increasing age of Web users.[4] Researchers routinely examine online dating processes[5] and online community building[6] but discourse analyses of gender ideologies in digital media remain rare.[7]

The use of the Internet to meet others has received both substantial hype and substantial criticism. Several features of online matchmaking distinguish the process fundamentally from other forms of matchmaking, particularly the placement of personal ads in classified sections of print media; other aspects of online matchmaking appear mostly an adaptation of more traditional processes to a new medium. Advantages of online matchmaking include relative ease of access, reduced cost, increased information about the other person, speed, and increased confidentiality. On the other hand, the possibility of concealing one's real identity has, in instances, resulted in dangerous situations for trusting individuals. The commonplace exploitation of lesbian sexual practices often leads to multiple messages from heterosexual men, frequently posing as lesbians. Searching for "lesbian" sites frequently "traps" the Web user in pornographic sites or search engines geared at heterosexual men. The commercial ability to track Web site access often leads to an onslaught of electronic commercial solicitation. Locally and nationally varying degrees of the illegality of pornography pose new challenges for the users and law enforcement. Government surveillance and commercial tracking of Web site use create potential threats or inconvenience for the users. To address such negative aspects, some sites have affiliated themselves with credible organizations or businesses. Others require a higher degree of private, verifiable information to gain access to the site. Some services charge fees; commercial sites have implemented strict legal guidelines for posting and use of their sites.

Relatively few communication scholars have examined identity presentations of individuals searching online for dates or romantic relationships,[8] especially when it comes to cross-cultural critical examinations. The theoretical framework of critical attitude formulated by Henrik Bang and Anders Esmark[9] guides this study. Bang and Esmark advocate for the merits of critical attitude, rather than traditional critical theory, in examinations of the public sphere. Although critical theory tends to conceive of a global public sphere as a democratic ideal, critical attitude tends to work from the notion of various, contingent, historical publics. This study approaches freely accessible online personal ads as a specific section of the public sphere. Critically analyzing these ads may assist with discerning individual, social, and cultural ideology formations.[10] According to Marti Gonzales and Sarah Meyers,[11] personal ads enable advertisers to represent themselves with agency and to specify a desired respondent, a finding that speaks to the need for more nuanced understandings of public discourse.[12] In the tradition of discourse analyses focusing on the centrality of language,[13] this study offers insight into the ways in which personal online ads construct understandings of self. Altogether, this analysis is based on 150 German ads and 150 Taiwanese ads posted by women seeking women. The types of relationship sought via these ads vary strongly. The sites were first visited and analyzed in 2003 and then again in 2007 and 2009. The personal ads were posted on matchmaking sites yielded by a variety of common Internet search engines such as Google, Yahoo, and Netscape and the keywords: *lesbisch, Sie Sucht Sie*, and *Frauenliebe* (*lesbian, she searching for her,* and *love of women*, respectively) for the German ads and *wan shan jiao yo* (*seeking friendship online*) for the Taiwanese ads. Over the time span of the study, some of the sites went defunct and some changed terms of access. Because of ethical considerations, only online personal ads that were publicly accessible, without registration, were examined.

Women Seeking Women Online in Germany

A drastic change, as measured from the starting point of post-World War II Germany, began occurring in the mid-1980s in Germany. Gay and lesbian community groups, youth groups, and political action committees were formed then, mostly in metro areas in then-West Germany. Organizing around HIV/AIDS education was one of the critical needs driving such organizing. By the early 1990s, many of these groups had successfully founded community centers. By the mid-1990s, such safe spaces were extended into the online environment, originally as a local adaptation of U.S. gay rights discourse, including its symbols, icons, and historical references. Within less than one generation, the discursive construction of lesbian, gay, bisexual, transgender, and queer (LGBTQ) identities radically changed in Germany. This transformation has been affected by and manifested itself in changes in understandings of self, external forms of self-representation, access, and availability of computer-mediated communication, and legislative changes resulting from regional, national, European, and worldwide equal rights lobbying. Hundreds of Web sites created by and aimed at LGBTQ people in small or large German communities exist today. Similar to heterosexual ad online services, accessibility varies. Often, a public shorter version of the personal ads is available to the nonregistered site visitor. In some instances, registration requires payment of a fee; in other instances, registration requires disclosing verifiable personal information, typically including first name and last name, age, postal code, a verifiable e-mail account, and sometimes a bank account number, passport, or national identity number. Registering visitors create a handle and password; registering from outside Germany or the European Union may be difficult or impossible. For this study, personal ads posted on the following Web sites were examined: www01.eurogay.de/kontakte/date, www.susi.de/cgi-bin/art/ba5b/#0, single.tiscali.de/p/kontakte/anzeigen, www.siegessaule.de/interaktiv/anzeigen, www.single-kontaktanzeigen.org, and gay.szene.de. (The tiscali and gay.szene.de websites are no longer active as of January 15, 2011.) Of these, Eurogay has been one of the most prominent gay online portals. Between 2003 and 2007, a search for personal ads on the Eurogay Web site led the visitor to an entry page that organized the personal ad entries and searches by postal code, a common way of organization of German personal online ads. The listings are typically arranged in chronological order beginning with the current day and, in descending order, the time of the day. Visitors selected personal ad entries based on a one-line teaser or headline that was hyperlinked to the actual ad text. Most personal ads were between 5 and 10 lines long and gave the original post date and time. Visitors had the choice of replying in public or in private. If public responses had been entered, they were listed by poster, date, and time below the personal ad. In 2003, visitors could select "Matchmaking" from the main menu, which led to a page detailing one's search criteria. By clicking on a hyperlink, visitors could learn more about the process, which was referred to as *Spielregeln* ("rules of the game"), a word choice indicative of the underlying self-representation of the site. The words "Sex und Fun" appeared frequently, and the photo illustrations showed people who were laughing, smirking, grinning, or smiling. This is noteworthy because the German unmarked facial expression does not include a smile. Visitors could mark one or several of the following search check boxes: gay (male) and single; gay (male) and committed; lesbian and single; lesbian and committed; bisexual and single, male; bisexual and single, female; gay male couple (2 men); lesbian couple (2 women); group (male); group (female); and group (mixed).

Site users then created a profile (*Steckbrief*) indicating the type of relationship they were interested in from the following options: relationship, friendship, e-mail/chat, sex as a couple, sex with others or in groups, and other activities. Optional self-descriptions included postal code, city, physical appearance, appearance (no entry, average, conservative, alternative, feminine, leather, athletic, fashionable, punk, or skin), age range, body height range, hair color, smoking status, sexual orientation, out status, role (no entry, active, passive, flexible, don't want to tell), safe sex practices, body hair, breasts/penis size, religion, and zodiac. This site required the most detailed personal information and offered the most specific matching service of all the sites reviewed. Between 2003 and 2009, the portal changed organization and design several times, evolving into a medium that is primarily geared at men and emphasizes media and product consumption. This trend occurred alongside the trend of the emergence of reputable online matchmaking organizations that specialize in lesbian long-term partnership connections. Germany's largest online commercial matchmaking site for long-term relationships is operated by Parship.[14] The site has several million users. The affiliated site for women seeking women[15] had more than 100,000 members in March 2007.[16] This matchmaking enterprise employs psychologists to create and evaluate online personality profiles, suggest matches, and offer telephone counseling. Three of the other sites adopted more restrictive personal ad access regulations or went defunct by 2009. Clearly, the preferred online personal posting for women seeking women for long-term, monogamous relationships has shifted from public community portals to commercially operated, gated sites.

The analysis reveals a multitude of rhetorical strategies employed, a wide diversity of goals, and a range of self-understandings reflected and created. These ads share the documented discursive features of print personal ads, such as simplified grammar, fewer personal pronouns, a high degree of linguistic creativity, and decreased adherence to spelling conventions to an extent, but, in distinction from print personal ads, they are not characterized by generic, less specific vocabularies, or fewer personal pronouns. Both the Web site formatting and the texts of the personal ads present the pursuit of various relationship constellations as parallel. In other words, the goals of flirting, finding friends, finding a lifetime companion, securing a one-night stand, initiating a secret affair, initiating an open affair, or locating a travel or sports companion are all equally legitimized. Not much different from the handles selected by heterosexual German women, e-mail addresses from women seeking women often draw from Internet World English, for example, *Moonlight, angeldream, B4dGirl, IndigoGirl, once-morewithfeeling, sweety,* and *raining-blues,* or fairly literal translations from German, for example, *Bikewitch, Sunheart.* The relative frequency of anglicized handles decreased between 2003 and 2009, with a majority of handles by then consisting of German words, or first name variations, or first name variations with numeric codes. In contrast to language used by men seeking men, ads by women seeking women rarely contained terms associated with the American English-driven LGBTQ speech register (i.e., *GAYspeedy*). The German personal ads frequently list the poster's home phone number on a publicly accessible site or state that texting is preferred. Some sites make reference to criminal prosecution, possible under German law, for men posing as women on gender-gated Web sites.

Normativity over Identification

These ads portray the engagement in same-sex sexual activity as not necessarily a matter of sexual-political identification. They often offer details about previous or concurrent relationships, whether lesbian, straight, or bisexual. Some posters are involved in marital or nonmarital heterosexual relationships that they intend to continue, and the purpose of posting ads is described as seeking a secret lesbian affair, exploring new sexual practices, or initiating lesbian sexual relationships in which the poster's male partner would observe or participate in the sexual activity. Although some women describe themselves or their desired match as "*eher maskulin*" (of a more masculine nature), there are no other expressions of role play, butch, or stonebutch sexualities. A greater number of personal ads stress desired attributes of feminine performance in the match, often by those who identified as feminine as well. The bulk of the ads do not contain information about femininity or masculinity but about one's own and the desired partner's personality traits, values, and interests. A common thread in personal ads, online or off-line, regardless of orientation, is the theme of loneliness. Notably absent from the ads included in this study are the self-representations of discrimination, victimization, perceived marginalization, or politically constructed understandings of sexual orientation. However, for lesbian ads, one particular form of marginalization is explicitly addressed: the presence of *fakes* among the posters and the respondents. Although there are essentially no female posters on the men-seeking-men sites, a number of male posters appear on the women-seeking-women site, despite webspinner's notices that inappropriate posts will be immediately removed. Some fake posts offer hyperlinks to lesbian porn sites geared at heterosexual men. The personal ads of women often contain strong language about potential fake responses, such as "men and couples don't need to respond," "no fakes," and "telephone check required."

Expressing Sincerity through Discursive Strategies

Rhetorical strategies employed in these personal ads vary, from one-line teasers to elaborated self-descriptions, to ads with photos of the poster, ads with cartoon illustration, ads with photos of models, and to poetry. Ethnicity, culture, and linguistic or national origin is only peripherally mentioned and only in self-description—a finding similar to that of a study examining Romanian men's personal ads online[17]—but regional location is an overriding criterion for posting and accepting responses. The provision of real weight, real height, real regional identifications, real age, and, in many instances, photos that stress a natural (i.e., nonglossy) look cocreates the discursive motif of sincerity. In a similar vein, not being too thin emerges as a positive physical characteristic and is constructed as a desirable trait. The strategy of self-deprecation or understatement is employed in various ways, for example, "nicht hässlich" (not ugly), "beziehungsgeschädigt" (relationally damaged), or "nicht schlank" (not thin). Many ads reference online space as a real spatial location and directly address, by the use of the second person, others who might be located in this space, for example, "Where are you?" "Somebody has to be here," "Why don't you respond?" and so on. In contrast to the Taiwanese ads, the German ads are marked by a complete absence of information regarding educational status, social class, income, and occupation. Smoking habits are sometimes indicated or requested; references to sexually transmitted diseases are entirely absent. The overriding quality stressed is sincerity. A marked difference in the discourses of 2003 and 2007–2009 is the increasingly frequent and positive mentioning of children, both by women who are mothers and by women seeking others who have children. Also increasing in this time period is the visibility of bisexuality, which is significant since the creation and posting of personal ads by bisexual women, in any medium, has received scant scholarly attention.[18] Enjoyment of mothering roles, monogamy, and bisexuality were traditionally anathema in German lesbian communities into the 1990s; the positive or neutral portrayal of these reflects a significant shift.

Women Seeking Women Online in Taiwan

Queer studies is one of the most transnational and multifaceted areas for cultural research in Taiwan.[19] Gay/lesbian issues were promoted within mass media around the late 1980s. During the mid-1990s, queer movements for political equality started in Taiwan with burgeoning terminologies such as "*Tongzhi*" and "queer."[20] Queers refer to "*tongzhi*" which means "comrades" in Chinese. As Yin-Kun Chang explains, *tong* means "the same" and *zhi* refers to "will, ideal, and orientation"—the term denotes a common desire for a shared struggle.[21] Queer activism proliferated in the elite realm of Taiwanese society and led to energetic and playful linguistic identifications.[22]

In addition, issues on (in)visibility have attracted much examination. Chang stresses the significance of the Internet in Taiwanese *tongzhi* movements in which boundaries between the private/public, reality/fiction, and individual/community are blurred.[23] The stigma of being identified as "lesbigay" has decreased significantly; a Web site on *tongzhi* life in Taiwan claims that "there is hardly an Asian country that has come out more than Taiwan."[24] However, the queer movement remains characterized by the comparative invisibility of its members.[25] Despite increased public exposure, the queer community remains a marginalized group facing potential consequences for coming out. Various localized strategies (e.g., wearing masks in demonstrations) and transnational connections (e.g., creating a global Chinese *tongzhi* network) are practiced.[26] Wearing a mask has become a unique characteristic of Taiwanese queer movements. It fulfills the comrades' desire of representing themselves to the public in a safe way. Cheng suggests that the Internet has served as a similar type of mask since the mid-1990s. The Internet has provided the comrades a safe meeting space[27] and a source of information about the queer community;[28] it has also allowed an assertive presence in the public. Although much has been written on *tongzhi* issues, studies on online relationship initiation are rare. The sites examined were "*Nu Tong Zhi Leow Tian Hseen*" (Lesbians' Chat Room), http://match.f1.com.tw/?MID=10001, and PChome *Gio You* (PChome Make-Friends), http://love.pchome.com.tw. The site "Lesbians' Chat Room" is one of the largest sites with more than 10,000 members. The homepage has an image of two overlapping hearts, on a pink and red pastel background, appearing next to the Chinese characters 交友 (make friends). The page for "*Tongzhi* friendship" on the "PChome Make-Friends" site has an image of a bird coming out of a cage toward a green apple. It has multiple soft colors such as pink, blue, green, and gray. Both sites have areas for personal information such as age, educational background, salary, and residential condition. Since 2003, there has been an obvious trend to include pictures and links to personal Web pages. Such a practice may indicate the more open atmosphere for the Taiwanese *tong-zhi* community and/or much increased technological convergence. Another feature new in 2009 is the selection of "Add to my favorite list," "Add to the Blacklist," "Message board," or "Diary." In addition, the PChome site allows viewers to respond to the advertiser. These practices create an immediate and interactive atmosphere. The analysis led to identification of three key discursive features: nickname selections, framing the self, and description of the preferred partnership.

Nickname Selection as Identification

A unique nickname functions as an attention getter. Nicknames construct and reinforce first impressions in terms of personality and information such as age and locations. For example, 寂寞空氣裡面缺氧~P (Short of Oxygen in the Lonesome Air~P) and 角落灰塵 (Dust at the Corner) express their sense of loss through poetic nicknames. Handles such as 保溫杯 (A Thermo Cup), 外表是公主的王子 (A Prince with a Princess' Appearance), and 擁有天使翅膀ㄉ惡魔 (The Devil Owns Wings of an Angel) metaphorically portray the personalities of the advertisers. Whether intended or not, these nicknames project a distinct individuality and are more dominant in the 2007 and 2009 ads. In the same time frame, another phenomenon emerges—usage of the "Martian language"—the incorporation of unintelligible Mandarin phonetic or Japanese symbols as part of one's nickname [e.g., Ω薄荷愛上貓Ω (Ω Mint Falls in Love with Cats Ω]. Martian language is popular among Taiwanese youth and is often ambiguous. Martian language may include misuse of correct characters, incorporation of pronounced English, Japanese, or phonetic symbols, combination of two words into one or similar pronunciation (e.g., 3Q for "Thank you"), and substituting characters with symbols (i.e., "↓" instead of "xia" which can mean either "down" or "scare"). As Liou points out, linguistic playfulness is a significant characteristic in queer literature.[29] The combination of linguistic performance and technology creates a unique local practice.

Self-Description as Identification

In 2003, most comrades indicated their sexual preferences as "T" (i.e., the traditional masculine party) or "P" (i.e., the female party). These codes specify the desired partner's sexual preference and project the type of (sexual) relationships she wishes to form. Most lesbians only designate themselves as T/P or both but rarely state that they would only date T or P in 2003. This practice remains visible yet much less prevalent in 2007. Being T or P is instead framed as something that is "naturally born" rather than a "personal choice." Several advertisers stated "I was born from my mother as a T" and "Although my appearance is unlike a T, I have T's blood stream." These descriptions indicate that the heterosexual paradigm remains dominant in ads in which looking for a T who is "clean . . . but is very Man" and for a P having "long hair with big eyes" is commonly announced. This convention is slightly changed in 2009 with terms such as 第三性 (The Third Sex) and 變性慾者 (Transvestite) being used. This suggests that the binary and stabilized sexes are being subverted although the dichotomy of "P" and "T" remains in place. Scholars have traced the development of "T" and "P" roles back to the 1950s and point out that this phenomenon, although unique in Taiwanese society, simultaneously subverts and furthers the binary gender roles in lesbian romances.[30] Such traditional divisions were challenged in some of the recent ads, as in the following example:

不分 不分 不分
WHY 一定要分 T or P
推：The L WoRd 超讚美國拉子影集 . . .
最大的願望：

1-可以跟我全部的好朋友來張大合照
2-組一個Les社區.大家可以住一起

No difference No difference No difference
Why must we differ T or [from] P
Recommend: The L Word [is] a superb American Les soap . . .
[My] Biggest wish:
1. have a group picture with all my close friends
2. organize a Les [nickname for lesbian] community for everyone to
live together

The advertiser laments the practice of categorization in her self-description and defies any stereotypical confinement of lesbian identity. She embraces the malleable and overlapping fluidity of identity. Finally, ~CHIAO~ bridges the contesting attitude through her desire to create a Taiwanese lesbian community; a vision seems to be partially influenced by the U.S. television series "The L Word." Inclusion is the recurrent theme here as she promotes linguistic and behavioral strategies for a more encompassing environment for solidarity. The Taiwanese queer community has strived for localizing its own identity while aligning with global movements.[31] ~CHIAO~'s longing for some sort of collective understanding is greatly shared by other comrades where statements such as "I wish to find some insiders [within the lesbian community] to share daily activities with" and "It is pathetic that there are so few les friends around me" repeatedly appear in all years.

Between 2003 and 2009, the ads are poetic and philosophical as in the following 2003 excerpt: "When it is the right time to meet the right person, it will bring forever happiness! When it is the right time to meet the wrong person, it will bring heartbreak!" The ad demonstrates the language game in which the same characters can be (re)organized in making new meanings to express intricate emotions. Such a practice remains visible in the 2007 and 2009 ads. Although Taiwanese online personal ads demonstrate an appreciation for language play, they ironically reflect distrust in language. These ads cast doubt in words as in the following example: "I am myself, I don't want to be confined by words!" Overlooking or purposefully down-playing positive self-descriptions indicates a way of protesting consumerism and resisting marketization through overly positive self-representation.[32]

Emphasis on Compatibility as Identification

Although the Taiwanese queer community seems to be influenced by global, particularly western, ideologies, some traditions such as the belief in *yuan* remains apparent in 2003 ads, for example, "am waiting for you who has *yuan* with me to call!!!!" and "having *yuan* is more important." As a philosophical concept, *yuan* connotes the transient and whimsical life in which human beings exist.[33] These ads suggest that holding on to the faith of *yuan* would bring lovers together. One salient phenomenon in the 2007 and 2009 ads is the emphasis on "feeling" as a way to determine the quality of the relationship. Statements such as "All depends on feeling!" and "Feeling is the most important" are the frequent response when asked to describe "ideal partner." The switch from awaiting *yuan* to rely on "feeling" indicates a more empowered position. Instead of waiting for *yuan* to arrive, the advertiser is keen to self-determine her feelings. Taiwanese lesbians expect themselves to have more control in their relationships and in their lives as this excerpt shows: "No men please! [I am] super individualistic, super hot temper." As a married female comrade explains, "Can a princess only turn into one when she meets a prince? Then I'll construct a castle for myself to complete the dream of becoming a 'princess'!" Many of the advertisements express their dissatisfaction of being harassed by heterosexual people; these ads exemplify the interwoven ideologies of feminism and queer politics at a local level.[34]

Conclusion

This analysis identifies dominant discourse practices and understandings of self embraced by these communities as well as the environment in which they take place. In addition to obvious linguistic differences, some marked differences emerge. The Taiwanese women seeking women online in this study are young, and their online discursive practices reflect their youth and technological proficiency. The German women seeking women included in this study tend to span across generations. The Taiwanese discourse speaks to the dominance of, and resistance to, heterosexism; the German discourse does so rarely. This is not to suggest that the German cultural context operates beyond heterosexism; rather, it suggests that sufficient political change and visibility have occurred to the degree that resistance no longer dominates the discourse in these ads of women seeking women. This is a significant change from personal ads of women seeking women just one or two decades ago. The analogous change has occurred in the perspective of researchers analyzing such ads, who just a decade or two ago approached such ads expecting to find discourses of feminism, counterhegemony, and resistance to beauty norms.[35] Resistance to beauty norms is still prominent, but rather than being characterized by a complete absence of references to physical attributes,[36] the German personal ads often contain explicit references to beauty standards that contrast those presented as desirable in commodity culture. Such ads either, somewhat defiantly, self-describe posters as "round," "voluptuous," and "soft" or describe such qualities as desired in others. The connections between linguistic practice and social practice, perhaps most evident in the use of Martian language by Taiwanese women, point to the significance of symbols, whether visual or textual, in the understanding of one's own sexuality.

Both Taiwanese and German women seeking women in these ads defy challenges to defend, justify, or explain the nature of their sexual orientation. They present it as taken for granted (particularly in the German ads), biologically based (particularly in the Taiwanese ads), and not subject to the other's interpretations (both German and Taiwanese ads). This discursive strategy constructs, in essence, a bridge between both discourses and appears conceptually related to a continuously evolving and strengthening global LGBTQ human rights discourse that eschews marginalization. LGBTQ human rights struggles have taken on a central role in global human rights discourse seeking to reconcile culture, identities, and rights. This study lends empirical evidence to this argument. The German and Taiwanese discourses of women seeking women online are culturally distinct and yet clearly could not function as presented in the public sphere without the larger context of a global LGBTQ human rights discourse manifested on the Internet. Jakob Linaa Jensen suggests that scholars must reconceptualize the public sphere in regard to place and function;[37] he points to the futility of clearly delineating boundaries between private and public spaces and the blurring of public space and public sphere. Extending that argument, Jensen argues that the public sphere is not at its most vibrant in either physical settings or citizen mindsets: "it is in the interplay between physical space and social constructions and actions amongst individuals. In short, the public sphere consists of social practices." Whether in Taiwan or in Germany, the personal ads women seeking women post online constitute social practices that offer insight into localized understandings of self, sexuality, and relational priorities amidst the universal search for a partner.

Endnotes

1. Patti M. Valkenburg and Jochen Peter, "Who Visits Online Dating Sites? Exploring Some Characteristics of Online Daters," *CyberPsychology & Behavior* 10, no. 6 (2007): 849.
2. Marissa Miley, "Dating Sites Still Attracting Users," *Advertising Age*, March 2009, 8.
3. Adam Arvidsson, "'Quality Singles': Internet Dating and the Work of Fantasy," *New Media & Society* 8, no. 4 (2006): 671.
4. Robert J. Stephure, Susan D. Boon, Stacey L. MacKinnon, and Vicki L. Deveau, "Internet Initiated Relationships: Associations Between Age and Involvement in Online Dating," *Journal of Computer-Mediated Communication* 14, no. 3 (2009): 658–9.
5. Jimmie Manning, review of *Double Click: Romance and Commitment Among Online Couples*, by A. J. Baker, *The Review of Communication* 7, no. 4 (2007): 430.

6. Jan Fernback, "Beyond the Diluted Community Concept: A Symbolic Interactionist Perspective on Online Social Relations," *New Media & Society* 9, no. 1 (2007): 49.

7. Amber Luce, review of *The Web: Social Control in a Lesbian Community*, by Christine M. Robinson, *Women's Studies in Communication* 32, no. 2 (2009): 255.

8. Valkenburg and Peter, "Who Visits," 849.

9. Henrik Bang and Anders Esmark, eds. *New Public With/out Democracy* (Frederiksberg: Samfundslitteratur, 2008), 33.

10. Rodney H. Jones, "'Potato Seeking Rice': Language, Culture, and Identity in Gay Personal Ads in Hong Kong," *International Journal of the Sociology of Language* 143 (2000): 35.

11. Marti H. Gonzales and Sarah A. Meyers, "'Your Mother Would Like Me': Self-presentation in the Personal Ads of Heterosexual and Homosexual Men and Women," *Personality and Social Psychology Bulletin* 19, no. 2 (1993): 131–42.

12. Jonathan Alexander, "Introduction to the Special Issue: Queer Webs: Representations of LGBT People and Communities on the World Wide Web," *International Journal of Sexuality and Gender Studies* 7, no. 2/3 (2002): 81.

13. Kirill Postoutenko, "Between 'I' and 'We': Studying the Grammar of Social Identity in Europe (1900–1950)," *Journal of Language and Politics* 8, no. 2 (2009): 200.

14. http://www.parship.de.

15. http://eurogay-girls.parship.de.

16. Now http://girls.parship.de.

17. Sebastian E. Bartos, Voon Chin Phua, and Erin Avery, "Differences in Romanian Men's Online Personals by Sexualities," *The Journal of Men's Studies* 7, no. 2 (2009): 154.

18. Christine A. Smith and Shannon Stillman, "What Do Women Want? The Effects of Gender and Sexual Orientation on the Desirability of Physical Attributes in the Personal Ads of Women," *Sex Roles* 46, no. 9/10 (2002): 338.

19. Fran Martin, *Situating Sexualities: Queer Representation in Taiwanese Fiction, Film and Public Culture* (Hong Kong: Hong Kong University Press, 2003), 94–100.

20. Antonia Chao, "A Reflection Upon Taiwan's Queer Studies: From a Viewpoint of Cultural Production and Reproduction," *Taiwan: A Radical Quarterly in Social Studies* 38 (2000): 210–17; Liang-ya Liou, "Queer Theory and Politics in Taiwan: The Cultural Translation and (Re)Production of Queerness in and Beyond Taiwan Lesbian/Gay/Queer Activism," *NTU Studies in Language and Literature* 123, no. 14 (2005): 125–33.

21. Yin-Kun Chang, "The Gay Right Movement in the Internet: Is It Possible or Not?" *Journal of Cyber Culture and Informational Technology* 4 (2003): 58.

22. Liang-ya Liou, "Queer Theory," 139–44.

23. Ming-hui Cheng, "The Internal and Oversea Lesbian Web Sites and the Trans-territorial Identity," *Cities and Design* 5/6 (1998): 203–8.

24. http://www.globalgayz.com/country/Taiwan/view/TWN/gay-taiwan-loving-and-living-gay-in-taiwan-the-up-side-part-1.

25. Fran Martin, *Situating Sexualities*, 223.

26. John N. Erni and Anthony Spires, "The Formation of a Queer-Imagined Community in Post-Martial Law Taiwan," in *Asian Media Studies: Politics of Subjectivities*, ed. John N. Erni and Anthony Spires (UK: Blackwell Publishing, 2005), 225–52.

27. Ming-hui Cheng, "The Internal," 204–8.

28. Chien Yo and Tong Jakob Linaa Jensen, "The Internet Omnopticon," in *New Publics With/out Democracy*, ed. Henrik Bang and Anders Esmark (Frederiksberg: Samfundslitteratur, 2007), 351; Yo Chien "Tongxinglian Gee Doo Too U Wan Lu Go Ton [Homosexual Christians and Internet Communication]," *Economic, Society, and Communication* 73 (2002): 114–16.

29. Liang-ya Liou, "Queer Theory," 130.

30. Jia-shin Gian, "Taiwanese Lesbians' Counter Culture Since 1990: Deconstruction, Reconstruction, and Transformation of 'T' Partner," *Thought and Words: Journal of the Humanities and Social Science* 35 (1997): 205–7.

31. Antonia Chao, "A Reflection," 236–7; Fran Martin, *Situating Sexualities*, 238–51.

32. Justine Coupland, "Dating Advertisements: Discourses of the Commodified Self," *Discourse & Society* 7, no. 2 (1996): 199–201.

33. Hui Ching Chang and Richard Holt, "The Concept of Yuan and Chinese Conflict Resolution," in *Chinese Conflict Management and Resolution*, ed. Guo-Ming Chen and Ringo Ma (Westport, CT: Ablex Publishing, 2002), 26–30.

34. Jia-shin Gian, "Taiwanese Lesbians' Identification Under the Queer Politics Since 1990," *Taiwan: A Radical Quarterly in Social Studies* 30 (1998): 90–106.

35. Christine A. Smith and Shannon Stillman, "What Do Women Want?" 340.

36. Ibid.

37. Jakob Linaa Jensen, "The Internet Omnopticon," in *New Publics With/out Democracy*, ed. Henrik Bang and Anders Esmark (Frederiksberg: Samfundslitteratur, 2007), 351.

CHAPTER 15

Marketing Empowerment?
Commodifying the "Other" through
Online Microfinance

RADHIKA GAJJALA, ANCA BIRZESCU, AND
FRANKLIN N. A. YARTEY*

Chapter Description

This chapter walks readers through the lending processes of Kiva.org, a transnational online microfinance lending site that serves the poorest of the poor around the world, especially in Third World countries. Online microfinance networks such as Kiva have been described by some scholars as representing a democratic public space where the poor in developing countries virtually meet the rich from developed countries for social and economic exchanges. Through a feminist critical lens, we examine Kiva's lending processes, as it relates to the representation of Third World bodies on global spaces like Kiva. We acknowledge the importance of online sociofinancial networks such as Kiva in empowering the poor around the world. We also point out some of the power imbalances that emerge on online networks such as Kiva and the reproduction of old and new postcolonial hierarchies that occur in the process of lending to the poor.

* * *

*We wish to thank Dr. V. Gajjala and Ms. Samara Anarbaeva for work on related articles (see for instance V. Gajjala, R. Gajjala, A. Birzescu, and S. Anarbaeva, forthcoming) that feeds into some of our observations in this paper.

Introduction

In 2002, Gayatri Spivak cautioned that while "cyberliteracy is an excellent, enticing and seductive wonderful thing . . . the invasion of unmediated, so-called, cyberliteracy in the subaltern[1] sphere is deeply frightening" (285).[2] It is the assumption of unmediated (which is of course why Spivak qualifies it with "so-called") cyberliteracy that is problematic. Implicit in notions of cyberliteracy and the eradication of digital divides is the perception of "unmediatedness." The assumption of transparency with regard to the transferring of cyberliteracy is an issue because this perception of the online world implies that such practices of literacy are untouched by power structures and dominant hierarchies. Technology, often meaning the "new" technology of the modern and postmodern, is thus viewed as transparently and inherently democratic and transferable across contexts. In this essay, we seek to question the generally optimistic view of the emergence of "global civil society" through such new technology and to argue the need to interrogate the marketing paradigm that frames such a civil society or democracy as a consumer-based global society. Our examination uses transnational feminist lenses, as we take into account the structural, technical, and ideological negotiations that development movements and social actors from within developing countries enact to access and participate in online network cultures. In this chapter, we draw from a study conducted by a team of collaborators including the co-authors of the present work. We examined Kiva.org in its current form about 4 years after it was first launched online in 2005 during the spring and summer of 2009. This essay is mainly theoretical, drawing on prior and continuing empirical examination of online social networking sites.

At present, we see that there are many nongovernmental organizations (NGOs), nonprofits, and social entrepreneurs springing up all over the world to champion some cause or the other, running the gamut of human issues from environmental protection to human rights to development assistance. Transnational social networks geared toward development goals are a phenomenon circumscribed by globalization. The well-meaning origins and attempts of individual and community actors in these contexts are unquestionable. However, these social networks need to be carefully examined so as to consider how they can effectively privilege the needs of the materially underprivileged in the world.

The interweaving of sociocultural and economic activity in relationship to e-commerce, philanthropy, and various other socioeconomic networks since the mid-1990s to the present in cyberspace invokes multiple connections and complicities within processes of globalization. As global spaces for financial transactions that rely on the production and continued fostering of social relationships through online networks emerge, there is also a simultaneous reproduction of old and new colonial and postcolonial power hierarchies.

Online Sociofinancial Interface/Networks

Online social networking tools as well as massive multiuser online game environments and associated virtual economies of microtransactions allow a renewed wave of celebration and euphoria regarding "the Internet." Fan-labor, game economies, and increased access to the Internet by women and people of the Third World (even if mostly as consumers of multinational brand name products) are touted as evidence of the potential for democratic public space online. Furthermore, the use of "Web 2.0" tools by such online sites shifts concepts such as microfinance into global visual and communicative spaces of the online social networking models popularized in Web 2.0 Internet culture modeled along the lines of social-networking sites such as Facebook, MySpace, Etsy, and Ravelry.

In such social networking sites, relationship building is centered in an oddly scattered, disembodied, and decontextualized manner that encourages the user to split their attention between multiple parallel worlds. The design of these networks—adapted from past designs for peer-to-peer commerce and peer-to-peer exchange of data and information—hide and obfuscate off-line hierarchies essential to the function of social systems and status quo. They hide—but do not necessarily shift the hierarchies. In fact, they may reinstate traditional imbalances and reinstate them insidiously in the name of the "new."

Thus, it might be argued that interesting social and financial relationships are indeed emerging, as in the case of Etsy.com and Ravelry.com[3] where the populations using them might be from a comparatively homogeneous layer of society. However, when the users are from vastly different contexts—socioeconomically, culturally, and geographically—the hiding of the hierarchies allows for a complex dynamic of Othering and implicit disempowerment at the interface of the global. In what follows, the authors of this chapter will discuss this issue in relationship to Kiva. The present examination extends other critical inquiries of the Internet from this perspective.[4]

A key factor to note in relationship to software is that, although the ways in which software is prevalent in urban locations can perhaps be mapped through circuits of software use, the hidden ways in which software is routed around certain geographic, sociocultural, and economic spaces is not as obvious. Therefore, the implication of software becoming a key technology of government and world economies, as well as for NGOs, nonprofits, and philanthropy, continues a "modern" and colonial legacy of eliminating skills and the dispersal of bodies from preexisting communities. Despite the fact that such preexisting communities (as in the case of farming, for instance) are formed around continuing and locally sustainable liveli-hoods, there is an insistence on their disruption through the introduction of "innovation." This innovation takes the form of "globalizing" of local resources through patenting and certification by so-called global standards that are in fact standards situated in hierarchies that privilege Westernized modes of existence. Thus, for instance, the agricultural company Monsanto claims to "apply innovation and technology to help farmers around the world produce more while conserving more" while taking away the local farmers' decision-making powers and ownership of seeds through their patenting process. Exemplifying a worldview that sees standardization as a tool of globalization, such companies are able to claim that "enforcing [their] *patents* is to ensure a level playing field."[5]

Although some may argue that, in 2009, we do not have the same issues of digital divides and lack of literacy and access as we did in 1999, we would like to point out that the divides are not merely a result of access and tech-nical and/or linguistic literacy. The issue is that even having access and literacy does not allow for active choices to be made by these Others. These are Others because the Center expands in the name of giving them access and allowing them voice through translation and transformation. Therefore, to further unpack the spirit of the quote from Spivak, the transmission, diffusion, and dissemination of these "unmediated so-called cyberlitera-cies" can still be considered an "invasion" that *dis*connects and disappears the Other from the global mainstreams.

The irony of course is that the disconnection potentially becomes more deeply embedded when nonprofits and social entrepreneurs use these very same social networking tools and practices as the for-profit corporations and for-profit marketing agencies. The social relationships encouraged by the hierarchies as well as the literacies privileged render specific socioeco-nomic locations as unspeakable and unrecognizable, or recognizable only in subordinate, disempowered modes. These contribute to "new" lexicons of empowerment.

Along with the "new" of new media and with gender-mainstreaming formats in multinational contexts, such lexicons of empowerment are per-formed within a multicultural, inclusive global village. However, this global village is routed around communities whose image and praxis of self-empowerment does not fit easily into the rhetoric of individual choice through consumption of the "West" and the modern. The communities thus made invisible are often part of hidden labor forces such as migrant farm labor, sex workers, sweat shop labor, workers producing computer hardware and software programmers doing backend work, and so on. However, the mobility, individual-appearing choices, and freedom of those that directly contribute to, and benefit from, multinational economic globalization rest on the social and economic immobility of these invisible labor forces.

Thus, our argument is centered around a continuing questioning of existing design of technological environments. This questioning allows us to understand how the process of technological change in the Internet era influences the organizing of economic activities transnationally. Such an understanding, we hope, might lead to the engagement with issues and concerns of marginalized populations all over the world. For, as things stand, the Internet as it is *still* does not work on their behalf.

Marketing Empowerment

Clifford Bob discusses how the marketing model provides the motivations for the disparate levels of international success and support or activism for local *challengers* or *insurgencies* or *movements*. He uses these three terms interchangeably to refer particularly to "domestically based social currents and organizations that oppose governments, elites, and other powerful institutions chiefly using protest and pressure outside conventional political channels."[6] Marketing concepts such as "demand and supply" and "marketing strategies" are applied to activities of local political movements, and their ability to be heard and noticed is framed by a global marketing logic. They are compelled to compete for entry into this global marketplace for support and popularity that transnational NGOs in the developed world have been granted. The competitive market paradigm is embedded in a discourse of empowerment and altruism. An "analytical blind spot" is produced through such an embedding. This blind spot perpetuates a deceivingly simple picture of the growth of transnational NGO assistance to the disempowered and off-line Other, whereas in actuality, "winning NGO support is neither easy nor automatic but instead competitive and uncertain."[7]

Bob's case analysis demonstrates that transnational success and growth of assistance to local political movements relies to an important extent on gaining international visibility. Such visibility is gained through framing strategies operated by local challengers in view of matching key characteristics of potential international supporters. Along with attempts at tapping the media for international awareness, local challengers embark on a process of promotional strategies where their "parochial demands, provincial conflicts, and particularistic identities" must be framed, so that they match interests, expectations, and agendas of prospective international supporters.[8] These framing strategies impact the tactical, cultural, ethical, and organizational attributes of the movements off-line as well. Thus, for instance, the movements' tactics to universalize their conflicts, or the movements' employment of a current (marketable) rhetoric that easily resonates abroad, become the off-line discourse that circulates locally as well. It is crucial to acknowledge that, even though framing is dynamic and mutual for local challengers and transnational NGOs, local groups are most likely to undergo a process of reinvention and alteration.

Bob's analysis also points to the politics of international NGOs where NGOs carefully calculate mutual interests and concerns, and where eventually the supporters' agendas do not necessarily answer the real needs of local movements. As they themselves compete for members and funding, NGOs often choose less needy local groups, seemingly more capable to use the aid successfully. Therefore, they shape a transnational political space that is more often marked by self-interest and competition than by altruism and cooperation, in view of a market where "many desperate groups demand scarce support from a relatively small number of NGO suppliers," and where, thus, transnational appeals will not "easily or invariably yield assistance."[9] Thus, in the case of the particular development frame of microfinance online, the concept of networked agency heralded and advocated by global actors such as transnational advocacy networks or NGOs requires us to map the problematic intersections of local or global circumscribed by current international politics.

We do not, however, simply discard what might be called mainstream analysis highlighting the achievements of microlending. Nor do we fully reject the potential of the Internet for marginalized populations in very specific global or local intersections. Thus, we do acknowledge that the "capacity of the Internet to handle micro-transactions and to cater to niche markets" is something that can and should be explored.[10] For instance, the ways in which off-line communities such as those who network through sites such as Ravelry.com and Etsy.com are worthy of further nuanced exploration. Furthermore, we do acknowledge the possibility that such programs as Kiva.org might assist potential strategies against poverty and toward empowerment. But a broader, more inclusive focus when assessing their outcomes and impact is necessary. The need to examine these sites closely arises whether we agree that this makes the world a better place or not. The tools are here and are being used. It is better we understand how they benefit and how they hinder specific kinds of empowerment projects, rather than blindly take for granted the ways in which this empowerment occurs.

The Kiva Model

Various grassroots organizations have linked independent indigenous producers to global markets through microfinance programs. Kiva.org is one such example with its promise of online microfinance—and it is a very high-profile example. It is a peer-to-peer microlending Web site that acts as an intermediary to bring the borrower and the lender together. Kiva partners with Microfinance Institutions (MFIs) to identify qualified potential borrowers (entrepreneurs). Lenders—using PayPal or credit cards—channel their microloans to the borrower through Kiva. Founded in 2005 and headquartered in San Francisco, Kiva's mission is to connect people, through lending, to alleviate poverty. More than half a million people have loaned more than US$ 76 million to 180,000 entrepreneurs in 45 countries through Kiva with a current repayment rate of 98%.[11]

The objective, for Kiva, is to empower people to be entrepreneurs, so that they may eventually lift themselves out of poverty. Thus, their mission is "to connect people through lending for the sake of alleviating poverty."[12] Referring to the growth and development of the microcredit and microfinance sector, Sengupta and Aubuchon contend that Kiva renders the microfinance movement "as accessible to lenders as the Grameen Bank made microcredit accessible to borrowers."[13]

Kiva's members consist of individuals from developing and developed countries. The members are in two categories—those who are in need of funding for their small businesses to enable them to make a livelihood and those who are willing to lend small amounts of money. Members can choose to lend money to entrepreneurs who are members of the site and thus, ideally, help that individual achieve economic independence.[14] The loans made through Kiva usually take 6–12 months to be repaid—during the currency of the loan, members get email updates and thus track periodic repayments. Once the loan is repaid, the member can relend to another person who is in need.

Kiva also works with specialized MFIs to gain access to deserving entrepreneurs from impoverished communities around the globe. These entrepreneurs are usually from developing nations who have a plan to succeed in their small businesses but do not have the funds to get started. The most qualified entrepreneurs thus are chosen locally through the services of these institutions. The MFI has a process of its own that determines how these qualified entrepreneurs are selected. The specialized MFIs that Kiva partners with are responsible for uploading their newly discovered entrepreneur profiles on to the Kiva site, where people can view the pictures and descriptions, and make decisions about who to lend money to.

Through Kiva, not only do people lend money to help the ones in need but they also get connected and build relationships. Loans vary in their sums and can start as low as US$ 25, but the effect of this amount can change the loan recipient's life forever. The Kiva Web site periodically has a featured entrepreneur with a profile. A prospective lender can read about this individual and lend money—if he or she wishes to do so—by choosing the amount in the drop box and clicking "lend now." Kiva also encourages its MFI partners to promote latent entrepreneurial skills among the poor by providing training and other assistance. In addition, Kiva has links to an online store, which sells goods ranging from gift certificates to items with Kiva's logo. Kiva's networking practices seek to do some social consciousness raising among individuals who are comparatively materially privileged. To assist in this, there are features such as the community forum, which lists the number of loans, number of team members, names of team members, and the total amount loaned in that particular thread. All these teams form Kiva's extended network.

One can also read journals of members online. The journals provide member descriptions, profiles, and pictures. Each member has ratings and recommendations. The timely repayment of a loan results in good recommendations and ratings of a loan recipient, which then improves that individual's chances of getting more loans in the future. Although an individual can do many things on Kiva—become a supporter and/or become a voluntary fellow—only an MFI can become a field partner.

The Kiva fellows are independent volunteers and they chronicle case studies that reveal the impact and results that the loans have on the economic status of the borrowers. This activity satisfies a main condition of Kiva, namely client impact transparency on the Internet. The Kiva interface and interactive technical tools that link various local sites to a global space seem to be successful—from what we see online at the site—in developing a sense of community ethics and thus of resensitization of the privileged toward poverty.

Thus, the actuality of the impact of the loans on borrowers' lives is established by means of Web 2.0 tools that the Kiva fellows make use of in their activities (blogging, YouTube uploaded interviews with the borrowers, etc.). The goal of this visualization of the actual impact of the loans through online text and imaging is to show lenders that these loans are not just a drop in the ocean. A paragraph from a Kiva fellow's journal in Peru explains the importance of journaling:

> Because a picture is worth a thousand words (or at least $ 25 minimum loan!) and the photos on Kiva's website that are taken of the women in their place of business, which is often their home as well, is what Kiva lenders have repeatedly indicated is what they want to see. While going to the community bank meetings assures that the women will be present, it doesn't allow their photos to be taken in their individual places of business.[15]

Indeed, the main theme throughout the fellows' online postings is precisely the narrative of the impact of the loans on the individual entrepreneurs. This is a way of showing the evidence of the empowering results. At the same time, it functions to assure the individual lenders that their loans have been put to the best possible use and to persuade other possible lenders to take part in the microfinance initiatives.

A Transnational Feminist Lens Focused on Kiva's Use of Web 2.0

Current global hegemonies are the outcome of global restructuring and neoliberal economic policies that lead to the reconfiguration and resurgence of imperial ambitions. In this sense empowerment seems given, but it is manifested through a neoliberal philosophy that emphasizes the individual. This does not sufficiently make apparent the structural inequalities that emerge as a result.

This neoliberal understanding fosters a one size fits all model of empowerment by disregarding the range of political, economic, and cultural contexts that allow for complex and sometimes contradictory possibilities for empowerment. This is why a transnational feminist perspective is also an analytical alternative to global feminism that is rather delineated by the same neoliberal stance, in that it has been criticized for propagating a eurocentric, Western hegemonic, and homogenizing feminism.[16] It is a feminism that carries with it the marks of imperialism, professing a North–South and top–down prescriptive model of feminism for the rest of the world. More specifically, in this narrow view on empowerment, gender is defined as having a universal, monolithic character worldwide, without acknowledging the reality that gender is simultaneously embedded within much more complex power dynamics alongside other social markers as race, class, religion, nation, and ethnicity. It is, therefore, an expected conclusion of this narrow premise that oppression is being addressed partially and inadequately, whereas the resulting empowerment has limited prospects. Elliott[17] describes the co-option of empowerment as a neoliberal strategy to fulfill other goals in the development realm:

> too often development agencies see empowerment as only an instrument for reaching other goals, just as contraception can serve the goal of population control rather than women's choices . . . program goals may be achieved, but without individual transformation it is not empowerment.
>
> (2008, 8)

Thus, ICTs employed in the global development activities, as in the case of the Web 2.0 tools used by microlending organizations online, need to be examined in an analytical framework that emphasizes the importance of everyday practices and sociocultural hierarchies. Such a framework would not only try to describe shaping of online identities but also would unpack hierarchies and processes of inclusion and exclusion (gendered, raced, and classed online subjectivities).[18]

For instance, Nakamura defines the concept of cybertyping as a process where "computer/human interfaces, the dynamics and economics of access, and the means by which users are able to express themselves online interact with the . . . ideologies regarding race that they bring with them into cyberspace."[19] The seemingly progressive nature of the Internet is shown to be contrasted by the practice of identity tourism on the Internet, which only reiterates gender and racial stereotypes and, even worse, evidences the consumption and commodification of racial difference. The visions of "postracial democracy," apparent in the discourse surrounding the Internet, are more often a device working toward a cosmetic cosmopolitanism or multiculturalism that seeks to mask the reality of racism.[20]

By the same token, Web sites and social networks targeting users from the developing world produce a monolithic, homogenizing imagery of Third World poverty. This is an image of poverty being marketed to, and being consumed by, the Western gaze. Poverty, as well as images of empowerment through the transcending of these conditions imaged as poverty, become instrumentalized as commodities.

Furthermore, it is precisely because they advocate for development and poverty alleviation through a model of "transnational investing" and not simply by charity that such online sites display a homogenized market of Third World microentrepreneurs for foreign investors from developed countries to invest in. In doing so, they end up displacing political subjectivities of the microentrepreneurs. They reinstate the discourse of Otherness globally, while limiting a process of empowerment locally. Referring to the erroneously homogeneous image of poor people, Lingam contends that

> there are attempts to discipline women and communities and functionally cobble together "social cohesion" among the poor as a class without working on the deep-seated caste difference. This is a bigger challenge that is not amenable to solution by micro-credit programs.[21]

For example, take the case of the borrowers on Kiva. There is a linear information flow, involving a three-layered mediation of the representation of the borrowers. The first layer involves the choosing of the actual individual in need of a loan and the vetting process that classifies him or her as adequate to be a borrower by the local MFI. The second layer of representation is through the Kiva fellows' descriptions and narratives on the Web site, and the third layer of representation comes from the Internet tools themselves that serve as filters which shape the final representation of the borrower to potential lenders and the world at large.

The sheer fact of direct access to the computer and Internet technologies that lenders have has positioned them in greater control of negotiating the representation of their borrowers. Through such a positioning of materially underprivileged Others, Kiva.org becomes a space for consumption[22] where Third World bodies are consumed through a Western gaze. Consumption spaces present various types of authenticities for different people, and the Third World bodies showcased on digital platforms such as Kiva.org could be authenticated through accompanying descriptions as true representations of off-line bodies.[23] For instance, the profile of one particular female borrower from Ghana is described in a way that illustrates what we have been arguing in this essay.

Adwoa Nyamekye is 45 years old. She is a married woman with two children. Both are currently in senior high school. She lives with her husband and children in a rented apartment in Nkawkaw, in the Eastern Region of Ghana. Her husband is a farmer.

Adwoa works to make some income to support her husband financially. She trades in food items such as tomatoes, corn dough, pepper, and so forth on a table top in the market square. She procures the goods from wholesalers in nearby towns at cost-effective prices. Adwoa sells the products mostly to food vendors in her community. She has been in business for 10 years. She wants a loan to procure goods in bulk to maximize her profit margin. She aspires to improve on her living standard and support her children's education.[24]

Adwoa appears to the Westernized gaze of the researchers as a middle-aged black woman sitting on the bottom of the stairs in a white plastic chair. Adwoa's hands are clasped together. She is wearing a green dress with white flowers and is accessorized with gold jewelry (watch, bracelet, and necklace with matching earrings). She is looking down in the picture, and her eyes are semi closed. Her face does not reveal emotion recognizable by the Westernized researchers and lenders—nor is she looking directly at the camera. This, read through the cultural understanding produced for us in the Westernized academic reading, implies to us that she is not active and in control but rather is passive and waiting. Adwoa's image is a strategic, performative tool that fits a certain "cybertype" meant to market her to the Western or global lender as an ideal borrower. Social cues, bodily posture, and clothing aesthetic are all carefully arranged. Adwoa and her implicit need are the commodity for the Western global consumer. The lender or consumer's desire to "consume" the Other's empowerment is fulfilled through the practice of giving to this image.

Though not all Africans or people from Third World countries are poor, globalized images of Africans have become synonymous with poverty and corruption. One may argue that prospective borrowers even from materially disadvantaged locations also have some form of agency in crafting their profiles on Kiva because they play a role in telling their stories. This is true; however, Kiva and its field partners have the rights of media production[25] and they have greater control over the representation of Third World bodies. Furthermore—it is not Kiva that actually has full control over the logic of interaction and objectification produced through the design and placement of the interface—it is a standardized social marketing interface adapted for Kiva. Thus, the practices are still clearly based in practices of shopping and consumption in a global mall.

Therefore, even in relationship to the Internet, we see the relationship between economic forms and cultural forms, which, as Raymond Williams has pointed out, is complex and multidirectional.[26] Through an examination of how social networking practices are unequally available and hierarchically framed through remediated images of Otherness, we can map the problematic intersections of local or global as circumscribed by current international politics. The framework that we use in this analysis, therefore, makes possible a clear consideration of images of empowerment and the complex ways in which these images lead us to conceptualize what it means to be empowered or to empower.

Although we do acknowledge that the "capacity of the Internet to handle micro-transactions and to cater to niche markets"[27] is something that can and should be explored to enhance the ways in which Web 2.0 tools might connect up marginalized communities to material empowerment, we would like to see this done with more consideration and a careful evaluation of actual choices made possible. Thus, we do acknowledge that perhaps such programs can provide potential strategies against poverty but under very specific conditions. We want to add to it a larger focus when assessing their outcomes, efficiency, as well as ethics, which takes into consideration multiple identities and social hierarchies formed through the layering of technological literacy, language, race, gender, class, caste, geographical location, and cultural context.

Endnotes

1. The term "subaltern" is a term used by the "Subaltern Studies Group," an interdisciplinary organization of South Asian scholars led by Ranajit Guha, and is a name for the general attribute of subordination in South Asian society whether this is expressed in terms of class, caste, age, gender, and office or in any other way.
2. Cited in Radha S. Hegde and Shome Radha, "Postcolonial Scholarship—Productions and Directions: An Interview with Gayatri Chakravorty Spivak," *Communication Theory* 23, no. 3 (2002): 271–86.

3. Sal Humphreys, "The Economies within an Online Social Network Market: A Case Study of Ravelry," in *ANZCA 09 Annual Conference: Communication, Creativity and Global Citizenship, July 8–10, 2009* (Brisbane: QUT, in press), 234–52.

4. See Radhika Gajjala, "Third-World Critiques of Cyberfeminism," *Development in Practice* 9, no. 5 (1999): 616–19; Radhika Gajjala, *Cyber Selves: Feminist Ethnographies of South Asian Women* (Walnut Creek, CA: AltaMira Press, 2004); Radhika Gajjala, Yahui Zhang, and Phyllis Dako-Gyeke, "Lexicons of Women's Empowerment Online," *Feminist Media Studies* 10, no. 1 (2010): 69–86.

5. "Monsanto Seed Patent Protection," *Monsanto*, http://www.monsanto.com (accessed December 16, 2009).

6. Clifford Bob, *The Marketing of Rebellion: Insurgents, Media and International Activism* (New York, NY: Cambridge University Press, 2005), 8.

7. Ibid., 4–5.

8. Ibid., 4.

9. Ibid., 192.

10. Humphreys, "The Economies within an Online Social Network Market," 234.

11. "Kiva Launches Online Microfinance in the United States: Opportunity to U.S. Entrepreneurs," *WebSite 101*, http://website101.com/finance/kiva-launches-online-microfinance-united-states-entrepreneurs/#ixzz0qS0sLh7C (accessed December 16, 2009).

12. "About Kiva," *Kiva*, http://www.kiva.org/about (accessed December 16, 2009).

13. Rajdeep Sengupta and Craig P. Aubuchon, "The Microfinance Revolution: An Overview," *Federal Reserve Bank of St. Louis Review* 90, no. 1 (2008): 9–30.

14. "How Kiva Works," *Kiva*, http://www.kiva.org/about/how (accessed December 16, 2009).

15. Emily Sweeney, "Are You My Entrepreneur?" *Kiva*, March 22, 2009, http://fellowsblog.kiva.org/2009/03/22/are-you-my-entrepreneur (accessed April 23, 2009).

16. See, for example, Chandra T. Mohanty, *Feminism without Borders: Decolonizing Theory, Practicing Solidarity* (Durham and London: Duke University Press, 2003); Uma Narayan, *Dislocating Cultures: Identities, Traditions, and Third-World Feminism* (New York, NY: Routledge, 1997); Radhika Parameswaran, "The Other Sides of Globalization: Communication, Culture, and Postcolonial Critique," *Communication, Culture and Critique* 1, no. 1 (2008): 116–25.

17. Carolyn M. Elliott, "Introduction: Markets, Communities, and Empowerment," in *Global Empowerment of Women: Responses to Globalization and Politicized Religions*, ed. Carolyn M. Elliott (New York, NY: Routledge, 2008), 1–23.

18. See Jilliana Enteen, "Spatial Conceptions of URLs: Tamil Eelam Networks on the World Wide Web," *New Media and Society* 8, no. 2 (2006): 229–49; Radhika Gajjala and Melissa Altman, "Producing Cyberselves through Technospatial Praxis: Studying through Doing," in *Health Research in Cyberspace*, ed. P. Liamputtong (New York, NY: Nova Science, 2006), 67–84; Beth E. Kolko, Lisa Nakamura, and Gilbert Rodman, "Race in Cyberspace: An Introduction," in *Race in Cyberspace*, ed. Beth E. Kolko, Lisa Nakamura, and Gilbert Rodman (New York, NY: Routledge, 2000), 1–14; Lisa Nakamura, *Cybertypes: Race, Ethnicity, and Identity on the Internet* (New York, NY: Routledge, 2002).

19. Nakamura, *Cybertypes*, 3.

20. Ibid., 14.

21. Lakshmi Lingam, "Domains of Empowerment: Women in Microcredit Groups Negotiating with Multiple Patriarchies," in *Global Empowerment of Women: Responses to Globalization and Politicized Religions*, ed. Carolyn M. Elliott (New York, NY: Routledge, 2008), 135.

22. Sharon Zukin, "Consuming Authenticity: From Outposts of Difference to Means of Exclusion," *Cultural Studies* 22, no. 5 (2008): 724–48.

23. Ibid., 734.

24. Adwoa Nyamekye, *Kiva*, March 2009, http://www.kiva.org/app.php?page=businesses&action=about&id=97791 (accessed December 16, 2009).

25. See Lisa Nakamura, "Don't Hate the Player, Hate the Game: The Racialization of Labor in World of Warcraft," *Critical Studies in Media Communication* 26, no. 2 (2009): 128–44. In this article, Nakamura discusses the privileges of media production available to those who are already empowered with the necessary technologies and the time to create content for media. We draw parallels with Kiva and argue that the privileges of media production belong to the Kiva partners (not the lenders) who have the final control of how these lenders will be represented on Kiva. They edit lender biographies and decide what is included or excluded, before the images and accompanying text is uploaded on Kiva.org.

26. Raymond Williams, *The Sociology of Culture* (Chicago: The University of Chicago Press, 1995).

27. Humphreys, "The Economies within an Online Social Network Market," 1.

Afterword
Media Identities in a "Post-American" World

DAYA THUSSU

The globalization of media has contributed to erasing as well as enriching our cultural identities. Although some fear that the creation of a uniform and homogeneous communication experience will lead to a loss of identity, others rejoice in the potential cultural diversity that the digital revolution has promised and, to some extent, delivered. In this multimedia age, more and more of us are learning to live with multiple identities—based on a mélange of gender, sex, nationality, race, ethnicity, class, cultures, and sub-cultures. As we enter the second decade of the twenty-first century, the world of global media and communication offers exciting challenges and possibilities of rethinking intercultural exchanges at a local, national, and transnational level.

The time-space compression in the 24/7 digitized media economy, with its localization and multiple and multivocal flows, visible in all shapes and sizes on such networks as MySpace and YouTube, has ensured that witnessing global events is becoming a pastime for a growing number of media consumers. Whether it is the closing ceremony of the 2008 Beijing Olympics, the Mumbai terrorist attacks later that year, or the inauguration of Barack Obama, these media events have become part of a global shared experience. At the same time, boundaries between media producers and consumers are being dissolved through the use of personal technologies to broadcast these events, such as the violent clampdown during Iran's 2009

Presidential elections when mobile telephones transmitted live pictures of the last moments of a student's life.

As contributors to this volume have amply demonstrated, the global media landscape is complex as well as contested, and a cosmopolitan theoretical framework that draws on the strengths of various strands—critical and liberal; Marxian and market-driven; past and post various "isms"—is needed to make sense of a rapidly changing scenario. The range of topics and case studies covered—from minority media channels (be they highbrow, such as Europe's Association Relative to European Televisions (ARTE), or popular, concerning the Chinese diaspora) to the dynamics of global/local film production to the world of online microfinance—brings a rich variety to the study of the temporal, spatial, and cultural dimensions of the global.

Much of this debate in the field tends to be framed within a discourse that has its roots in Western, or more specifically Anglo-American, academia, where to a substantial degree globalization continues to be equated with the notions of "modernization" and "Westernization." Given that the dominant discourse of globalization developed in the West, particularly within the US academy, US approaches were adopted in universities around the world, aided by some European input. The trajectory is not very different from the historical study of media and communication when the "modernization paradigm" influenced the theoretical framework for media and communication studies in much of the global South. Its revised version for the internet age—and championed by the digital democracy brigade—can tend toward an unwavering faith in the potential of new information and communication technologies as agents for development and empowerment. This "neo-developmentalist" view, under the banner of the globalization of the information society, legitimized an advanced telecommunication and computing infrastructure through transnational corporations.

The critical tradition—with its critiques of media and cultural imperialism—largely failed to take into account the rich tapestry of cultural complexity and dynamism beyond the rather deterministic view of commodity culture, a lacuna that indirectly led to the bourgeoning of cultural studies programs, informed by postcolonial and poststructuralist frameworks. The growth of this type of scholarship opened up new ways of thinking about media and communication consumption and of media "effects," going beyond the behaviorist or psychological approaches dominant in the United States.

With the end of Cold War-induced ideological turf wars and the demise of such disciplines as "Sovietology," critical research lost some of its political edge as postmodern, identity-driven media and communication discourses gained momentum. Their globalization since the 1990s is a testimony to the hegemony of English language scholarship now entering hitherto uncharted territories such as the former Soviet Union and China, embedded as it is, at least since World War II, within an American-led global capitalism with its formidable media, cultural, and communication networks.

The US–UK "duopoly" in global media and communication is reflected in the study of media, largely because of the dominance of English as the language of global communication, combined with the fact that the field emerged in the United States and is home to the majority of textbook and journal publishing in the area, closely followed by Britain.

A significant—albeit largely unrecognized in the academic world— change in relation to the globalization of media and communication is the rise of China and India as global players. In 2010, China bypassed Japan to become the world's second largest economy after the United States. The world's two ancient civilizations with the largest populations and fast growing economies—coinciding with cracks within the neoliberal model of US-led Western capitalism—have a huge potential to influence the way we have traditionally theorized media, culture, and notions of the "global." According to Goldman Sachs' estimates, within a generation China and India will become the largest and the third largest world economies, respectively, in terms of purchasing power parity.[1] Together they will account for nearly 40% of world trade. This "rise," or as some have argued, "return," of Asia as a major global power offers exciting research possibilities: until the eighteenth century, as Angus Maddison has shown, China and India were the largest economies in the world, accounting for more than 60% of global GDP.[2]

In the "post-American" world, globalization is much more than merely a euphemism for "Americanization." With the rise of China and India, we are likely to see globalization with an Asian orientation. This might give a new meaning to the phrase "alter-globalization," a term associated with the World Social Forum. How will this affect discourses of mediated identity and culture? Will their combined economic and cultural impact, aided by extensive and increasingly vocal and visible global diasporas, create globalization with an Asian accent? Already, China has the planet's biggest blogger population, whereas India boasts the world's most linguistically diverse media landscape as well as its largest film factory. Would a Chinese media perspective on events in Africa be less affected by the colonial mindset and therefore more representative of African realities? Would the "development" discourse be different if it were shaped and influenced by Gandhian philosophy? What if international NGOs and major alternative media networks were emanating from Beijing and New Delhi rather than from New York, Geneva, or London?

The banking crisis that hit the United States in 2008 has arguably eroded the credibility of Western governments to set the global agenda and, in the words of one senior analyst in a recent article in *Foreign Affairs*, created "a geopolitical setback for the West," as power begins to shift from G8 to G20.[3] In addition, one of those untold stories of the "other" globalization, taking place away from the Western media spotlight, concerns the growing economic links between India and China with the potential to reconfigure the global economy: trade between the two countries—negligible at the beginning of the 1990s—had grown to US$ 60 billion by 2010, making India's eastern neighbor its largest trading partner.

The rise of these two countries offers new incentives to "reorient" the global media research paradigm. One could draw inspiration from such works as John Hobson's *The Eastern Origins of Western Civilization*, which provide a historical context in which to reevaluate the role countries such as China had in an earlier version of globalization.[4] Such comparative and innovative research and scholarship will inform and invoke a transnational and transdisciplinary conversation on how we might contribute to a fuller and culturally richer understanding of what is global media and how we might study it in a multipolar world no longer shaped by the West.

Endnotes

1. Goldman Sachs, *BRICs and Beyond* (New York, NY: Goldman Sachs Global Economics Department, 2007).
2. Angus Maddison, *The World Economy: A Millennial Perspective* (Paris: OECD, 2001), 28.
3. Roger C. Altman, "The Great Crash 2008: A Geopolitical Setback for the West," *Foreign Affairs*, January/February 2009, http://www.foreignaffairs.com/articles/63714/roger-c-altman/the-great-crash-2008 (accessed September 6, 2010).
4. John M. Hobson, *The Eastern Origins of Western Civilization* (Cambridge, United Kingdom: Cambridge University Press, 2004).

Bibliography

Foreword—Emile McAnany

Appadurai, Arjun. "Disjuncture and Difference in the Global Cultural Economy." In *Global Culture: Nationalism, Globalization and Modernity*, edited by Mike Featherstone, 295–310. London: Sage Publications, 1990.

Barker, Chris. *Global Television*. Malden, MA: Blackwell, 1997.

Lerner, Daniel. *The Passing of Traditional Society: Modernizing the Middle East*. New York, NY: Free Press, 1964.

Lull, James. *Media, Communication, Culture: A Global Approach*. New York, NY: Columbia University Press, 1995.

Rogers, Everett M. *A History of Communication Study: A Biographical Approach*. New York, NY: Free Press, 1994.

Chapter 1—Rohit Chopra

Appadurai, Arjun. *Modernity at Large: Cultural Dimensions of Globalization*. Minnesota: University of Minnesota Press, 1996.

Bacon, Jr., Perry. "Foes Use Obama's Muslim Ties to Fuel Rumors About Him." *Washington Post*, November 29, 2007. http://www.washingtonpost.com/wp-dyn/content/article/2007/11/28/AR2007112802757.html (accessed February 2, 2009).

Baudrillard, Jean. *Jean Baudrillard, Selected Writings*, edited by Mark Poster. Stanford, CA: Stanford University Press, 1988.

Bennett, Tony, Lawrence Grossberg, and Meaghan Morris, eds. *New Keywords: A Revised Vocabulary of Culture and Society*. Malden, MA: Blackwell, 2005.

Bourdieu, Pierre. *On Television*, trans. Priscilla Parkhurst Ferguson. New York, NY: The New Press, 1999.

Boyd-Barrett, Oliver. "Media Imperialism Reformulated." In *Electronic Empires: Global Media and Local Resistance*, edited by Daya Kishan Thussu, 157–76. London: Arnold, 1998.

Castells, Manuel. *The Rise of the Network Society*. 2nd ed. Oxford: Blackwell, 2000.

Cooper, Frederick (with Rogers Brubakers). "Identity." In *Colonialism in Question: Theory, Knowledge, History*, by Frederick Cooper, 59–90. Berkeley: University of California Press, 2005.

Derrida, Jacques. *Of Grammatology*, trans. Gayatri Chakravorty Spivak. Baltimore, MA: Johns Hopkins University Press, 1998.

Erlanger, Steve. "After U.S. Breakthrough, Europe Looks in Mirror." *New York Times*, November 11, 2008. http://www.nytimes.com/2008/11/12/world/europe/12europe.html?_r=1&scp=3&sq=europe%20on%20obama%20victory&st=cse (accessed February 7, 2009).

Foucault, Michel. *Discipline and Punish: The Birth of the Prison*. 2nd ed. New York, NY: Vintage, 1995.

——. *History of Sexuality*. Vol. 1. New York, NY: Vintage, 1990.

——. *The Order of Things: An Archaeology of the Human Sciences*. 2nd ed. New York, NY: Routledge, 2001.

Ghosh, Amitav. "India's 9/11? Not Exactly." *New York Times*, December 2, 2008. http://www.nytimes.com/2008/12/03/opinion/03ghosh.html (accessed February 4, 2010).

"The Inauguration of President Barack Obama." *Boston Globe*, January 21, 2009. http://www.boston.com/bigpicture/2009/01/the_inauguration_of_president.html (accessed February 2, 2009).

Lechner, Frank J., and John Boli, eds. *The Globalization Reader*. 3rd ed. Malden, MA: Blackwell, 2008.

Luckett, Moya. "Postnational Television: *Goodness Gracious Me* and the Britasian Diaspora." In *Planet TV: A Global Television Reader*, edited by Lisa Parks and Shanti Kumar, 402–22. New York: New York University Press, 2003.

Lyotard, Jean-François. *The Postmodern Condition: A Report on Knowledge*. Translated by Geoff Bennington and Brian Massumi. Minneapolis: University of Minnesota, 1984.

McAnany, Emile. "Globalization and the Media: The Debate Continues." *Communication Research Trends* 21, no. 4 (2003): 3–19.

Morley, David. "Globalisation and Cultural Imperialism Reconsidered: Old Questions in New Guises." In *Media and Cultural Theory*, edited by James Curran and David Morley, 30–42. New York, NY: Routledge, 2006.

"Obama Race Speech." *Huffington Post*, March 18, 2008. http://www.huffingtonpost.com/2008/03/18/obama-race-speech-read-th_n_92077.html (accessed February 2, 2009).

Robertson, Ronald. "Globalization as a Problem." In *The Globalization Reader*, edited by Frank J. Lechner and John Boli, 87–94. 3rd ed. Malden, MA: Blackwell, 2008.

Robinson, Eugene. "The Moment for This Messenger?" *Washington Post*, March 13, 2007. http://www.washingtonpost.com/wp-dyn/content/article/2007/03/12/AR2007031200983.html (accessed January 19, 2007).

Said, Edward. *Orientalism*. New York, NY: Vintage, 1994.

Schwoch, James. "Television, Chechnya, and National Identity after the Cold War: Whose Imagined Community?" In *Planet TV: A Global Television Reader*, edited by Lisa Parks and Shanti Kumar, 226–42. New York: New York University Press, 2003.

Shohat, Ella, and Robert Stam. *Unthinking Eurocentrism: Multiculturalism and the Media*. New York, NY: Routledge, 1994.

Shome, Raka, and Radha S. Hegde. "Postcolonial Approaches to Communication: Charting the Terrain, Engaging the Intersections." In *International Communication: A Reader*, edited by Daya Kishan Thussu, 89–104. New York, NY: Routledge, 2010.

Singh, Madhur. "*Slumdog Millionaire*, an Oscar Favorite, Is No Hit in India." *Time*, January 26, 2009. http://www.time.com/time/arts/article/0,8599,1873926,00.html (accessed May 11, 2009).

Smith, Ben. "Muslims Barred from Picture at Obama Event." *Politico*, June 18, 2006. http://www.politico.com/news/stories/0608/11168.html (accessed February 3, 2009).

Sreberny-Mohammadi, Annabelle. "The Many Cultural Faces of Imperialism." In *Beyond Cultural Imperialism: Globalization, Communication and the New International Order*, edited by Peter Golding and Phil Harris, 49–68. London: Sage, 1997.

Thussu, Daya Kishan. *International Communication: Continuity and Change*. London: Arnold, 2000.

Tomlinson, John. *Cultural Imperialism: A Critical Introduction*. Baltimore, MD: Johns Hopkins Press, 1991.

Wallerstein, Immanuel. "The Modern World-System as a Capitalist World-Economy." In *The Globalization Reader*, edited by Frank J. Lechner and John Boli, 55–61. 3rd ed. Malden, MA: Blackwell, 2008.

Williams, Raymond. *Keywords: A Vocabulary of Culture and Society*. Rev. ed. New York, NY: Oxford University Press, 1983.

——. *Marxism and Literature*. New York, NY: Oxford University Press, 1977.

——. *Politics of Modernism: Against the New Conformists*. London: Verso, 2007.

Win, Hannah Ingberger. "'Slumdog Millionaire' Payment Controversy Provokes Union Debate." *Huffington Post*, January 28, 2009. http://www.huffingtonpost.com/2009/01/28/slumdog-millionaire-payme_n_161954.html (accessed May 11, 2009).

Young, Robert J. C. *Postcolonialism: An Historical Introduction*. Oxford: Blackwell, 2001.

Chapter 2—Cindy Patton

Crimp, Douglas, ed. "AIDS: Cultural Analysis, Cultural Activism." Special issue. *October* 43 (1987).

Epstein, Steven. *Impure Science: AIDS, Activism, and the Politics of Knowledge*. Berkeley: University of California Press, 1998.

Fleck, Ludwick. *Genesis and Development of a Scientific Fact*. Edited by Thaddeus J. Trenn and Robert K. Merton. Translated by Frederick Bradley and Thaddeus J. Trenn. Chicago: University of Chicago Press, 1979.

Kuhn, Thomas. *The Structure of Scientific Revolutions*. 3rd ed. Chicago: University of Chicago Press, 1996.

May, Robert M. "The Scientific Wealth of Nations." Office of Science and Technology, Albany House, 94–98 Petty France, London SW1H 9ST, UK.

National Science Board. "Science and Engineering Indicators, 2004." Arlington, VA, 2004.

Patton, Cindy. *Globalizing AIDS*. Minneapolis: University of Minnesota, 2002.

——. *Inventing AIDS*. New York, NY: Routledge, 1990.

——. *Sex and Germs: The Politics of AIDS*. Boston, MA: South End Press, 1985.

——. "Talking to Tina." In *Fractals: Body/State/Media*. Minneapolis: Minnesota University Press, forthcoming.

Penney, Shelley. "Swine Flu—Made in America?" http://www.swineflu-information.com/commentary/swine-flu-made-in-america (accessed May 13, 2010).

Triechler, Paula. *How to Have Theory in an Epidemic: Cultural Chronicles of AIDS*. Durham, NC: Duke University Press, 1999.

Watney, Simon. *Policing Desire: Pornography, AIDS, and the Media*. London: Cassell, 1986.

World Health Organization Pacific Region. "WHO Key Messages—Conflict of Interest Issues." January 11, 2010. http://www.wpro.who.int/vietnam/media_centre/press_releases/h1n1_8jan2010.htm (accessed May 13, 2010).

Chapter 3—Joseph Sciorra

Appadurai, Arjun. *Modernity at Large: Cultural Dimensions of Globalization*. Minneapolis: University of Minnesota Press, 2003.

Barker, Hugh, and Yuval Taylor. *Faking It: The Quest for Authenticity in Popular Music*. New York, NY: W. W. Norton & Company, 2007.

Cannistraro, Philip V. "The Duce and the Prominenti: Fascism and the Crisis of Italian American Leadership." *Altreitalie* 31 (2005): 76–86.

da MetroGnome. "Interview with JoJo Pellegrino." *SoundSlam.* http://soundslam.com/articles/print_page.php?id=in_jojope&type=interviews (accessed October 3, 2007).

Della Piana, Libero. "Are Italians the New Anti-Racist Front?" RaceWire blog, 2004. http://www.arc.org/racewire/041006l_piana.html (accessed April 4, 2006).

De Stefano, George. *An Offer We Can't Refuse: The Mafia in the Mind of America.* New York, NY: Faber & Faber, 2006.

di Leonardo, Micaela. *The Varieties of Ethnic Experience: Kinship, Class, and Gender Among California Italian-Americans.* Ithaca, NY: Cornell University Press, 1984.

Eddy, Chuck. "Spaghetti Eastern." *Village Voice*, August 23–29, 2006.

Gardaphé, Fred L. *From Wiseguys to Wise Men: The Gangster and Italian American Masculinities.* New York, NY: Routledge, 2006, 209–14.

George, Nelson. *Hip Hop America.* New York, NY: Penguin Books, 1998.

Ferraro, Thomas J. *Feeling Italian: The Art of Ethnicity in America.* New York: New York University Press, 2005.

Fields, Ingrid Walker. "Family Values and Feudal Codes: The Social Politics of America's Twenty-First Century Gangster." *The Journal of Popular Culture* 37, no. 4 (2004): 611–33.

Forman, Murray. *The 'Hood Comes First: Race, Space, and Place in Rap and Hip-Hop.* Middletown, CT: Wesleyan University Press, 2002.

Gennari, John. "Passing for Italian: Crooners and Gangsters in Crossover Culture." In *Frank Sinatra: History, Identity, and Italian American Culture*, edited by Stanislao G. Pugliese, 147–54. New York, NY: Palgrave, 2004.

Ghost Dog: The Way of the Samurai. DVD. Directed by Jim Jarmusch. Santa Monica, CA: Lions Gate Entertainment, 2001.

Guglielmo, Jennifer, and Salvatore Salerno, eds. *Are Italians White?: How Race is Made in America.* New York, NY: Routledge, 2003.

"Image & Identity." *National Italian American Foundation.* http://www.niaf.org/image_identity/summer2004.asp (accessed April 29, 2010).

Kayser, Brian. "Interview with JoJo Pellegrino." *Hip Hop Game*, March 17, 2008. http://www.hiphopgame.com/index2.php3?pahe=jjp (accessed March 18, 2008).

Kenna, Laura Cook. "Dangerous Men, Dangerous Media: Constructing Ethnicity, Race, and Media's Impact Through the Gangster Image, 1959–2007." PhD diss., George Washington University, 2008.

Koslow, Jessica. "JoJo Pellegrino." *The Source*, October 2000, 104.

Magliocco, Sabina. "Imagining the Strega: Folklore Reclamation and the Construction of Italian-American Witchcraft." *The Italian American Review* 8, no. 2 (2001): 57–81.

Mikie Da Poet. "Interview." Original Italian Soul MySpace blog, January 6, 2008. http://blogs.myspace.com/originalitaliansoul (accessed May 28, 2009).

Pellegrino, JoJo. "About JoJo Pellegrino 'Pella.'" JoJo Pellegrino MySpace profile, November 11, 2007. http://profile.myspace.com/index.cfm?fuseaction=user.viewprofile&friendid=44584748 (accessed March 18, 2008).

——. "JoJo Pellegrino Journal," July 30, 2007. *Hip Hop Game.* http://www.hiphopgame.com/index2.php3?page=jojojournal (accessed October 12, 2007).

Perkins, William Eric. "The Rap Attack: An Introduction." In *Droppin' Science: Critical Essays on Rap Music and Hip Hop Culture*, edited by William Eric Perkins, 1–45. Philadelphia, PA: Temple University Press, 1995.

Roediger, David R. *Colored White: Transcending the Racial Past.* Berkeley: University of California Press, 2002.

Sciorra, Joseph. "'Hip Hop from Italy and the Italian Diaspora': A Report from the 41st Parallel." *Altreitalie* 24 (January to June 2002): 86–104.

——. "'Took a Bird to the Boot': Hip Hop Expressions of Italian Diasporic Consciousness." Paper presented at the conference "The Land of our Return: Diasporic Encounters with Italy," John D. Calandra Italian American Institute, New York, NY, April 23–25, 2009.

Taussig, Michael. *Mimesis and Alterity: A Particular History of the Senses.* New York, NY: Routledge, 1993.

Tricarico, Donald. "Guido: Fashioning an Italian American Youth Subculture." *The Journal of Ethnic Studies* 19, no. 1 (Spring 1991): 41–66.

Troy D. "Jo Jo Pellegrino." *Rap Scene.* http://www.rapscene.com/JOJO.htm (accessed October 12, 2007).

White, Armond. "Who Wants to See Ten Niggers Play Basketball?" In *Droppin' Science: Critical Essays on Rap Music and Hip Hop Culture*, edited by William Eric Perkins, 192–208. Philadelphia, PA: Temple University Press, 1996.

Wikipedia contributors. "Gangsta rap." *Wikipedia, The Free Encyclopedia.* http://en.wikipedia.org/wiki/Gangsta_rap (accessed May 28, 2009).

Chapter 4—Michael Jenson

Bartram, Robert. "Visuality, Dromology and Time Compression: Paul Virilio's New Ocularcentrism." *Time & Society* 13, no. 2–3 (2006): 285–300.

Harvey, David. "The Social and Geographical Imaginations." *The International Journal of Political and Cultural Sociology* 18 (2005): 211–55.

Heidegger, Martin. *Discourse on Thinking.* New York, NY: Harper & Row, 1966.

Massey, Doreen, and Pat Jess. "Introduction." In *The Shape of the World: Explorations in Human Geography*, Vol. 4, edited by Doreen Massey and Pat Jess, 1–4. Oxford: Oxford University Press, 1995.

Miller, Vincent. "The Unmappable: Vagueness and Spatial Experience." *Space and Culture* 9, no. 4 (2006): 453–67.

Mugerauer, Robert. *Interpretations on Behalf of Place: Environmental Displacements and Alternative Responses.* New York: State University of New York Press, 1994.

Norberg-Shultz, Christian. *Genius Loci: Towards a Phenomenology of Architecture.* New York, NY: Rizzoli, 1979.

Relph, Edward. *Rational Landscapes and Humanistic Geography.* Totowa, NJ: Barnes and Noble Books, 1981.

Ricoeur, Paul. "Universal Civilization and National Cultures." In *History and Truth*, translated by Chas A. Kelbley, 271–84. Evanston, IL: Northwestern University Press, 1965.

Robinson, Eugene. "The Moment for This Messenger?" *Washington Post*, March 13, 2007. http://www.washingtonpost.com/wpdyn/content/article/2007/03/12/AR2007031200983.tml.

Ruskin, John. *The Modern Painters. Vol. IV: Of Mountain Beauty.* London: G. Allen, 1906.

Scholte, Jan Aart. *Globalization: A Critical Introduction.* New York, NY: St. Martin's Press, 2000.

Schwarzer, Mitchell. *Zoomscape: Architecture in Motion and Media.* New York, NY: Princeton Architectural Press, 2004.

Virilio, Paul. *Open Sky.* Translated by Julie Rose. New York, NY: Verso, 1997.

——. *The Paul Virilio Reader.* Edited by Steve Redhead. New York, NY: Columbia University Press, 2004.

——. *Virilio Live.* Edited by John Armitage. London: Sage Publications, 2001.

Virilio, Paul and Sylvère Lotringer. *Pure War.* New York, NY: Semiotexte, 1997.

Chapter 5—David Kenley

Anderson, Benedict. *Imagined Communities.* London: Verso, 1980.

Bailey, Paul. "The Chinese Work-Study Movement in France." *The China Quarterly* 115 (September 1988): 454.

Calhoun, Craig. "Nationalism and Ethnicity." *Annual Review of Sociology* 19 (1993): 211–39.

Chen Mong Hock. *The Early Chinese Newspapers of Singapore, 1881–1912*. Singapore: University of Malaya Press, 1967.

Chen, Shehong. *Being Chinese, Becoming Chinese American*. Urbana: University of Illinois Press, 2006.

Cui Guiqiang. *Xinjiapo huawen baokan yü baoren*. Singapore: Huo hua wen xin wen ye ji jin can jü, 1993.

Fang Xiu, comp. *Mahua xin wenxue da xi*. Xinjiapo: Xing zhou shi jie shu jü yu xian gong si, 1972.

Guo Min Bao (National Daily) [Tokyo], multiple issues between October 1907 and June 1908.

He Shumin, *Xinjiapo zui zao de huawen ribao—Le Bao (1881–1932)*. Singapore: Nanyang bianze-suo chuban, 1978.

Huang Fu-ch'ing. *Chinese Students in Japan in the Late Ch'ing Period*, East Asian cultural studies series, no. 22. Tokyo: The Centre for East Asian Cultural Studies, 1982.

Lü Ou Zhou Kan (Weekly Chinese Journal or Journal Chinois Hebdomadarie) [Paris], multiple issues between 15 November 1919 and 18 December 1920.

Müller, Gotelind and Gregor Benton. "Esperanto and Chinese Anarchism, 1907–1920." *Language Problems and Language Planning* 30, no. 1 (2006): 45–73.

Reynolds, Douglas R. "A Golden Decade Forgotten: Japan–China Relations, 1898–1907." *Transactions of the Asiatic Society of Japan*, 4th ser., 2 (1987): 105.

Shaonian Zhongguo (Young China) [San Francisco], multiple issues between 30 October 1911 and 3 February 1924.

Shijie Ribao (Chinese World or Sai Gai Yat Bo) [San Francisco], multiple issues between 16 October 1911 and 9 January 1923.

Tölölyan, Khachig. "The Nation-State and Its Others." *Diaspora* 1 (Spring 1991): 3–7.

Xin Shi Ji (New Century or Le Tempoj Novaj) [Paris], multiple issues between 22 June 1907 and 3 August 1907.

Zhong Xi Ribao (Western Daily or Chung Sai Yat Po) [San Francisco], multiple issues between 14 January 1911 and 5 January 1923.

Chapter 6—Nayantara Sheoran

Bureau Report, Hindu Business Line. "Mankind Pharma Mulls New Wing." *The Hindu—Business Line*, March 30, 2007, epaper edition. http://www.thehindubusinessline.com/2007/03/30/stories/200703300524030.htm (accessed January 14, 2009).

Dumit, Joseph. "Pharmaceutical Witnessing: Drugs for Life in an Era of Direct-to-Consumer Advertising." Unpublished essay.

Foucault, Michel. *The Birth of the Clinic: An Archaeology of Medical Perception*. New York, NY: Vintage Books, 1975.

——. "The Order of Discourse. Inaugural Lecture at the Collège de France, Given 2 December 1970." In Robert Young, ed. *Untying the Text: A Post-Structuralist Reader*, 48–78. Boston, MA: Routledge and Kegan Paul, 1981.

Gagnon, Marc-André, and Joel Lexchin. "The Cost of Pushing Pills: A New Estimate of Pharmaceutical Promotion Expenditures in the United States." *Public Library of Science (Medicine)* 5, no. 1 (2008): 29–33.

Goffman, Erving. *Gender Advertisements*. 1st ed. New York, NY: Harper & Row, 1979.

Goldman, Robert, and Michael Montagne. "Marketing 'Mind Mechanics': Decoding Antidepressant Drug Advertisements." *Social Science and Medicine* 22, no. 10 (1986): 1047–58.

Harish, B. "Marketing Practice: i-pill: Get Back to Life." E-blogger. *Marketing Practice*, August 17, 2007. http://marketingpractice.blogspot.com/2007/08/i-pill-get-back-to-life.html (accessed January 14, 2009).

Hodges, Sarah. *Contraception, Colonialism and Commerce: Birth Control in South India, 1920–1940.* Aldershot, England: Ashgate, 2008.

——. *Reproductive Health in India: History, Politics, Controversies.* New Delhi: Orient Longman, 2006.

Horkheimer, Max, and Theodor W. Adorno. "The Culture Industry: Enlightenment as Mass Deception." In *Dialectic of Enlightenment*, edited by Max Horkheimer and Theodor W. Adorno, translated by John Cumming, 120–67. New York, NY: Continuum, 1997.

Lutz, Catherine, and Jane Lou Collins. *Reading National Geographic.* Chicago: University of Chicago Press, 1993.

Mankekar, Purnima. "Dangerous Desires: Television and Erotics in Late Twentieth-Century India." *The Journal of Asian Studies* 63, no. 2 (2004): 403–31.

——. *Screening Culture, Viewing Politics: An Ethnography of Television, Womanhood, and Nation in Postcolonial India.* Durham, NC: Duke University Press, 1999.

Mazzarella, William. *Shoveling Smoke: Advertising and Globalization in Contemporary India.* Durham, NC: Duke University Press, 2003.

——. "'Very Bombay': Contending with the Global in an Indian Advertising Agency." *Cultural Anthropology* 18, no. 1 (February 2003): 33–71.

Perlitz, Uwe. "India's Pharmaceutical Industry Goes Global (Deutsche Bank Research)" May 6, 2008. http://www.euractiv.com/en/health/india-pharmaceutical-industry-goes-global/article-172137# (accessed January 14, 2009).

Petryna, Adriana, and Arthur Kleinman. "The Pharmaceutical Nexus." In *Global Pharmaceuticals: Ethics, Markets, Practices*, edited by Adriana Petryna, Andrew Lakoff, and Arthur Kleinman, 1–31. Durham, NC: Duke University Press, 2006.

Rajan, Kaushik Sunder. *Biocapital: The Constitution of Postgenomic Life.* Durham, NC: Duke University Press, 2006.

Soni, Veena. "Thirty Years of the Indian Family Planning Program: Past Performance, Future Prospects." *International Family Planning Perspectives* 9, no. 2 (June 1983): 35–45.

Talreja, Vishakha. "Morning After, Men Try to Find What's i-pill." *Economic Times*, September 29, 2007. http://economictimes.indiatimes.com/Morning_after_men_try_to_find_whats_i-pill/articleshow/2413553.cms (accessed January 14, 2009).

Tone, Andrea. *Devices and Desires: A History of Contraceptives in America.* 1st ed. New York, NY: Hill and Wang, 2001.

United States Congress. House of Representatives. The House Committee on Energy and Commerce Democrats: The Public Record: Detail Page. "The House Committee on Energy and Commerce: The Public Record: Subcommittee on Oversight and Investigations Hearing Entitled, 'Direct-To-Consumer Advertising: Marketing, Education or Deception?'" May 28, 2008. Text. http://energycommerce.house.gov/Press_110/110st162.shtml (accessed January 14, 2009).

Unnikrishnan, C. H. "Patents Carve up Drug Market." *Business Standard*, July 29, 2005. http://www.business-standard.com/india/news/patents-carvedrug-market/217607 (accessed January 14, 2009).

van der Geest, Sjaak, Susan Reynolds Whyte, and Anita Hardon. "The Anthropology of Pharmaceuticals: A Biographical Approach." *Annual Review of Anthropology* 25, no. 1 (1996): 153–78.

Williams, Raymond. "Advertising: The Magic System." In *The Cultural Studies Reader*, edited by Simon During, 410–23. London: Routledge, 1999.

Williamson, Judith. *Decoding Advertisements: Ideology and Meaning in Advertising.* New York, NY: Boyars, 1984.

Chapter 7—Frederike Felcht

Andersen, Hans C. *The Complete Andersen.* Edited by Jean Hersholt. New York, NY: The Limited Editions Club, 1949. The Complete Andersen. http://www.andersen.sdu.dk/vaerk/hersholt.

——. *Eventyr og Historier*. Edited by Det Danske Sprog- og Litteraturselskab. 3 vols. Copenhagen: Gyldendal, 2003.

Anderson, Benedict. *Imagined Communities: Reflections on the Origin and Spread of Nationalism*. London: Verso, 1983.

Appadurai, Arjun. "Disjuncture and Difference in the Global Cultural Economy." In *Global Culture: Nationalism, Globalization and Modernity*, edited by Mike Featherstone, 295–310. London: Sage Publications, 1990.

——. "Introduction: Commodities and the Politics of Value." In *The Social Life of Things: Commodities in Cultural Perspective*, edited by Arjun Appadurai, 3–63. Cambridge: Cambridge University Press, 1986.

Balibar, Etienne, and Immanuel Wallerstein. *Rasse Klasse Nation: Ambivalente Identitäten*. 2nd ed. Hamburg: Argument, 1992.

Barth, Volker. *Mensch versus Welt: Die Pariser Weltausstellung von 1867*. Darmstadt: Wissenschaftliche Buchgesellschaft, 2007.

Beck, Ulrich. *Was ist Globalisierung? Irrtümer des Globalismus—Antworten auf die Globalisierung*. Frankfurt/Main: Suhrkamp, 1997.

Böhme, Hartmut. *Fetischismus und Kultur: Eine andere Theorie der Moderne*. 2nd ed. Reinbek: Rowohlt, 2006.

Borges, Jorge L. "Tausendundeine Nacht." In *Die letzte Reise des Odysseus: Vorträge und Essays 1978-1982*. Edited by Gisbert Haefs, 116–31. Frankfurt/Main: Fischer, 2001.

Brandes, Georg. "Adam Oehlenschläger." In *Samlede Skrifter*. Vol. 1, 215–65. Copenhagen: Gyldendalske Boghandels Forlag, 1899. http://adl.dk/adl_pub/vaerker/cv/e_vaerk/e_vaerk. xsql?ff_id=2&id=615&hist=fmAnn oc=adl_pub.

Bredsdorff, Thomas. "Oehlenschläger's Aesthetics: Allegory and Symbolism in 'The Golden Horns' and a Note on 20th Century Eulogy of the Allegory." *Edda* 3 (1999): 211–21.

Casanova, Pascale. *The World Republic of Letters*. Cambridge, MA: Harvard University Press, 2004.

Chakrabarty, Dipesh. *Provincializing Europe: Postcolonial Thought and Historical Difference*. Reissue. Princeton, NJ: Princeton University Press, 2008.

Conrad, Sebastian, and Andreas Eckert. "Globalgeschichte, Globalisierung, Multiple Modernen." In *Globalgeschichte: Theorien, Ansätze, Themen*, edited by Sebastian Conrad, Andreas Eckert, and Ulrike Freitag, 7–49. Frankfurt/Main: Campus, 2007.

Fäßler, Peter E. *Globalisierung: Ein historisches Kompendium*. Köln: Böhlau, 2007.

Fischer, Wolfram. *Expansion, Integration, Globalisierung: Studien zur Geschichte der Weltwirtschaft*. Göttingen: Vandenhoeck & Ruprecht, 1998.

Foucault, Michel. *Les mots et les choses: Une archéologie des sciences humaines*. Paris: Éditions Gallimard, 1966.

Kraidy, Marwan M. *Hybridity, or the Cultural Logic of Globalization*. Philadelphia, PA: Temple University Press, 2005.

Kretschmer, Winfried. *Geschichte der Weltausstellungen*. Frankfurt/Main: Campus, 1999.

Latour, Bruno. *Eine neue Soziologie für eine neue Gesellschaft: Einführung indie Akteur-Netzwerk-Theorie*. Frankfurt/Main: Suhrkamp, 2007.

——. *Wir sind nie modern gewesen: Versuch einer symmetrischen Anthropologie*. Berlin: Akademie, 1995.

Lund, Jørn, ed. *Den Store Danske Encyclopædi*. Copenhagen: Gyldendal, 1994–2001.

Mackie, Erin. "Red Shoes and Bloody Stumps." In *Footnotes: On Shoes*, edited by Shari Benstock and Suzanne Ferriss, 233–47. New Brunswick, NJ: Rutgers University Press, 1994.

Marx, Karl. *Das Kapital*. Vol. 1, *Kritik der politischen Ökonomie*. Berlin: Dietz, 1962.

Müller-Wille, Klaus. "Romantik-Biedermeier-Realismus (1800–1870)." In *Skandinavische Literaturgeschichte*, edited by Jürg Glauser, 131–82. Stuttgart: Metzler, 2006.

Nyborg, Eigil. *Den indre linie i H.C. Andersens eventyr: En psykologisk studie*. Copenhagen: Gyldendal, 1962.

Oehlenschläger, Adam. *Oehlenschlæger Poetiske Skrifter*, edited by Helge Topsøe-Jensen. 5 vols. Copenhagen: J. Jørgensen & Co., 1926–1930. http://www.adl.dk/adl_pub/udgave/udgave_menu.xsql?ff_id=58&nnoc=adl_pub.

Oxfeldt, Elisabeth. *Nordic Orientalism: Paris and the Cosmopolitan Imagination 1800–1900*. Copenhagen: Museum Tusculanum Press, 2005.

Paul, Fritz. "Romantik und Poetischer Realismus." In *Grundzüge der neueren skandinavischen Literaturen*, edited by Fritz Paul, 86–146. Darmstadt: Wissenschaftliche Buchgesellschaft, 1991.

Prendergast, Christopher. "The World Republic of Letters." In *Debating World Literature*, edited by Christopher Prendergast, 1–25. London: Verso, 2004.

Rossel, Sven H. *A History of Danish Literature*. Lincoln: University of Nebraska Press, 1992.

Said, Edward W. *Orientalism*. New York, NY: Vintage Books, 2004.

Sassen, Saskia. *Das Paradox des Nationalen: Territorium, Autorität und Rechte im globalen Zeitalter*. Frankfurt/Main: Suhrkamp, 2008.

Serres, Michel. *Der Parasit*. Frankfurt/Main: Suhrkamp, 2007.

Sørensen, Peer E. *H. C. Andersen & Herskabet: Studier i borgerlig krisebevidsthed*. Grenaa: GMT, 1973.

Steiner, Uwe. "Widerstand im Gegenstand. Das literarische Wissen vom Ding am Beispiel Franz Kafkas." In *Literatur, Wissenschaft und Wissen seit der Epochenschwelle um 1800*, edited by Thomas Klinkert and Monika Neuhofer, 237–52. Berlin: de Gruyter, 2008.

Thastum Leffers, Gerda. *Kunstnerproblematikken hos H. C. Andersen belyst gennem eventyrene*. Copenhagen: C. A. Reitzel, 1994.

Wallerstein, Immanuel. *The Modern World-System*. 3 vols. New York, NY: Academic Press, 1974–1989.

Zerlang, Martin. "Orientalism and Modernity: Tivoli in Copenhagen." *Nineteenth-Century Contexts* 20, no. 1 (1997): 81–110.

Chapter 8—Ivan Kwek

Ang, Ien. "Desperately Guarding Borders: Media Globalization, 'Cultural Imperialism', and the Rise of 'Asia.'" In *House of Glass: Culture, Modernity and the State in Southeast Asia*, edited by Yao Souchou, 27–45. Singapore: Institute of Southeast Asia Studies, 2001.

Appadurai, Arjun. "Disjuncture and Difference in the Global Cultural Economy." In *Modernity at Large: Cultural Dimensions of Globalization*, edited by Arjun Appadurai, 27–47. Minneapolis: University of Minnesota Press, 1996.

Birch, David. *Singapore Media: Communication Strategies and Practices*. Cheshire: Longman, 1993.

Channel NewsAsia. *Singapore Tonight*, January 30, 2000. Broadcast News Program.

Datamonitor. *Media in Singapore: Industry Profile*. Sydney: Datamonitor, October 2008.

Erni, John Nyuyet, and Chua Siew Keng, eds. *Asian Media Studies: Politics of Subjectivities*. Malden, MA: Blackwell, 2004.

Featherstone, Mike. "Genealogies of the Global." *Theory, Culture & Society* 23, no. 2–3 (2006): 387–92.

Friedman, Jonathan. "Globalization and the Making of a Global Imaginary." In *Global Encounters: Media and Cultural Transformation*, edited by Gitte Stald and Thomas Tufte, 13–32. Luton, UK: University of Luton Press, 2002.

Gomez, James. *Self-Censorship: Singapore's Shame*. Singapore: Think Centre, 2000.

Iwabuchi, Koichi. "Contra-flows or the Cultural Logic of Uneven Globalization? Japanese Media in the Global Agora." In *Media on the Move: Global Flow and Contra-flow*, edited by Daya Kishan Thussu, 61–75. London: Routledge, 2007.

Kim, Youna. "The Rising East Asian 'Wave': Korean Media Go Global." In *Media on the Move: Global Flow and Contra-flow*, edited by Daya Kishan Thussu, 121–35. London: Routledge, 2007.

Kearney, Michael. " The Local and the Global." *Annual Review of Anthropology* 24 (1995): 547–65.

Rahim, Lily Zubaidah. *Singapore in the Malay World: Building and Breaching Regional Bridges.* Oxono. New York: Routledge, 2009.

Singapore. *Singapore Parliamentary Debates Official Report* 70, no. 6 (March 12, 1999): 680–8.

Singapore Department of Statistics, Ministry of Trade and Industry. *Population Trends 2009.* Singapore: Singapore Department of Statistics, 2009.

Slack, Jennifer Daryl. "The Theory and Method of Articulation in Cultural Studies." In *Stuart Hall: Critical Dialogues in Cultural Studies,* edited by David Morley and Kuan-Hsing Chen, 112–27. London: Routledge, 1996.

Straubhaar, Joseph Dean. "Beyond Media Imperialism: Asymmetrical Interdependence and Cultural Proximity." *Critical Studies in Mass Communication* 8 (1991): 39–59.

Suria. "About Us." http://www.suria.sg/about_us (accessed November 2008).

Chapter 9—Aalok Khandekar and Grant Jun Otsuki

Aditya Birla Group. "Taking India to the World." http://www.vgc.in/film2006/home.html, 2006 (accessed March 27, 2009).

Anderson, Benedict. *Imagined Communities: Reflections on the Origin and Spread of Nationalism.* Rev. ed. New York, NY: Verso, 2006.

Beech, Hannah. "Eurasian Invasion." *Time Magazine,* April 4, 2001.

Bolter, Jay David, and Richard Grusin. *Remediation: Understanding New Media.* Cambridge, MA: MIT Press, 1999.

Chiba Stearns, Jeff. *What Are You Anyways?* Meditating Bunny Studio, 2005.

Fulbeck, Kip. *Part Asian, 100% Hapa.* San Francisco, CA: Chronicle Books, 2006.

Hegde, Atul. "The Making of an Epic." http://www.vgc.in/film2006/home.html, 2006 (accessed March 1, 2009).

National Geographic 196, no. 2 (August 1999): cover.

Pukui, Mary Kawena, and Samuel H. Elbert. *Hawaiian Dictionary: Hawaiian-English, English-Hawaiian.* Revised and enlarged ed. Hawaii: University of Hawaii Press, 1986.

Silvio, Teri. "Remediation and Local Globalizations: How Taiwan's 'Digital Video Knights-Errant Puppetry' Writes the History of the New Media in Chinese." *Cultural Anthropology* 22, no. 2 (2007): 285–313.

Strassler, Karen. "The Face of Money: Currency, Crisis, and Remediation in Post-Suharto Indonesia." *Cultural Anthropology* 24, no. 1 (2009): 68–103.

Tsing, Anna Lowenhaupt. *Friction: An Ethnography of Global Connection.* Princeton, NJ: Princeton University Press, 2005.

Videocon. "Gayatri Mantra." http://www. youtube.com/watch?v=-iuEOUhdxqs (accessed January 14, 2011).

Chapter 10—Nolwenn Mingant

"Alien, la Résurrection." *Positif,* no. 442, December 1997.

Allen, Michael. *Contemporary US Cinema.* New York, NY: Longman/Pearson Education, 2003.

——. "From *Bwana Devil* to *Batman Forever*: Technology in Contemporary Hollywood Cinema." In *Contemporary Hollywood Cinema,* edited by Steve Neale and Murray Smith, 109–29. London: Routledge, 1998.

Allen, Robert. "Home Alone Together: Hollywood and the 'Family Film.'" In *Identifying Hollywood's Audiences: Cultural Identity and the Films,* edited by Melvyn Stokes and Richard Maltby, 109–34. London: BFI, 1999.

Barber, Benjamin. "Jihad vs McWorld." *The Atlantic Monthly,* March 1992.

Bidaud, Anne-Marie. *Hollywood et le rêve américain: Cinéma et idéologie.* Paris: Masson, 1994.

Bourget, Jean-Loup. *Hollywood: Un rêve européen.* Paris: Armand Colin Cinéma, 2006.

"Broken Arrow." *Cahiers du cinéma*, no. 500, March 1996.

"Fewer Stars Lay Claim to Fame." *Variety*, February 13, 1998.

Croué, Charles. *Marketing international: Un consommateur local dans un monde global*, 5th ed. Brussels: De Boeck, Perspectives Marketing, 2006.

Guback, Thomas. *The International Film Industry: Western Europe and America since 1945*. Bloomington: Indiana University Press, 1969.

Mattelart, Armand. "La nouvelle idéologie globalitaire." In *La Mondialisation au-delà des mythes*, edited by Serge Cordellier, 81–92. Paris: La Découverte/Poche, 2000.

Meers, Philippe. "'It's the Language of Film!': Young Film Audiences on Hollywood and Europe." In *Hollywood Abroad: Audiences and Cultural Exchanges*, edited by Melvyn Stokes and Richard Maltby, 158–75. London: BFI Publishing, 2004.

Michalet, Charles-Albert. *Le Drôle de drame du cinéma mondial*. Paris: La Découverte/Centre fédéral FEN, 1987.

Miller, Toby, Nitin Govil, John McMurria, and Richard Maxwell. *Global Hollywood*. London: BFI Publishing, 2001.

Miller, Toby, Nitin Govil, and John McMurria. *Global Hollywood 2*. London: British Film Institute, 2005.

Mingant, Nolwenn. *Hollywood à la conquête du monde: Marchés, stratégies, influences*. Paris: CNRS Editions, 2010.

——. "Les Stratégies d'exportation du cinéma hollywoodien (1966–2004)." PhD diss., Université Paris X-Nanterre, 2008.

MPAA. *2007 International Theatrical Snapshot*. http://www.mpaa.org/International%20 Theatrical%20Snapshot.pdf (retrieved January 16, 2008).

——. *Theatrical Market Statistics*, 2009.

Phillips, Joseph D. "Film Conglomerate Blockbusters: International Appeal and Product Homogenization." In *The American Film Industry*, edited by Gorham Kindem, 325–35. Carbondale: Southern Illinois University Press, 1982.

Rosenbaum, Jonathan. *Movie War: How Hollywood and the Media Conspire to Limit What Films We Can See*. Chicago, IL: A Capella Press, 2000.

Tomlinson, John. *Cultural Imperialism: A Critical Introduction*. Baltimore, MD: Johns Hopkins University Press, 1991.

Van Elteren, Mel. "Conceptualizing the Impact of US Popular Culture Globally." *Journal of Popular Culture* 30 (1996): 47–89.

Wasko, Janet. *How Hollywood Works*. London: Sage, 2005.

Chapter 11—Damien Stankiewicz

Abu-Lughod, Lila. *Dramas of Nationhood: The Politics of Television in Egypt*. Chicago: University of Chicago Press, 2005.

Appadurai, Arjun. "Disjuncture and Difference in the Global Cultural Economy." In *Modernity at Large: Cultural Dimensions of Globalization*, edited by Arjun Appadurai, 27–47. Minneapolis: University of Minnesota Press, 1996.

Born, Georgina. *Uncertain Vision: Birt, Dyke and the Reinvention of the BBC*. London: Secker & Warburg, 2004.

Bouvet, Laurent. *France-Allemagne: Le bond en avant*. Paris: O. Jacob, 1998.

Caldwell, John. *Production Culture: Industrial Reflexivity and Critical Practice in Film and Television*. Durham, NC: Duke University Press, 2008.

Chalaby, Jean K. *Transnational Television Worldwide: Towards a New Media Order*. New York, NY: I. B. Tauris, 2009.

——. *Transnational Television in Europe: Reconfiguring Global Communications Networks*. New York, NY: I. B. Tauris, 2009.

Cherribi, Sam. "From Baghdad to Paris: Al-Jazeera and the Veil." *Harvard International Journal of Press and Politics* 11 (2006): 121–38.

Clément, Jérôme. "ARTE, enfin l' Europe!" *Le Monde*, September 26, 1992.

Creeber, Glen."'Hideously White: British Television, Glocalization, and National Identity.'" *Television and New Media* 5 (2004): 27–39.

Da Lage, Olivier. "The Politics of Al Jazeera or the Diplomacy of Doha." In *The Al Jazeera Phenomenon*, edited by M. Zayani, 49–65. Boulder, CO: Paradigm Publishers, 2005.

Elasmar, Michael G. *The Impact of International Television: A Paradigm Shift*. Mahwah, NJ: L. Erlbaum Associates, 2003.

Fumaroli, Marc. *L'Etat Culturel: Une religion moderne*. Paris: Fallois, 1991.

Geertz, Clifford. *The Interpretation of Cultures: Selected Essays*. New York, NY: Basic Books, 1973.

Ginsburg, Faye D., Lila Abu-Lughod, and Brian Larkin, eds. *Media Worlds: Anthropology on New Terrain*. Berkeley: University of California Press, 2002.

Glick-Schiller, Nina. "Racialized Nations, Evangelizing Christianity, Police States, and Imperial Power: Missing in Action in Bunzl's New Europe." *American Ethnologist* 32, no. 4 (2005): 526–32.

Herman, Edward S., and Robert Waterman McChesney. *The Global Media: The New Missionaries of Corporate Capitalism*. Washington, DC: Cassell, 1997.

Kearney, Michael. "The Local and the Global: The Anthropology of Globalization and Transnationalism." *Annual Review of Anthropology* 24 (1995): 547–65.

Larkin, Brian. *Signal and Noise: Media, Infrastructure, and Urban Culture in Nigeria*. Durham, NC: Duke University Press, 2008.

Li, Jinquan. *Chinese Media, Global Contexts*. New York, NY: Routledge, 2003.

Lloyd, David, and Paul Thomas. *Culture and the State*. New York, NY: Routledge, 1998.

Lutz, Wolfgang, Brian C. O'Neill, and Sergei Scherbov. "Europe's Population at a Turning Point." *Science* 299, no. 5615 (2003): 1991–2.

MacDougall, David. *Transcultural Cinema*. Princeton, NJ: Princeton University Press, 1998.

Mahon, Maureen. "The Visible Evidence of Cultural Producers." *Annual Review of Anthropology* 29 (2000): 467–92.

Mandel, Ruth. "A Marshall Plan of the Mind: The Political Economy of a Kazakh Soap Opera." In *Media Worlds: Anthropology on New Terrain*, edited by F. D. Ginsburg, L. Abu-Lughod, and B. Larkin, 211–28. Berkeley: University of California Press, 2002.

Mazzarella, William. "Culture, Globalization, Mediation." *Annual Review of Anthropology* 33 (2004): 345–67.

——. "'Very Bombay': Contending with the Global in an Indian Advertising Agency." *Cultural Anthropology* 18, no. 1 (2005): 33–71.

Mazzucelli, Colette. *France and Germany at Maastricht: Politics and Negotiations to Create the European Union*. New York, NY: Garland, 1997.

Messina, Anthony M. *West European Immigration and Immigrant Policy in the New Century*. Westport, CT: Praeger, 2002.

Parks, Lisa, and Shanti Kumar, eds. *Planet TV: A Global Television Reader*. New York: New York University Press, 2003.

Regourd, Serge. *L'Exception Culturelle*. Paris: Presses Universitaires de France, 2002.

Silverstein, Paul A. "Immigrant Racialization and the New Savage Slot: Race, Migration, and Immigration in the New Europe." *Annual Review of Anthropology* 34 (2005): 363–84.

Tsing, Anna. *Friction: An Ethnography of Global Connection*. Princeton, NJ: Princeton University Press, 2005.

——. "The Global Situation." *Cultural Anthropology* 15, no. 3 (2000): 327–60.

Tylor, Edward. *Primitive Culture*. New York, NY: G. P. Putnam's Sons, 1920 [1871].

Wilk, Richard R. "Television, Time and the National Imaginary in Belize." In *Media Worlds: Anthropology on New Terrain*, edited by F. D. Ginsburg, L. Abu-Lughod, and B. Larkin, 171–86. Berkeley: University of California Press, 2002.

Yang, Mayfair Mei-hui. "Mass Media and Transnational Subjectivity in Shanghai: Notes on 6's (Re)Cosmopolitanism in a Chinese Metropolis." In *Media Worlds: Anthropology on New Terrain*, edited by F. D. Ginsburg, L. Abu-Lughod, and B. Larkin, 189–210. Berkeley: University of California Press, 2002.

Chapter 12—Paul Longley Arthur

American National Biography. http://www.anb.org (accessed December 1, 2009).

"America's Highway: Oral Histories of Route 66." http://sites.google.com/site/route66map (accessed August 28, 2009).

Australian Dictionary of Biography. http://adbonline.anu.edu.au/adbonline.htm (accessed January 15, 2011).

Ayers, Edward L. "The Pasts and Futures of Digital History" (1999). http://www.vcdh.virginia.edu/PastsFutures.html (accessed February 22, 2010).

Barbrook, Richard, and Andy Cameron. "The Californian Ideology" (1995). *Alamut*. http://www.alamut.com/subj/ideologies/pessimism/califIdeo_I.html (accessed September 13, 2009).

Blue, Carroll Parrott, Kristy H. A. Kang, and The Labyrinth Project. *The Dawn at My Back: Memoir of a Black Texas Upbringing. An Interactive Cultural History* [DVD]. Annenberg Center for Communication, University of Southern California, 2003.

Burton, Orville Vernon. "American Digital History." *Social Science Computer Review* 23, no. 2 (2005): 206–20.

Carr, E. H. *What is History?* London: Penguin, 1961.

Cohen, Dan, and Roy Rosenzweig. *Digital History: A Guide to Gathering, Preserving, and Presenting the Past on the Web* (2005). http://chnm.gmu.edu/digitalhistory (accessed December 12, 2009).

Coventry, Michael. "Moving beyond 'the Essay': Evaluating Historical Analysis and Argument in Multimedia Presentations." *Journal of American History* (March 2006). http://www.indiana.edu/~jah/textbooks/2006/coventry.shtml (accessed August 15, 2009).

Dictionary of Sydney. http://www.dictionaryofsydney.org (accessed November 1, 2009).

Encyclopedia of Melbourne. http://www.emelbourne.net.au/home.html (accessed November 1, 2009).

"Gallipoli: The First Day." http://www.abc.net.au/innovation/gallipoli (accessed November 12, 2009).

Himmelfarb, Gertrude. "A Neo-Luddite Reflects on the Internet." *Chronicle of Higher Education*, November 1, 1996, A56. Quoted in Dan Cohen and Roy Rosenzweig, *Digital History: A Guide to Gathering, Preserving, and Presenting the Past on the Web* (2005). http://chnm.gmu.edu/digitalhistory/introduction/#_ednref3 (accessed December 20, 2009).

Hurricane Digital Memory Bank. http://911digitalarchive.org (accessed December 18, 2009).

Kinder, Marsha, and John Rechy. *Mysteries and Desire: Searching the Worlds of John Rechy* [CD-ROM]. Annenberg Center for Communication, University of Southern California, 2000.

Klein, Norman. *The Vatican to Vegas: A History of Special Effects*. New York, NY: The New Press, 2004.

Manning, Patrick. "Navigating World History: A Synopsis." http://www.historycooperative.org/journals/whc/1.1/manning.html (accessed December 28, 2009).

Manovich, Lev, and Andreas Kratky. *Soft Cinema: Navigating the Database* [pamphlet with accompanying DVD-ROM]. Cambridge, MA: MIT Press, 2005.

Mattelart, A. *Networking the World, 1794–2000*. Minneapolis: University of Minnesota Press, 2000.

Oxford Dictionary of National Biography. http://www.oxforddnb.com (accessed December 1, 2009).

Rosenzweig, Roy. "So, What's Next for Clio?: CD-ROM and Historians." *Journal of American History* 81 (1995): 1621–40.

September 11 Digital Archive. http://911digitalarchive.org (accessed December 18, 2009).

Te Ara Encyclopedia of New Zealand. http://www.teara.govt.nz (accessed November 1, 2009).

"Texas Slavery Project." http://www.texasslaveryproject.org/maps/hb (accessed September 10, 2009).

Thomas, William. "Computing and the Historical Imagination." In *A Companion to Digital Humanities*, edited by Susan Schreibman, Ray Siemens, and John Unsworth, 61. Oxford: Blackwell, 2004.

"The Valley of the Shadow: Two Communities in the American Civil War." http://valley.vcdh. virginia.edu (accessed December 12, 2009).

"Who Built America?" http://ashp.cuny.edu/who-america (accessed December 12, 2009).

Chapter 13—Hudson Moura

Appadurai, Arjun. "Disjuncture and Difference in the Global Cultural Economy." In *Media and Cultural Studies: Keyworks*, edited by Meenakshi Gigi Durham and Douglas Kellner, 584–603. Malden, MA: Blackwell Publishers, 2006.

Deleuze, Gilles. *Cinema 1: The Movement-Image.* Minneapolis: University of Minnesota Press, 1986.

Ebert, Roger. "The World." *Chicago Sun-Times*, July 29, 2005, 5.

Havis, Richard James. "Illusory Worlds: An Interview with Jia Zhangke." *Cineaste*, Fall 2005, 58–9.

Jaffee, Valerie. "An Interview with Jia Zhangke." *Senses of Cinema*, June 2004. http://www.senses ofcinema.com/contents/04/32/jia_zhangke.html (accessed January 30, 2008).

Lee, Kevin. "Jia Zhang-Ke". *Senses of Cinema.* 2003. http://www.sensesofcinema.com/contents/ directors/03/jia.html (accessed January 30, 2008).

Lo Kwai-Cheun. *Chinese Face/Off: Transnational Popular Culture of Hong Kong.* Urbana: University of Illinois Press, 2005.

MacDougall, David. *Transcultural Cinema.* Princeton, NJ: Princeton University Press, 1998.

Naficy, Hamid. "Epistolarity and Textuality in Accented Films." In *Subtitles on the Foreignness of Film*, edited by Atom Egoyan and Ian Balfour, 131–52. Cambridge/London: MIT Press, 2004.

Nancy, Jean-Luc. *The Creation of the World or Globalization.* Albany: State University of New York Press, 2007.

Rosenbaum, Jonathan. "Workers' Playtime." *Sight & Sound* 16, no. 9 (2005): 92.

Yi Sicheng. "A Window to Our Times: China's Independent Film since the Late 1990's." PhD diss., Kiel University, 2006.

Yiman Wang. "The Amateur's Lightning Rod: DV Documentary in Postsocialist China." *Film Quarterly* 58, no. 4 (2005): 16–26.

Yingjin Zhang. "Styles, Subjects and Special Points of View: A Study of Contemporary Chinese Independent Documentary." *New Cinemas: Journal of Contemporary Film* 2, no. 2 (2004): 2.

Chapter 14—Matthew Heinz and Hsin-I Cheng

Alexander, Jonathan. "Introduction to the Special Issue: Queer Webs: Representations of LGBT People and Communities on the World Wide Web." *International Journal of Sexuality and Gender Studies* 7, no. 2/3 (2002): 77–84.

Arvidsson, Adam. "'Quality Singles': Internet Dating and the Work of Fantasy." *New Media & Society* 8, no. 4 (2006): 671–90.

Bang, Henrik, and Anders Esmark, eds. *New Public With/out Democracy.* Frederiksberg, DK: Samfundslitteratur, 2008.

Bartos, Sebastian E., Voon Chin Phua, and Erin Avery. "Differences in Romanian Men's Online Personals by Sexualities." *The Journal of Men's Studies* 7, no. 2 (2009): 145–54.

Chang, Hui Ching, and Richard Holt. "The Concept of Yuan and Chinese Conflict Resolution." In *Chinese Conflict Management and Resolution*, edited by Guo-Ming Chen and Ringo Ma, 19–38. Westport, CT: Ablex Publishing, 2002.

Chang, Yin-Kun. "The Gay Right Movement in the Internet: Is It Possible or Not?" *Journal of Cyber Culture and Informational Technology* 4 (2003): 53–86.

Chao, Antonia. "A Reflection Upon Taiwan's Queer Studies: From a Viewpoint of Cultural Production and Reproduction." *Taiwan: A Radical Quarterly in Social Studies* 38 (2000): 207–44.

Cheng, Ming-hui. "The Internal and Oversea Lesbian Web Sites and the Trans-territorial Identity." *Cities and Design* 5/6 (1998): 199–209.

Coupland, Justine. "Dating Advertisements: Discourses of the Commodified Self." *Discourse & Society* 7, no. 2 (1996): 187–207.

Erni, John N., and Anthony Spires, "The Formation of a Queer-Imagined Community in Post-Martial Law Taiwan." In *Asian Media Studies: Politics of Subjectivities*, edited by John N. Erni and Anthony Spires, 225–52. UK: Blackwell Publishing, 2005.

Fernback, Jan. "Beyond the Diluted Community Concept: A Symbolic Interactionist Perspective on Online Social Relations." *New Media & Society* 9, no. 1 (2007): 49–69.

Gian, Jia-shin. "Taiwanese Lesbians' Counter Culture Since 1990: Deconstruction, Reconstruction, and Transformation of 'T' Partner." *Thought and Words: Journal of the Humanities and Social Science* 35 (1997): 145–209.

——. "Taiwanese Lesbians' Identification Under the Queer Politics Since 1990." *Taiwan: A Radical Quarterly in Social Studies* 30 (1998): 63–115.

Gonzales, Marti H., and Sarah A. Meyers. "'Your Mother Would Like Me': Self-presentation in the Personal Ads of Heterosexual and Homosexual Men and Women." *Personality and Social Psychology Bulletin* 19, no. 2 (1993): 135.

Jensen, Jakob Linaa. "The Internet Omnopticon." In *New Publics With/out Democracy*, edited by Henrik Bang and Anders Esmark, 351–80. Frederiksberg: Samfundslitteratur, 2007.

Jones, Rodney H. "'Potato Seeking Rice': Language, Culture, and Identity in Gay Personal Ads in Hong Kong." *International Journal of the Sociology of Language* 143 (2000): 33–61.

Liou, Liang-ya. "Queer Theory and Politics in Taiwan: The Cultural Translation and (Re)Production of Queerness in and beyond Taiwan Lesbian/Gay/Queer Activism." *NTU Studies in Language and Literature* 123, no. 14 (2005): 123–54.

Luce, Amber. Review of *The Web: Social Control in a Lesbian Community*, by Christine M. Robinson. *Women's Studies in Communication* 32, no. 2 (2009): 255–8.

Manning, Jimmie. Review of *Double Click: Romance and Commitment Among Online Couples*, by A. J. Baker. *The Review of Communication* 7, no. 4 (2007): 427–30.

Martin, Fran. *Situating Sexualities: Queer Representation in Taiwanese Fiction, Film and Public Culture*. Hong Kong: Hong Kong University Press, 2003.

Miley, Marissa. "Dating Sites Still Attracting Users." *Advertising Age* 80, no. 8 (March 2, 2009): 8.

Postoutenko, Kirill. "Between 'I' and 'We': Studying the Grammar of Social Identity in Europe (1900–1950)." *Journal of Language and Politics* 8, no. 2 (2009): 195–222.

Smith, Christine A., and Shannon Stillman. "What Do Women Want? The Effects of Gender and Sexual Orientation on the Desirability of Physical Attributes in the Personal Ads of Women." *Sex Roles* 46, no. 9/10 (2002): 337–42.

Stephure, Robert J., Susan D. Boon, Stacey L. MacKinnon, and Vicki L. Deveau. "Internet Initiated Relationships: Associations Between Age and Involvement in Online Dating." *Journal of Computer-Mediated Communication* 14, no. 3 (2009): 658–81.

Valkenburg, Patti M., and Jochen Peter. "Who Visits Online Dating Sites? Exploring Some Characteristics of Online Daters." *CyberPsychology & Behavior* 10, no. 6 (2007): 849–52.

Yo, Chien. "Tongxinglian Gee Doo Too U Wan Lu Go Ton [Homosexual Christians and Internet Communication]." *Economic, Society, and Communication* 73 (2002): 114–20.

Chapter 15—Radhika Gajjala, Anca Birzescu, and Franklin N. A. Yartey

"About Kiva." *Kiva*. http://www.kiva.org/about (accessed December 16, 2009).

Bob, Clifford. *The Marketing of Rebellion: Insurgents, Media and International Activism*. New York, NY: Cambridge University Press, 2005.

Elliott, Carolyn M. "Introduction: Markets, Communities, and Empowerment." In *Global Empowerment of Women: Responses to Globalization and Politicized Religions*, edited by Carolyn M. Elliott, 1–23. New York, NY: Routledge, 2008.

Enteen, Jilliana. "Spatial Conceptions of URLs: Tamil Eelam Networks on the World Wide Web." *New Media and Society* 8, no. 2 (2006): 229–49.

Gajjala, Radhika. *Cyber Selves: Feminist Ethnographies of South Asian Women*. Walnut Creek, CA: AltaMira Press, 2004.

Bibliography

Third-World Critiques of Cyberfeminism." *Development in Practice* 9, no. 5 (1999): 616–19.

ı, Radhika, and Melissa Altman. "Producing Cyberselves through Technospatial Praxis: Studying through Doing." *Health Research in Cyberspace*, edited by P. Liamputtong, 67–84. New York, NY: Nova Science, 2006.

Gajjala, Radhika, Yahui Zhang, and Phyllis Dako-Gyeke. "Lexicons of Women's Empowerment Online." *Feminist Media Studies* 10, no. 1 (2010): 69–86.

Hegde, Radha S., and Shome Radha. "Postcolonial Scholarship—Productions and Directions: An Interview with Gayatri Chakravorty Spivak." *Communication Theory* 23, no. 3 (2002): 271–86.

"How Kiva Works." *Kiva*. http://www.kiva.org/about/how (accessed December 16, 2009).

Humphreys, Sal. "The Economies within an Online Social Network Market: A Case Study of Ravelry." In *ANZCA 09 Annual Conference: Communication, Creativity and Global Citizenship*, 234–52. Brisbane: QUT, July 8–10, 2009.

"Kiva Launches Online Microfinance in the United States: Opportunity to U.S. Entrepreneurs." *WebSite 101*. http://website101.com/finance/kiva-launches-online-microfinance-united-states-entrepreneurs/#ixzz0qS0sLh7C (accessed December 16, 2009).

Kolko, Beth E., Lisa Nakamura, and Gilbert Rodman. "Race in Cyberspace: An Introduction." In *Race in Cyberspace*, edited by Beth E. Kolko, Lisa Nakamura, and Gilbert Rodman, 1–14. New York, NY: Routledge, 2000.

Lingam, Lakshmi, "Domains of Empowerment: Women in Microcredit Groups Negotiating with Multiple Patriarchies." In *Global Empowerment of Women: Responses to Globalization and Politicized Religions*, edited by Carolyn M. Elliott, 119–40. New York, NY: Routledge, 2008.

Mohanty, Chandra T. *Feminism without Borders: Decolonizing Theory, Practicing Solidarity*. Durham, NC: Duke University Press, 2003.

"Monsanto Seed Patent Protection." *Monsanto*. http://www.monsanto.com (accessed December 16, 2009).

Nakamura, Lisa. "Don't Hate the Player, Hate the Game: The Racialization of Labor in World of Warcraft." *Critical Studies in Media Communication* 26, no. 2 (2009): 128–44.

Narayan, Uma. "The Project of Feminist Epistemology: Perspectives from a Nonwestern Feminist." In *Feminist Theory Reader: Local and Global Perspectives*, edited by Carole R. McCann and Seung Kyung Kim, 308–17. New York, NY: Routledge, 2003.

Nyamekye, Adwoa. *Kiva*. http://www.kiva.org/app.php?page=businesses&action=about&id=97791 (accessed December 16, 2009).

Parameswaran, Radhika. "The Other Sides of Globalization: Communication, Culture, and Postcolonial Critique." *Communication, Culture and Critique* 1, no. 1 (2008): 116–25.

Sengupta, Rajdeep, and Craig P. Aubuchon. "The Microfinance Revolution: An Overview." *Federal Reserve Bank of St. Louis Review* 90, no. 1 (2008): 9–30.

Sweeney, Emily. "Are You My Entrepreneur?" *Kiva*. March 22, 2009. http://fellowsblog. Kiva/2009/03/22/are-you-my-entrepreneur (accessed April 23, 2009).

Williams, Raymond. *The Sociology of Culture*. Chicago: The University of Chicago Press, 1995.

Zukin, Sharon. "Consuming Authenticity: From Outposts of Difference to Means of Exclusion." *Cultural Studies* 22, no. 5 (2008): 724–48.

Afterword—Daya Thussu

Altman, Roger C. "The Great Crash 2008: A Geopolitical Setback for the West." *Foreign Affairs*, January/February 2009. http://www.foreignaffairs.com/articles/63714/roger-c-altman/the-great-crash-2008 (accessed September 6, 2010).

Goldman Sachs. *BRICs and Beyond*. New York, NY: Goldman Sachs Global Economics Department, 2007.

Hobson, John M. *The Eastern Origins of Western Civilization*. Cambridge, UK: Cambridge University Press, 2004.

Maddison, Angus. *The World Economy: A Millennial Perspective*. Paris: OECD, 2001.

Index

251